Race, Racism and Sports Journalism

Beginning with a theoretical discussion of race, sport and media, this book critically examines issues of race, racism and sports journalism and offers practical advice on sports reporting, including a discussion of guidelines for ethical journalism.

In a series of case studies, representations of race are explored through historical and contemporary analysis of international media coverage, including online and digital platforms. The background and impacts of these representations is also discussed through interviews with athletes and sports journalists. Subjects covered include:

- cricket in the UK, Australian and Asian media, with particular focus on Pakistan;
- athletics and media representations of athletes, including a study of the reporting of South African runner Caster Semenya;
- football and the under-representation of British Asians, with an analysis of how race is constructed in the digital arena;
- boxing with particular reference to Muhammad Ali, America and Islam;
- Formula One and analysis of the media reporting, international spectator response and racism towards Lewis Hamilton, described in the media as the first black driver.

Finally, the book analyses the make-up of sports journalism, examining the causes and consequences of a lack of diversity within the profession.

Neil Farrington is a senior lecturer in sports journalism at the University of Sunderland, and a multi award-nominated sports journalist with 18 years of experience.

Daniel Kilvington lectures at the University of Sunderland and is studying for a PhD in media and cultural studies.

Dr John Price is a senior lecturer and programme leader for sports journalism at the University of Sunderland.

Dr Amir Saeed is programme leader for media, culture and communication at the University of Sunderland and online tutor for MA mass communication theory at the University of Leicester.

Race, Racism and Sports Journalism

Neil Farrington, Daniel Kilvington,
John Price and Amir Saeed

 Routledge
Taylor & Francis Group

LONDON AND NEW YORK

First published 2012
by Routledge
2 Park Square, Milton Park, Abingdon, Oxon OX14 4RN

Simultaneously published in the USA and Canada
by Routledge
711 Third Avenue, New York, NY 10017

Routledge is an imprint of the Taylor & Francis Group, an informa business

British Library Cataloguing in Publication Data
A catalogue record for this book is available from the British Library

Library of Congress Cataloging in Publication Data
Race, racism and sports journalism / by Daniel Kilvington. [et al.].
p. cm.
Includes bibliographical references and index.
1. Sports journalism–Great Britain. 2. Racism in the press–Great Britain.
3. Minorities–Press coverage–Great Britain. I. Kilvington, Daniel.
PN5124.S65R33 2012
070.4'49796089–dc23
2011039543

ISBN: 978-0-415-67639-7 (hbk)
ISBN: 978-0-415-67640-3 (pbk)
ISBN: 978-0-203-14630-9 (ebk)

Typeset in Sabon
by Taylor & Francis Books

MIX
Paper from
responsible sources
FSC
www.fsc.org FSC® C004839

Printed and bound in Great Britain by the MPG Books Group

Contents

List of figures

Acknowledgements

The authors would like to thank the people and organizations who have contributed their time, cooperation and expertise to the production of this book. Without their help, this book could not have been written.

List of acronyms and abbreviations

ANC	African National Congress
ASA	Athletics South Africa
BAWA	British Athletics Writers Association
BBC	British Broadcasting Corporation
BCOMS	Black Collective of Media in Sport
BME	black or minority ethnic
BNP	British National Party
BOA	British Olympic Association
CRT	critical race theory
F1	Formula One
FA	Football Association
FC	Football Club
IAAF	International Association of Athletics Federations
ICC	International Cricket Council
IFJ	International Federation of Journalists
IRA	Irish Republican Army
MP	Member of Parliament
NCTJ	National Council for the Training of Journalists
NFL	National Football League
NOI	Nation of Islam
NUJ	National Union of Journalists
OCA	Otago Cricket Association
PCB	Pakistan Cricket Board
PCC	Press Complaints Commission
PFA	Professional Footballers Association
PR	public relations
SJA	Sports Journalists' Association
TKO	technical knockout

UK	United Kingdom
US	United States
WBC	World Boxing Council
WCM	*Wisden Cricket Monthly*
ZRF	Zesh Rehman Foundation

Chapter 1

Introduction

Sports reporting has a long tradition in the press, but has often been seen as 'soft' journalism. However, during recent times, sports journalism has moved from the toy department to the finance department. Where once the profession was looked upon with amusement or scorn, it is now seen as crucial to the incomes and audiences of many media organizations. As Steen (2008, p21) says: 'Newspaper editors once referred to their sports desks as the toy department. In recognition of the seemingly unslakeable public thirst for information, and the profits engendered by satisfying that demand, the sneering has all but abated.'

Colin Gibson, former sports editor at the *Sunday Telegraph* and the *Daily Mail*, has noted that:

> Sports and papers have both changed. Gone are the days when sports just meant filling up a couple of pages at the back. Sport is now high profile. It's a serious business involving corporate finance, so papers have to treat it with more seriousness, while appreciating that it's part of the entertainment industry as well.
>
> (cited in Boyle, 2006a, p92)

Sport has become increasingly important to the media (Rowe, 2009). Recent years have witnessed a huge growth in the amount and prominence of sports coverage across broadcast, print and online media. Perhaps the most notable example of this is to be found in the quality press, where there have been huge increases in the numbers of pages and proportion of editorial space devoted to sports coverage. For example, sports reporting in *The Times* almost doubled between 1974 and 2004, rising from 11 per cent of editorial to 21 per cent. Similarly, *The Guardian*'s coverage increased from 11 to 17 per cent during the same period (Boyle, 2006a). Sport has also moved from the back pages to the news pages with stories about corruption, Olympic legacies and financial takeovers becoming staples of television and newspaper headlines. Furthermore, with the rise of celebrity culture, sports stars are no longer confined to the back pages. Increasingly, they find themselves open to public and media scrutiny of their private and social lives.

For some, these changes provide further evidence of the *dumbing down* of our media, in which the trivial, entertaining and ephemeral are given ever greater attention (Franklin, 1997). This perspective taps into a traditional view of sports journalists as being nothing more than 'fans with typewriters'. For example, Harcup (2004, p61), in a discussion about journalism's relationship with 'truth', makes the following assessment: 'We might expect sports journalism to be informed by the subjective, even though we trust journalists to be accurate when giving us the score. At the end of the day, it's not a matter of life and death – it's just entertainment. News reporting is different.' Journalism as a whole has long faced questions about its status and whether it can truly be classed as a profession or, rather, as a trade or craft (Tumber and Prentoulis, 2005). Such questions can equally be asked of sports journalists – both in the way that they perceive themselves, and the way in which they are perceived by fellow journalists.

However, there is evidence to suggest that sports journalism is becoming more and more professionalized. A growing number of sports reporters are being professionally trained, using specialist skills and being required to work across different sections of media organizations (Boyle, 2006b). Such characteristics increasingly help to set the professional sports journalist apart from the part-time blogger, citizen journalist or 'fan with an i-phone'. These changes have coincided with the increased economic importance of sport to media outlets. As Boyle (2006a, p167) comments: 'As more space is devoted to sports journalism at the broadsheet/compact end of the market, this area increasingly demands that sports journalists are coming with a strong journalistic background as opposed to simply a passion for sport.'

These changes in the quantity, prominence and perception of sports journalism are due to a number of factors. In the case of newspapers, they must be viewed as part of attempts to gain new and loyal audiences in an ever-more competitive market. As Andrews (2005, p2) says: 'The British newspaper market is the most competitive in the world, and increasingly, that competition takes place on the sports pages.' Investment in sports pages is aimed at attracting younger, professional male readerships (Boyle, 2006a, p51).

This investment has coincided with wider cultural shifts in the popularity and positioning of sport within society. With the ever increasing globalization of media and culture, combined with the global diaspora of peoples, sporting passions have transcended national boundaries. This has led to sport becoming ever more appealing to the media as it has become increasingly interesting to a global audience. For example, more than 16 million people attended UK Football League matches in the 2010/2011 season, compared to 10 million in 1992. The Premier League was also followed by a global television audience of billions, particularly in the Far East, Middle East and Caribbean. Of course, this public appeal is, in part, a consequence of increased media coverage. As Rowe (2004,

2005) has observed, the boundaries of sport and the sports media have become increasingly blurred and their fortunes entwined. In fact, he claims: 'Newspapers and the wider media have become so intimately involved in sport – and vice versa – as to suggest a convergence of these formally (and formerly) separate institutions' (Rowe, 2005, p127).

The third character in this marriage of mutual benefit is television. Andrews (2005, p6) observes: 'Much of the recent growth of interest in sport has been driven by the media, in particular satellite television, which has bought rights to major sporting events and promoted them vigorously as one of the most effective ways of selling subscriptions to its services.' The influx of money into sport (particularly football) in the form of broadcasting rights has created a lucrative feeding ground on which sports stars, sports journalism and broadcasters can all grow fat together. Rather than providing further competition for sports journalism, television has helped to create a culture in which sport, and sports stars as both athletes and celebrities, increasingly take centre stage. The emergence of online, social and interactive media further fuels this appetite for sports news. As Boyle (2006a, p52) says: 'Far from crippling sports journalism in the print media, the growth of sports broadcasting and online coverage has actually helped drive readers to the print media.'

However, despite its increasing prominence, sports journalism has received relatively little academic attention to date. There are some practical guides to sports journalism (Andrews, 2005; Steen, 2008) that provide functional advice on techniques such as match reporting and sourcing. There have also been some limited attempts to place sports reporting in wider social contexts (Boyle, 2006a; Rowe, 2009). However, issues of 'race' and racism, and how they are reported, have received very little attention in these texts. For example, Andrews (2005) in *Sports Journalism: A Practical Introduction* notes that sports journalists should avoid 'isms' such as sexism, racism and ageism. While the tone of this is commendable, it does not really acknowledge the complex nature of 'race' and racism. Once again, these categories are given only fleeting attention.

In contrast, the relationships between sport and 'race' have received far more analysis (Carrington and McDonald, 2001b; Ross, 2005; Hylton, 2009; Burdsey, 2010; Carrington, 2010; Hundley and Billings, 2010; Spracklen and Long, 2010). However, most of these studies only give passing attention to the role of the media. Where the media has been more foregrounded, studies have tended to come from the wider fields of sociological, media and communications research rather than journalism studies directly (Wenner, 1998; Brookes, 2002; Bernstein and Blain, 2003; Rowe, 2004; Boyle and Haynes, 2009; Kennedy and Hills, 2009). Research in this area has tended to focus on certain elements within sports coverage, such as stereotyping, portrayals of national identity and representations of gender. Researchers have done empirical work looking at 'race' and racisms in sport, analysing issues such as participation and spectatorship, and interviewing professional athletes. Significantly, though, few studies have historically analysed the shifting nature of 'race' and racism in *sports journalism* with the aid of extensive empirical work. This is an important gap in research given the increasing social and cultural prominence of sports journalism and the fact that sports reporting has the power and ability to shape people's opinions on contentious issues such as 'race', racism, ethnicity, nationalism and belonging (Boyle and Haynes, 2009). It is a gap which this book seeks to start to address.

Reporting 'race': Guidelines and regulation

In the UK, the Press Complaints Commission (PCC) sets out guidelines for the reporting of 'race' in its code of practice. The guideline on discrimination states the following:

1   The press must avoid prejudicial or pejorative reference to an individual's race, colour, religion, gender, sexual orientation or to any physical or mental illness or disability.
2   Details of an individual's race, colour, religion, sexual orientation, physical or mental illness or disability must be avoided unless genuinely relevant to the story.

There are three key aspects of this for journalists to have in mind. First, reference to someone's 'race' must only be made if it is deemed 'genuinely relevant' to the story. Second, if such reference is made, it must not be 'prejudicial or pejorative'. Third, the regulation only applies to the reporting of an individual and therefore does not cover, for example, references to groups or nations of people.

This third aspect of the guideline is contentious and has provoked criticism of the PCC. As Frost (2004, p114) commented:

> The PCC's insistence that only discrimination against individuals breaches the code and that complaints about racism affecting groups of people are really a matter of taste and decency, and therefore not something on which it can adjudicate, begins to look perverse at a time when there is considerable public concern about perceived racism in some reporting of asylum seekers, the Iraq war and terrorism.

Some of the most controversial reporting of this kind surrounded England's match against Germany in the Euro 96 football tournament. A number of tabloids used the discourse and metaphor of war in their coverage, including *The Mirror*'s infamous headline:

> ACHTUNG! SURRENDER For you Fritz, ze Euro 96 Championship is over.

The PCC received hundreds of complaints about the coverage, but ruled that it could not uphold them on the grounds the reporting was not directed at an individual. Instead, it issued guidance to editors in an attempt to avoid similar coverage during the 1998 World Cup. The statement, by then PCC Chairman Lord Wakeham, said:

> Of course newspapers have every right to report on events in a robust and partisan fashion; indeed, the Code of Practice protects that right. But that right must be balanced by responsibility. Editors should therefore seek to ensure that their reporting and their comment does nothing to incite violence, disorder or other unlawful behaviour, or to foster any form of xenophobia that could contribute directly to such incitement.

The PCC claims that the guidance had a positive impact upon toning down the nature of reporting and reducing the levels of 'jingoistic' journalism. However, it did not prevent the *Daily Star* from running a leader comment headlined: 'Frogs need a good kicking' (*Daily Star*, 2 March 1998). The leader argued that the fact that the French had 'grabbed the lion's share of World Cup tickets is typical of their slimy continental ways … As we proved at Agincourt and Waterloo, a good kicking on their Gallic derrieres is the only language the greedy frogs understand.' Again, the PCC received complaints about the story and, again, it rejected them. Its ruling stated:

> Sporting events – and matters relating to them, such as ticketing arrangements – are bound to excite considerable emotion. Newspapers will inevitably reflect that – even if they do so in a way which some people will find offensive … The Code is not intended to stop such robust comment. Indeed, the purpose is to protect individuals from prejudice – not to restrain partisan comment about other nations.
>
> (PCC: Report 42, http://www.pcc.org.uk/news/index.html?
> article=MjAwMg==)

The PCC's position is that to rule on generalized comments about groups of people 'would involve subjective views, often based on political correctness or taste, and be difficult to adjudicate upon without infringing the freedom of expression of others'. However, such arguments could be used against its existing regulations. All reporting guidelines, to some extent, 'infringe' on freedom of expression. Furthermore, decisions about whether a reference to someone's 'race' is 'genuinely relevant' or, indeed, 'pejorative or prejudiced' are inherently subjective. The fact that the PCC chooses to apply them to individuals, rather than groups, does not make them less so.

Another potential criticism of the PCC lies in the number of 'race' discrimination cases that it has addressed throughout its history. In 2010, just over 3 per cent of the 7,000-plus complaints made to the PCC were on the grounds of discrimination. Yet, despite receiving dozens of such complaints each year, the PCC has never upheld a complaint made about discrimination in terms of 'race'.

Chris Frost (2004) made a similar observation in his review of the first ten years of the PCC. During that period, complaints about discrimination in the press rose from 1.7 per cent of PCC complaints to 10.6 per cent. But Frost found that out of an estimated 1440 complaints about discrimination, only 38 were adjudicated by the PCC, and only 6 were upheld. Three of these were about sexuality and three related to the reporting of mental health.

An explanation for this lies partly in the way that the PCC operates. It declines many complaints on the grounds that they do not properly fall within the remit of its code. Furthermore, it seeks to informally reach agreement between the complainant and publications, meaning that many do not reach the stage of being officially ruled upon. For example, in 2010, of the 7,000-plus complaints received, the PCC accepted that 750 fell within its remit and managed to successfully mediate an agreement in 544 of these cases. A spokesman for the PCC said: 'The PCC attempts wherever possible to successfully resolve complaints by mediating between complainants and publications. Whether there is an "upheld adjudication" is therefore only one small part of an overall picture.'

Another factor is that complaints which may be thought matters of discrimination are sometimes dealt with in relation to other parts of the PCC code, such as accuracy. For example, the commission has upheld a number of complaints against publications for using the term 'illegal asylum seeker' on the grounds that this is an inaccurate and nonsensical phrase.

So what does lie behind the PCC's lack of rulings on 'race' issues? Is it a case of *institutional racism*? Or does the lack of rulings reflect a lack of *overt racism* in media coverage? If this is the case, is the PCC missing more instances of *inferential* or *covert racism* within the media? These concepts will be defined and explained in the following chapter and the questions discussed throughout this book.

Outline of the book

This book examines the extent to which 'race' and racism remain live issues in the sports media and analyses how they are handled across a range of sports journalism. In approach, it seeks to combine theoretical perspectives with more practical aspects of the subject. The authors believe that theory and practice can, and should, be mutually beneficial to our understanding of the world. Theory taking no account of practice can be hollow, while practice blind to theory can be parochial. To understand concepts such as 'race' and racism, or even racial categories, one must examine the historical, social and cultural contexts in which these terms have been constructed. For example, it could be argued that the term 'negro' was acceptable up until the 1960s as a racial description; however, in a contemporary context one now realizes that this term was based on racist understanding of human difference.

Previous literature on journalism has been 'too often polarised between journalists (practitioners) who feel academics have little to teach them, and academics whose focus on theory is in danger of denying journalists any degree of autonomy' (Harcup, 2004, p7). This book seeks to address such weaknesses in its approach. It is aided in this by the diverse backgrounds of its authors. Two of its authors come from a traditional academic background and are steeped in the theories of media and 'race'. Its other two authors come from a background of practising journalism and combine the discourses of the newsroom with those of the lecture theatre.

In this spirit, the book combines practical advice, with discussion of the sports journalism profession and its practices, and an examination of their wider social and cultural implications. New empirical material in the book comprises analysis of a range of media texts and interviews with journalists, athletes, campaigners and politicians.

The thoughts and opinions of the following people will appear throughout the book:

- Steve Cram, BBC athletics commentator, 5 April 2011;
- Steven Downes, secretary of the Sports Journalists' Association, 15 August 2011;
- Greg Gobere, sports journalist, 18 January 2011;
- Rodney Hinds, *The Voice* sports editor, 18 January 2011;
- Anna Kessel, *The Guardian* sports journalist, 10 March 2011;
- Danny Lynch, *Kick It Out*'s media and communications officer, 19 January 2011;
- Leon Mann, sports journalist and founder of the Black Collective of Media in Sport (BCOMS), 19 August 2011;
- Dean Morse, *Mirror* Newspapers head of sport, 20 August 2011;
- Lord Herman Ouseley, chair of *Kick It Out*, 18 April 2011;
- Simon Parker, *Telegraph and Argus* sports journalist, 27 April 2011;
- Rob Steen, sports journalist and senior lecturer, 6 July 2011;
- Rob Tanner, *Leicester Mercury* sports journalist, 5 May 2011;
- Simon Turnbull, *The Independent* athletics correspondent, 24 February 2011;
- Anwar Uddin, Barnet FC Anglo-Asian footballer, 7 April 2011;
- Dean Wilson, *The Mirror* cricket correspondent, 19 July 2011.

The following off-the-record interviews have also been conducted:

- British Asian journalist, 6 April 2011;
- white British scout, 2 June 2011;
- British Asian scout, 27 May 2011;
- former professional British Pakistani footballer, 19 March 2011;

- British Indian semi-professional footballer, 3 May 2011;
- British Pakistani coach, 8 June 2011;
- British Indian semi-professional footballer, 6 May 2011;
- British Indian grassroots coach, 4 April 2011.

Chapter 2 of the book provides a theoretical foundation for discussions in later chapters. It seeks to define and discuss concepts of 'race', racisms and national identity, and to contextualize them within the fields of sport and sports journalism. The chapter highlights how such terms have evolved and examines the interconnections between them. Following this, it looks at the relationships between media and minorities and theorizes how minorities, non-whites or 'Others' are represented within sport and the sports media.

Chapter 3 examines the issue of diversity, or lack of it, within sports journalism. It provides the latest statistics on the numbers of black and minority ethnic people working as journalists and taking part in journalism education. Then, through a series of interviews with reporters, editors and campaigners, it discusses the reasons behind the lack of diversity in sports journalism and looks at what can, and is, being done to improve the situation.

Chapter 4 looks at athletics. The stereotype of the 'natural' black athlete has been prevalent in the sport for decades and the chapter explores the extent to which 'race' remains an issue in contemporary reporting. It does this through three case studies. The first discusses coverage of 800m runner Caster Semenya and claims of racism from South Africa over her gender testing. The second examines reporting of sprinter Christophe Lemaitre, dubbed the 'fastest white man' after running under 10 seconds for the 100m. The section questions whether such reporting can be justified. Finally, the chapter looks at the case of Christine Ohuruogu and the extent to which 'race' played a role in some coverage of her return from a drugs ban.

Chapter 5 explores the changing representations of 'race' throughout the history of boxing. It does this through case studies analysing the discourses around three boxers from different eras: Jack Johnson, Muhammad Ali and Amir Khan. The chapter explores how each athlete has been discussed within popular culture and the sports media, analysing how each has taken a different approach to their complex, and often problematic, racial portrayals.

Chapter 6 looks at issues of colonialism, 'race' and racism, ethnicity, national identity and religion within cricket and its coverage in the media. It examines how cricket journalism was initially informed by the overt, albeit paternalistic, racism of Empire and discusses the extent to which mediated cultural and physiological stereotypes have contributed to the decline of black English cricketers during the last 10 to 15 years. In contrast, the recent emergence of

British Asian cricketers will be explored, with their success at apparent odds with the creeping Islamophobia in evidence within post-9/11 Britain, within which Asian cricketers run the risk of being depicted as a homogeneous 'Other'. This, in turn, leads the chapter to examine media reports of corruption within Pakistani cricket which betrays a moral double standard and, when combined with an event such as the death of Pakistan cricket coach Bob Woolmer, go further in demonizing Islam, and hark directly back to the myths and stereotypes of colonial discourse to draw spurious and damaging links between Muslim cricketers and terrorism. Finally, we will ask if such examples of mediated Islamophobia could come to undermine the progress made by British Asian players, or whether that progress can yet help to progress cricket's media discourse from its frequently problematic preoccupation with issues of 'race' and religion.

Chapter 7 examines the complex interconnections between 'race', nation, ethnicity, religion and culture in the reporting of British Asian footballers. It discusses the origins and characteristics of stereotypes such as the 'physical inferiority' of British Asian footballers, and analyses how the 'Other' culture of these players is represented within the media. The portrayals of potential Asian 'role models' in the media is explored, along with the trend of over-hyping young British Asian players.

Chapter 8 focuses on Formula One as a traditionally multicultural but historically white-dominated sport, and examines media representations of emerging non-white drivers. It looks at the breakthrough of Lewis Hamilton, discussing how important or newsworthy his 'race' or skin colour has been deemed by the media. The chapter explores two case studies in particular: the racist taunts directed at Hamilton in Spain, 2008; and his more recent 'maybe it's because I'm black' comments to journalists at the Monaco Grand Prix. Notions of 'race', racism, national identity and class will be examined, including the extent to which these concepts have become interconnected and why this 'overlapping' may be problematic.

Chapter 9 presents an overall conclusion to the book, drawing together its key themes and findings.

Consider the following research hypothesis or proposal. Are European Caucasians innately good at golf because of biological characteristics associated with their white skin? Such a proposition would be subject to ridicule and scorn. In contrast, researchers from a variety of academic disciplines have tried to scientifically reason the sporting success of certain ethnic groups based on a biological understanding of the concept of 'race'. The classification of racial categories is so entrenched within culture and society that people can debate and reason as to why black people are innately good at sprinting, and the topic has been the subject of much academic, scientific and political enquiry.

Figure 1.1 The Europe Ryder Cup team pose for pictures, 4 October 2010
(Source: Glyn Kirk/AFP/Getty Images)

Figure 1.2 Usain Bolt wins the Beijing Men's 100m Final, 16 August 2008
(Source: Vladimir Rys/Bongarts/Getty Images)

This book seeks to establish that our understandings of so-called racial categories, consciously and subconsciously, are evident in everyday discourses, including those of sport and sports journalism. It matters because these are not merely descriptive categories, but carry powerful connotations that can have actual negative impacts upon people's lives.

Chapter 2

Theories of 'race' and racism in sport and the media

Theory is always a detour on the way to something more important.

(Hall, 1991, p42)

'Race' exists as a conceptual reality, but it is a lie – a myth which leads to the direct and indirect discrimination, abuse and suffering of billions of people on Earth on a daily, hourly and secondly basis. Across the globe, racism manifests itself in various ways that ensure that people are victimized on the basis of some negative biological and/or cultural trait which they are supposed to possess. Any attempt to explain comprehensively global accounts of the immediacy, currency and future of racism is virtually impossible, since the institutional structures, types, targets and experiences are potentially so vast and full of regional, local and national variations that dispute and debate will be inevitable. What cannot be disputed is that human beings will suffer. In short, the racism encountered by an asylum seeker on the streets of north-east England from a fascist group will be visibly different from the persecution faced by a Palestinian woman from the occupying Israeli army in the Gaza strip. Both situations may have the essential requirements that allow racism and prejudice to manifest; but both are also dependent upon varying sociocultural circumstances.

Although there is a growing body of evidence that discredits the notion of 'race', 'race' thinking still permeates much of Western culture. It is routinely used by politicians, media workers, academics and laypeople from a variety of backgrounds to describe, ascribe and, at times, disparage groups of people. As Malik (1996, p2) argues:

> Race seems to be both everywhere and nowhere ... We continually categorise people according to their 'race' – Afro-Caribbean, white, Jewish. Discussions of culture, history or art often seem to centre around race – 'Asian culture', 'black history', 'African art'. Everything from criminality to the entrepreneurial spirit is given a racial connotation – witness the stereotypes of 'black muggers' or 'Asian shopkeepers'.

Hall (1996) has suggested that 'race' has become a 'floating signifier'; as a result, it has become entwined within elements of biology, culture, religion and nation, making it difficult to expel from everyday discourse. Although we cannot all agree on a common explanation of 'race', it is clear that it remains a pervasive force in society. One could suggest that if 'race' discourse is upheld in everyday language, the problematic ideology of racial difference will continue to live on. What we must remember is that 'racial' differences are social inventions, not natural or scientific constructions. Thus, 'races do not exist outside representation but are formed in and by it in a process of social and political struggle' (Barker 1999, p61). This has led some to argue that 'today the race concept is more problematic than ever before' (Winant, 2009, p678).

Where there is 'race', there is racism. If 'race' and racism have strong currency in today's world, then the study of their impacts upon society is of vital importance. As Solomos (2003, p1) eloquently notes:

> At the beginning of the twenty first century it is clear that there has been a major transformation in this field and a noticeable flowering of theorising and research on race and racism. It is also evident that the study of race and racism is now of some importance in a wide range of academic disciplines, including sociology, politics, cultural studies, history, anthropology, geography and literary theory.

The disciplines of media and sport can be added to this list and form the focus of this book, which seeks to better understand how issues of 'race' and racism are represented in the mediated reporting of sport. This current chapter provides theoretical foundations for subsequent chapters analysing reporting across a range of sports. The chapter attempts to define and discuss a number of key concepts, including 'race', racisms and national identity, before applying these concepts to sport and the sports media.

'Race'

The concept of 'race' is arguably one of the most difficult terms to explain and fully understand. 'Race' has been analysed and critiqued by elite thinkers from a vast range of disciplines, including social science, biology and socio-biology. Although the concept has been rigorously analysed for centuries, we still cannot provide a single definition of what a 'race' really is. As Malik (1996, pp1–2) suggests: 'everyone knows what a race is but no one can quite define it'. Thus, one has to question why 'race' is still used in everyday discourse despite the fact that it does not actually have a concrete meaning. Its complexity is further highlighted by Malik (1996, p265), who argues 'that the meaning of "race" cannot be confined to a simple definition or reduced to a single property or relationship'. Hence, it has been argued that 'race' is not only ambiguous, but can only be understood when located within its social and historical context (Pilkington, 2003). Put simply, 'race' does not stay static and monolithic in its meaning; it evolves and changes along with society (Back and Solomos, 1996).

What can be agreed, however, is that 'race' attempts to draw 'boundaries between people' (Pilkington, 2003, p11). In short, 'race' is a 'coding' based on the belief that the perceived difference is permanent and fixed. Historically, this categorization is based on the perceived differences of bodily appearance, primarily skin colour. The notion of 'race' as 'colour' is a powerful metaphor. Aime Cesaire (cited in Fanon, 1986, p118) argues: 'As colour is the most obvious outward manifestation of race it has been made the criterion by which men are judged.'

The ideological connotations that attach themselves to these 'constructed' differences are also of great significance. Cashmore (1996, p294) suggests that 'the main issue is not what a "race" is but the way it is used'. For example, skin pigmentation has been used to differentiate between groups; however, it is the ideological connotations that accompany this difference that present the most significant problems.

Almost 250 years since its arrival, we still cannot define 'race' in simple terms because of its complex and mutating nature (Goldberg, 1990). The concept of 'race' is 'fundamentally flawed' from a biological point of view (Fleming, 2001a, p115) and its relevance today creates debate among academics. For Miles (1989, p72), 'race' is 'an idea that should be explicitly and consistently confined to the dustbin of analytically useless terms'. Montagu (1974, p62) adds that 'race' should be dropped from the vocabulary completely due to its 'unjustifiable generalisations'. Nevertheless, although some academics have criticized the usage of 'race', others argue that it still serves a purpose. Mason (2000) indicates that racially stereotyped images of 'Others' work to protect the positions of power of dominant groups. Cashmore and Troyna (1990, p32) examine the fragile nature of 'race' from a scientific perspective, but then highlight that 'race' has been and still is a powerful ideology. Carrington and McDonald (2001b) go further and argue that 'race' science has by no means been completely destroyed, especially within a sporting context.

For many, then, the concept of 'race' still holds great power as it has the ability to single out individuals and groups in a meaningful and problematic fashion. It is important that we seek to understand how these processes work. In other words, 'race' still matters (Alexander and Knowles, 2005; Winant, 2009).

Racisms

While the concept of 'race' has a long history, the term racism only entered popular discourse following the Second World War and partly in response to the genocide carried out by the Nazis (who partly justified their atrocities by pseudo-scientific thinking). For Mason (2000, p9), the term racism is almost as contentious as 'race'. 'It is used both as an analytic concept and as a popular political epithet; more often than not in an untheorized and sloppy way' (Mason, 2000, p9).

For some writers, racism is an ideology (Miles, 1989), while for others it is a system of practice evident in social actions and structures more commonly known as institutional racism. Benedict (1983) explained racism as unfounded beliefs about the superiority of one race over another justified by inherent biological traits. For example:

> We can define racism as any set of claims or arguments which signify some aspect of the physical features of an individual or group as a sign of permanent distinctiveness and which attribute additional negative characteristics and or consequences to the individual's or group's presence.
> (Miles, 1989, p149)

This emphasis on physical/biological traits that underpins racist thinking is further elaborated upon by Cashmore (1982, p27), who notes that the consequence of this is an 'ordering' of human populations:

> Racism is the doctrine that the world's population is divisible into categories based on physical differences which can be transmitted genetically. Invariably, this leads to the conception that the categories are ordered hierarchically so that some elements of the world's population are superior to others.

Pilkington (2003, p189) defines racism as a discourse. First, one must identify groups based on physical markers; see essential differences between them; associate 'Others' with negative characteristics; and visualize the dissolution of the boundaries as undesirable. For Pilkington (2003), 'race' thinking has advanced; however, contemporary society very rarely attempts to showcase racial superiority. Even so, the debate about racism continues to persist due to its unstable and ambiguous meaning. Cashmore (1996, p298) poses a contemporary view of racism as he articulates that 'societies that recognize social races are invariably racist societies, in the sense that people, especially members of the dominant racial group, believe that physical phenotype is linked with intellectual, moral, behavioural characteristics. Race and racism thus go hand in hand.'

It has been argued that new forms of racism have emerged within contemporary society (Barker, 1981; Todorov, 1986; Gilroy, 1993a; Mason, 2000). Goldberg (1990, pxiii) argues that 'the presumption of a single monolithic racism is being displaced by a mapping of the multifarious historical formulations of racisms'. Thus, traditional forms of racism linked to biological difference have perhaps become outdated as racism has now attached itself to cultural differences between racial or ethnic groups. Therefore, Pilkington (2003, p18) notes that 'in the case of new racism race is coded as culture'. Hence, 'the question of cultural production and the politics of identity are fast becoming an important area of contemporary debate' (Back and Solomos, 1996, p17).

Although new cultural forms of racism are said to have emerged, Huyssen (1995) suggests that national identity and images of culture have always been linked with racism despite the emphasis during the nineteenth and twentieth centuries being on biological 'superiority'. If we take an historical approach here, not only has alleged racial 'superiority' been based on phenotypical features, but also on social class, too. Hence, one has to acknowledge that 'race' and racism have always been broad and complex concepts. It is therefore quite clear that, historically, racism as an exclusionary practice has always taken various forms. This has led some to suggest that symbolic racism is now evident (Gilroy, 1987; van Dijk, 1993).

One could define symbolic racism as ethnic or racial symbols that 'out-groups' display, which work to construct their homogeneous group identity. Significantly, it is the homogenization of 'Others' that is the issue here as ethnic features, dress and foods work to group together all those who visually express their religion and culture. As a result, 'Others' are grouped as one, problematically possessing no individuality. Furthermore, such cultural features are perhaps seen to clash with 'homeland values'. This arguably results in a feeling of 'us' versus 'them', the 'insiders' against the 'outsiders'. Hence, within the 'new racisms' framework, the concepts of national identity and ethnicity have become closely linked because it is through these notions that one's identity is created. In short, it is in this complex context that racism truly highlights its multiplicity.

What is clear is that racism is not just a passing phenomenon; it changes and mutates as new meanings are constantly being created. Malcolm X once used a metaphor from popular culture to eloquently describe its shifting meaning: 'Racism is like a Cadillac. The 1960 Cadillac doesn't look like the 1921 Cadillac, but it is still a Cadillac; it has simply changed form' (cited in Otis, 1993, p151). This metaphor arguably highlights that racism has changed from a biological to a cultural meaning within a relatively short period of time. However, whatever the detours may be, one constant remains: 'ultimately, the goal of racism is dominance' (Memmi, 2009, p131).

Hall (1990a, pp12–13) categorizes racism into two categories. He defines *overt racism* as:

> Those many occasions when open and favourable coverage is given to arguments, positions and spokespersons who are in the business of elaborating an openly racist argument or advancing a racist policy or view.

For example, this term could be applied to extreme right-wing groups who wish to repatriate all non-white communities from Western countries to their country of ancestral origin, or individuals and groups who actively seek out and verbally and physically abuse non-white minority groups. This type of racism is very visible and almost clear cut. The *racist skinhead* can be easily identified. Some racist groups also continue to employ biological reasoning in their arguments that blacks are less intelligent, etc. Indeed, if one looks at the increase in racist attacks throughout Western Europe on stigmatized minority groups, it could be argued that overt racism is widespread and rising. Witness, for example, the rise of the openly far-right British National Party in Britain, the National Front in France and the shift to populist right-wing governments in Denmark (*European Race Bulletin*, 2007).

However, even this definition is open to interpretation. For example, those who oppose immigration, especially from countries who have a non-white population, may construct their argument on cultural difference or economic necessity rather than racial origin and deny that they are racist. Indeed, it may be the case that these individuals only categorize real racists and real racism as being exclusive to extreme right-wing views. This feeling may be summarized as: 'I am not racist, but … '. Even the right-wing British National Party claim not to be racist and to welcome non-white members, but to be worried about the identity of British culture. However, a closer analysis of their politics reveals more a public relations makeover rather than a deep ideological shift (Kundnani, 2007).

Hall (1990a, p13) suggests that more covert or subtle racism can be classified as *inferential racism*, which refers to:

> … those apparently naturalised representations of events and situations relating to race, whether 'factual' or 'fictional', which have racist premises and propositions inscribed in them as a set of unquestioned assumptions. These enable racist statements to be formulated without ever bringing into awareness the racist predicates on which the statements are grounded … inferential racism is more widespread – and in many ways, more insidious [than overt racism], because it is largely invisible even to those who formulate the world in its terms.

In many ways, inferential racism is based on 'common-sense' thinking. For example, if black athletes do well in sports, it is because they are naturally good at sport. This form of racism is sometimes referred to as 'new' or 'symbolic' racism.

It could be argued that inferential, symbolic and new racisms are ideologies and beliefs that influence social actions and structures. In society, this can manifest itself in what has been termed *institutional racism* (Solomos, 2003). While this term entered British popular discourse (Cottle, 2004) with the publication of the *Macpherson Report* in 1999 (following the murder of black teenager Stephen Lawrence), the concept can originally be found in the writings of black activists Stokely Carmichael and Charles Hamilton. Writing in

1967 about the conditions of blacks in America, they argued that racism was not just the attitudes of a few white people but was intrinsic to US society. They note that institutional racism is harder to challenge, but in many ways is more pervasive than overt racism:

> When a black family moves into a house in a white neighbourhood and is stoned, burned or routed out, they are victims of an overt act of individual racism which many people will condemn – at least in words. But it is institutional racism that keeps black people locked in dilapidated slum tenements ... The society either pretends it does not know of this latter situation ...
>
> (Carmichael and Hamilton, 1967, p4)

This suggests that racism, as well as being an individual act, is also a part of the fabric of society and can be seen in various settings, including the media and sport. At times, this manifestation is overt; but more often it is covert and less likely to gain public condemnation or even acknowledgement. This suggests that the foundations of contemporary racism are to be found disguised within institutions and organizations. Carmichael and Hamilton (1967, p112) note that those with racist beliefs may 'not stone a black family', nor would they be involved in any other personal racist activity; but they may continue to support and involve themselves with institutions that perpetrate racist policies.

Examples of institutional racism in sport could include the lack of black people in positions of authority, both on and off the field, in different sports. For example, Owusu (2008) identified that until 2006, there had been only 10 black head coaches in the history of American football, compared to more than 310 white head coaches. This was despite the facts that black players comprised approximately 69 per cent of those in the game (Owusu, 2008, p6). Similarly, a number of studies (Blalock, 1962; Loy and McElvogue, 1970) have identified a disproportionate allocation of players to specific team positions on the basis of their race or ethnicity. Majority group players typically occupied positions considered as central, which involved most communication and interaction with others, as well as control over others, decision-making and leadership potential (Blalock, 1962; Loy and McElvogue, 1970). Minority group members occupied those positions considered as peripheral, involving mainly athleticism and 'instinct' (Blalock, 1962; Loy and McElvogue, 1970). One can see 'race' thinking here. Blacks are not mentally intelligent or astute enough for the central positions, but can perform the physical, less mentally demanding, tasks.

As many researchers have pointed out (Balibar, 1991; Gilroy, 1987, 1993a; Miles, 1993; Pilkington, 2003; Solomos, 2003), it is no longer relevant to talk of racism as a fixed, static, all-encompassing concept, but rather to examine it in terms of specific racisms. In short, the focus should be on how different racisms manifest themselves as they affect specific groups in various locations and times.

One could suggest that the continuation of hierarchical sporting stereotypes, or classical racism, has hindered the performances of some ethnic groups in sport. The 'natural ability' stereotype implies that some 'races' are more genetically and anatomically adept to some sporting actions over others. Problematically, though, this unfounded ideology harbours a darker meaning, indicating that those with 'natural ability' are not only lazier, but are physiologically closer to nature, less evolved and, ultimately, intellectually lacking (Hoberman, 1997).

One could suggest that longstanding colonial stereotypes referring to black intellectual inferiority have potentially exacerbated their exclusion from management and senior positions within sport. Back et al (2001, p180) argue that 'prospective black managers have to face preconceptions about their assumed incapacity to manage multi-racial teams even handedly, or cope with the organizational load of football management and its associated responsibilities'. Put simply, mediated stereotypes can and do have a real impact upon ethnic minority groups within sport.

Despite 'race' science being deemed invalid, Hoberman (1997) argues that the benign 'natural ability' stereotype, based upon classically racist ideals, has problematically been internalized by both white and non-white communities. Allison (1998, p146) argues that the real problem 'is not that whites classify blacks as "physical" beings, but that blacks accept this classification. If black people defined themselves as intellectuals, white prejudice would no longer prevent them from achieving the elusively "normal" levels of social mobility.' Problematically, then, a number of black athletes, including ex-footballer Garry Thompson (Cashmore, 1982) and former boxer Jimmy Dublin (Hoberman, 1997), have spoken out, insisting that blacks are the most athletically gifted 'race'.

Similarly, Vijay Amritraj, a former tennis player turned Hollywood star, said: 'As a race, we are also handsomely endowed with hand-to-eye co-ordination, which is why so many of our youngsters excel naturally at ball sports like cricket, squash and tennis' (Amritraj and Evans, 1990, cited in Fleming, 2001b, p116). 'Race' becomes an explanation of sporting success which overlooks other important inclusionary and exclusionary factors, such as cultural background, social segregation, education and economic wealth, as well as 'racisms'. Hence, notions of classical racism have arguably permeated the consciousness of elite sporting figures, athletes, fans and media consumers, which has impacted upon some racial or ethnic groups' relationships with sport.

Although sporting stereotypes can digress into acts of racialism (Cashmore, 2005), sport can also provide a platform to combat 'racisms'. Initiatives such as *Kick It Out*, *Show Racism the Red Card* and *Hit Racism for Six* have been established in a bid to achieve equality through tackling racism, homophobia and xenophobia, among other discriminatory practices.

National identity

For some, the evolution of racism is now witnessed in debates surrounding national identity and belonging. Thus, Solomos and Back (1996, p18) indicate that many studies have begun to explore the 'interconnections between race and nationhood, patriotism and nationalism rather than ideas about biological inferiority'. Barker (1982) argues that the 'new racism' essentially attempted to link 'race' with nation and culture. Brah (1996) does make the point that even 'old-fashioned' racism employed notions of cultural difference as signifiers of innate 'racial difference'. However, 'the new racism' was different in that, on the one hand, it combined a disavowal of biological racism while articulating this in a 'New Right' discourse on 'nation and family' (Hall and Jacques, 1983).

Nations only emerged as mass phenomena during the eighteenth and nineteenth centuries as a result of 'complex economic, political and cultural changes which encouraged their formation and made it possible for national identities to be widely disseminated' (Pilkington, 2003, p176). McCrone (1998, p24) notes that 'nation', which is derived from the Roman term '*natio*', meaning a breed or 'race', came into popular discourse to ultimately describe 'a distinct group of people characterised by common descent, language or history'. Thus, it is evident that there are overlapping similarities between 'race', ethnicity and national identity. Nevertheless, the simplest way to differentiate between these concepts is related to the degree of permanency that they hold. 'Race' is argued to be fixed at birth, permanent and commonly related to skin colour; ethnicity, which is coded as culture, is not fixed as one's identity is always in process (Hall, 1992a); while one's national identity is unchangeable, bound by blood and steeped in tradition through continuous exposure to historical and patriotic symbols (Miles, 1989; McCrone, 1998).

Anderson (1991) observed that the boundaries assembled in the construction of nations were possible only in particular historical contexts – namely, the emergence of print media and the onset of industrial capitalism. These facilitated the production of 'imagined communities' whereby people within man-made physical boundaries were compelled to rally themselves around integrative symbols that evoke feelings of solidarity, simultaneity and unison (Anderson, 1991, p145). Although most people within such 'communities' have little or nothing in common with their fellow compatriots (and will never even meet or hear about the vast majority of them), they remain connected by their shared recognition of constructed 'national' symbols, such as the national anthem (Anderson, 1991, p160).

They are constituted out of the historical heritage that they make their own, and they transform themselves in terms of the material provided to them from this heritage. As Smith (1996, p385, cited in McCrone, 1998, p16) comments:

> There is considerable evidence that modern nations are connected with earlier ethnic categories and communities and are created out of pre-existing

origin myths, ethnic cultures and shared memories; and that those nations with a vivid, widespread sense of an ethnic past are likely to be more unified and distinctive than those which lack that sense.

Therefore, our individual or group identities are arguably formed and strengthened as a result of constant exposure to historical symbols and references. For Hall (1996), then, the 'narrative' of a nation can be told and retold through national histories, literatures, images and rituals; through these stories, national identity is presented as primordial and constant. The definitions of a nation can be inclusive or exclusive, and this can be represented through the media.

National identity, like ethnicity and 'race', is a situational entity that is constructed upon socially defined cultural representations. This can be clearly exemplified within the socially constructed concepts of 'Englishness' and 'Britishness'. Various authors (Gilroy, 1987; Hall, 1992a; Modood, 1997) have pointed out that the homogenized view of Englishness and Britishness as being a synonym for 'whiteness' has led to the terms being classified away from ethnic boundaries. Modood (1997) calls 'British' a 'quasi-ethnic' term that does not allow for the inclusion of ethnic minorities such as black British or Pakistani-British. Hall (1992a, p257) discredits 'Englishness' as an ethnicity altogether. Solomos (2003, p240) refers to the Parekh report's findings on the two terms:

> Britishness, as much as Englishness, has systematic, largely unspoken, racial connotations. Whiteness nowhere features as an explicit condition of being British, but it is widely understood that Englishness, and therefore by extension Britishness are racially coded.

One of the most effective strategies followed by those hostile to a black presence in Britain has been to argue that blackness and Britishness are mutually exclusive categories (Gilroy 1987). Growing ethnic diversity is portrayed as a threat to the order and cohesiveness of the 'British way of life'. Analysis of political debates about race reveals that this argument has taken a variety of forms (Solomos, 2003); indeed, attempts to develop policies of 'anti-racism' are portrayed as un-British and evidence of the incompatibility of cultures and the unwillingness or inability of migrants to become British (van Dijk, 1993).

It can be seen from the previous discussion, then, that national identity is a much debated concept and that it has a relationship to issues of 'race', racism and identity. Gilroy (1993b) argues that sporting discourse helps to shape our national identities that, in turn, influence our understanding of 'race' and racism. Sport is sociologically important to nationalism because it represents the highly emotional ritual out of which imagined national communities arise. The importance of sport's contribution to the development and promotion of national identity has been discussed by a number of writers (see Billig, 1995; Boyle and Haynes, 2009; Blain et al, 1993). Sport and certain sporting contests in many ways are seen as a celebration or support of national identity. Creedon (1994, p27) suggest that athletes become symbolic warriors. At times of great sporting events, feelings of national identity can lead to outcries of nationalism. Elias (cited in Bernstein and Blain, 2003, p13) notes that 'sport continues to constitute an area of social activity in which overt emotional engagement remains purely acceptable'.

According to Gellner (1964), the force of nationalism can help to characterize and engender a nation. Whannel (1992) notes that various sporting studies have shown that there is a small step from outbursts of nationalism to the reliance on national stereotypes and, at times, outright racism. At this point, the uneasy relationship between national identity, belonging and minority groups can come to the fore. Young (2011), in an analysis of how national identity emotions were highlighted through the English football team at the 2010 World Cup, summarizes how issues of 'imagined community', symbolic flags and 'race' and ethnicity combine to include debates of inclusion and exclusion:

> For better or worse, every other team in the World Cup, from North Korea to Paraguay, boasts the basic tropes of nationhood: a state, a leader, an anthem and an army. Their identification with the national team emerges from their national identity ... The problem with this is that English identity is a very fragile thing. The re-emergence of the St George's cross as a popular symbol is relatively recent and completely contested. Some have an ambivalent relationship to it. The journey from rightwing totem to national emblem is by no means complete. Whether it signifies a grievance at the absence of nationhood, or a desire for racial and ethnic exclusion, depends on who is waving it and the experience of those who see it. Only in sport does it have any hope of sending a consensual, coherent message. Unfortunately, English football is an inadequate conduit for such a crucial conversation.

For Carrington and McDonald (2001b, p4), 'the inclusion of Asian and black communities into the lived cultures of contemporary Britain, including Britain's sporting culture, has decidedly re-shaped questions of local, regional and national identity for *all* Britons'. Thus, we need to accept that Britain is not a mono-cultural entity as people should be allowed to be British on their own terms. In short, 'a multicultural society that requires the prevailing view of national identity should allow its members to entertain dual and even multiple identities' (Parekh, 2000, p205, cited in Burdsey, 2006, p22). Problematically, though, if national identity is steeped in history and tradition, one could argue that within a sorting context it may exclude those who are deemed not to belong.

One could argue that some groups are deterred from sport at any level due to exclusionary policies or a feeling of 'not belonging'. Significantly, then, a poll conducted by the black British newspaper *New Nation* (cited in Burdsey, 2007a, p88) tested notions of nationalism through sport. They asked participants: if it came down to a choice between England and Nigeria, who would they prefer to be knocked out of the World Cup? The results showed that 33 per cent wanted England to fail, thus highlighting the black British populations' affiliation to Africa over England. One could argue that this result is highly surprising considering that black Britons have become a commonality within English football. For Carrington (1998a, p118, cited in Burdsey, 2007a, p88):

> The fact that the majority of the black population living in England had either a large degree of ambivalence towards England or openly supported 'anyone but England' underscores the point being made that the form of national identity produced failed to be inclusive and actually alienated large sections of the nation from view.

National belonging was famously tested via sport in 1990 when conservative British politician Norman (now Lord) Tebbit's infamous 'cricket test' called on diasporic ethnic minorities to prove their loyalty and desire to integrate within Britain by showing support for the English cricket team (Werbner, 2005, p756). Tebbit diagnosed multiculturalism as a threat and demanded allegiance to a supposedly mono-cultural British nation (Hesse, 2000, p4), represented by the England cricket team.

Carrington (1998) and Williams (2001) have shown that black Britons have used cricket to express an explicit anti-racism platform. Recreational cricket offers an opportunity to eschew exclusion from elite leagues, overturn hierarchies of dominance, subvert police harassment, and destabilize class subordination while athletes connect to their homeland, language, ethnic pride and community. Stoddart (2006, p803) found that international Test cricket spectatorship offered the same openings. In 1984, when the black Windies team executed an historic massacre of a white English team in England (5–0 in five matches), with the result repeated at home in the Caribbean four years later, celebrations abounded in black inner-city areas from Bristol to Leeds. The wins were labelled by these supporters as a 'blackwash' (as opposed to a whitewash).

The role of the media

The reason that the mass media are so important in contemporary society is because it is all around us. Various authors, such as Bagdikian (1997), Sparks and Tulloch (2000) and Lewis (2001), argue that there is no alternative to the mass media for knowing about the world outside of our immediate surroundings. Its influence on public opinion is the most important factor in how the public define their opinions. It provides the window to the outside world.

Hall (1978) and van Dijk (1991) note that the media, in all forms, have an important mediating role in creating public opinion. In 'race' and ethnic relations, the media provides information where public knowledge is fragmentary. Research into the media's treatment of 'race' over the years has suggested that its reporting has been limited in its themes and negative in its content. Research into minority representation in the British context can be summarized in two distinct but complementary stages. First, immigration issues have been formulated as a 'problem' or in terms of a fear of 'swamping'. Second, minorities who were born in Britain have also been perceived to be 'problems'. From the criminal mentality of the Afro-Caribbeans (Hall, 1978), the cheating Asians (Sivanandan, 1986), to the Islamic fundamentalists (Ahmed, 1993), minority communities tend to be represented in negative ways.

The role of the media in the increasingly multicultural and multi-ethnic societies of Europe is crucial. Whereas many, if not most, native citizens in most countries have no or little daily interaction with immigrants, information about immigration and ethnic minorities is largely based on information from the mass media, or from informal everyday conversations that are, in turn, based on information from the media (van Dijk, 1991). The critical role that media play within multi-ethnic contemporary societies has also been recognized within the world of journalism and the media themselves. Some active attempts to address the challenge already exist, such as the work of the International Federation of Journalists (IFJ) and their Media Working Group against Racism and Xenophobia. The working group Migrants and the Media of The Netherlands Association of Journalists has published a booklet entitled *Balance and Blunder*, which provides recommendations for reporting migrants. The National Union of Journalists in Britain has conducted substantial work and published *Guidelines on Race Reporting*.

In many respects, the media representation of minority groups is a 'double-edged sword'. First, it marginalizes minority voices, who are virtually ignored or invisible (Saeed, 1999). Simultaneously, actual representation of minority groups is often construed in negative discourses (Hartmann and Husband, 1974). When these frameworks are applied to audiences who have little social contact with minority groups, the role of the media as sole provider (or primary definer; see Hall, 1978) becomes crucial (van Dijk, 1991). Cottle (2000b, 2006) argues that the media hold a powerful position in conveying, explaining and articulating specific discourses that help to represent (and misrepresent) minority groups.

Within the sporting world, discussion about media representations are basically about issues of power and status. For example, Whannel (1992, p206) suggests in relation to British sporting representations that 'blacks are not quite full Britons'. Sabo et al (1996, p182) summarize the sporting media relationship with 'race' as: 'sport media are complicit in ... the larger institutional and cultural processes that reproduce and exonerate white men's domination over black men'. Arguably, the continuation and internalization of sporting stereotypes not only keeps alive the ideology of genetic difference, but also maintains the 'racial' status quo or hierarchy, whereby white identities are 'the principal site of efficiency and productivity' (Hoberman, 1997, p116). What is clear from the debate is that sporting stereotypes are far from innocent as they can easily transgress into 'out-and-out racism' (Bernstein and Blain, 2003, p15). As a result, it is vital that the future generation of aspiring sports journalists and commentators acknowledge that racial stereotypes can influence media consumers.

It has been argued that the media often present ideas about biological difference without challenging them; this is particularly true within the realm of sports reporting. As a result, sport media could be said to uphold rather than contest the ideology of biological difference between 'races' (Hoberman, 1997). Thus, it is necessary to investigate this claim in a bid to understand if, and how, the media keep, construct and reproduce these ideologies.

This 'problematizing' of non-white communities by the mainstream media has been replicated across Western countries. Non-white immigrant and even non-white indigenous communities have been represented in a narrow set of negative discourses. Within sport media, the same discourse can be found when representing athletes from minority groups. Brookes (2002) employs the notion of 'role models' and 'bad boys' and seems to imply that media representations of minority sportsmen fall into these categories.

It has been suggested that sport, with the media's help, can bring the world together (Brookes, 2002; Bernstein and Blain, 2003; Rowe, 2003b; Boyle and Haynes, 2009). One only has to witness the Football World Cup or the Olympic Games to see how sporting competitions can unite people from all over the planet. Conversely, sport can also separate nations and exclude 'Others'. For Boyle and Haynes (2009, p147), the media play a pivotal role in formulating national identities, as in many instances discourses of identity 'can be constructed or even at times invented, if the political or economic climate is suitable'. Hence, the media hold a highly influential position as they have the power to influence ideologies on contentious issues which, for example, can affect notions of belonging.

Hylton (2009, p1), in a concise summary of 'race' thinking in sport, notes:

> There is a popular perception in sport that our genes and to a degree our cultural background dictates the prowess of an individual sportsman or woman. This discourse of advantage and of course disadvantage in sport is invariably reduced to 'harmless' racial differences, a reduction that suggests, however, a more sinister undercurrent.

Although 'race' has become popularly coded as culture during recent times, it has been argued that physicality could be the reason behind the black domination of the 100m dash or the Kenyan success in long-distance running (Kane, 1971; Goldberg, 1990). Hence, 'stereotypes of the "natural" black athlete have been used to explain the apparent over representation of black people in sports' (Boyle and Haynes, 2009, p112). In its mass-produced and consumed form, the media is defined as key in circulating assumptions of 'blackness'. Carrington and McDonald (2001b, p6) argue it as a paramount force in 'validating popular beliefs about the existence of "race" and racial difference'. The same ideology has been positioned alongside South Asians because of their healthy participation in 'stick' sports, such as cricket and hockey. In spite of 'race' science being critically challenged within wider society, in sport this problematic ideology is still alive and kicking as over half the respondents to a 1991 poll agreed that 'blacks have more natural athletic ability' (Hoberman, 1997, p50).

Black sporting success was, at times, 'explained' through racial connotations. Although one could suggest that sporting representations may primarily appear harmless, Hoberman (1997, p116) states that the 'theory of sportive stereotypes depicts a Eurocentric discourse that identifies North-western (Europe) as the principal site of efficiency and productivity and Africa as the exemplary sinkhole of inefficiency and underdevelopment'. Hence, at the bottom of the racial hierarchy lie the Africans, whose stereotype appears to 'perpetuate the image of underdevelopment' (Hoberman, 1997, p117). Linked to this is the assumption that blacks were 'naturally' gifted in terms of physical ability.

Dyson (1993, p66) clearly summarizes this argument as follows:

> Coupled with this fear of superior black physical prowess was the notion that inferior black intelligence limited the ability of blacks to perform excellently in those sports activities that required mental concentration and agility. These two forces – the presumed lack of sophisticated black cognitive skills and the fear of superior black physical prowess – restricted black sports participation to thriving but financially handicapped subcultures of black athletic activity.

Although it may sound innocent, or even a compliment, to suggest that some racial groups possess some form of 'natural' sporting ability; in reality, it borders on outright racism. The 'natural athlete' stereotype, which will be investigated throughout this book, implies that black athletes have some form of natural inborn ability for certain tasks. Thus, one could argue that this stereotype almost indicates that some 'racial' groups, who possess this 'gift', do not have to work as hard as white groups in order to achieve success.

A number of academic studies and empirical research suggests that young blacks, especially men, actually believe that the black body is superior when it comes to certain sports. This false assumption encourages some young people to believe that it is innate biological ability that compels them to excel at certain sports. This attitude is further strengthened when young black men feel marginalized or socially excluded in other sections of society, hence assuming that sport is the only viable avenue (Harrison and Lawrence, 2004; Lawrence, 2005).

Despite the contentious academic debates about the suitability of the concept of 'race' and the burden of racial stereotypes, a number of recent studies have argued that the way the myth of the 'natural black athlete' is promoted in the media and wider culture is very persuasive in society, and difficult to challenge (Hayes and Sugden, 1999; Stone et al, 1999; Carrington and McDonald, 2001b; Harrison and Lawrence, 2004; Azzarito and Solomon, 2006).

Harrison and Lawrence's (2004) research showed that college students in an overwhelmingly white Midwestern university in the US accepted the racial stereotype that black athletes are superior in certain sports to whites due to their 'race'. Furthermore, in the UK (Hayes and Sugden, 1999; Carrington and McDonald, 2001b), research demonstrated that even older physical education teachers of different ethnic backgrounds believed in blacks' natural or intrinsic physical superiority. This raises urgent questions about the role of schooling and education in challenging the social and racial inequalities that inform young people's physicality.

Hoberman (1997) notes that some black athletes themselves have such belief in these stereotypes that it has a major influence on their occupational and aspiration life choices. This is similar to the work of Stone et al (1999), who argue how black and white individuals' embodiment of negative stereotypes about the body can further adversely affect their performance in sport. Likewise, Stone et al (1997) found that college students (predominantly white participants) accepted the 'white men can't jump' stereotype, and this racialized thinking informed their opinions of basketball players' skills and performances.

Implicit assumptions about 'race' are evident in both the sociology and media coverage of sport. When athletes are white, racial thinking becomes invisible. Success is determined and discussed on social and cultural factors, such as individual hard work and perseverance. This is why social scientists rarely do studies attempting to identify the genes amongst white British golfers or white Eastern European weightlifters. In speed skating, white men and women lead the sport, yet race-related genetic ancestry and racial similarity of the skaters is not studied from a racial perspective. In the same way, there have been no assertions that white Canadians should argue that their success in hockey is due to naturally strong ankle joints, natural eye–hand–foot coordination or a native tendency not to sweat so that they can preserve body heat in cold weather. Yet, black sporting success has been investigated and studied and writers have attempted to explain the superiority of West Africans in sprinting or East Africans in long-distance running. However, when black athletes excel in certain sports, many people seek to explain their success in terms of natural or instinctive qualities or weakness, rather than experience, strategy, motivation and intelligence. Some even suggest that success should be feared.

This is an indication of institutional racism or 'whitecentrism' (Hylton, 2009, p89) where 'whiteness can be seen as allocation of structural advantage or a way to see self and others'. We must continually remember that there is a lack of hard evidence to suggest that there are any significant biological differences between 'races' that could explain why one 'race' has outperformed another in a sport.

Research has shown that successes of black athletes have tended to be portrayed in a distorted way. While reporters and fans praised white athletes for their tactical skill, their strategy and their intelligence, black athletes have been celebrated for speed, power, leg power and stamina. According to much sports reporting, their performances have been due to uncontrollable external forces, while performances of white athletes were due to controllable internal forces (Davis and Harris, 1998, p158).

Studies have found that even sports commentary has ironically described black athletes as 'naturally gifted' (Staples and Jones, 1985; Jackson, 1989; Whannel, 1992; Harris, 1998), while drawing notice to white athletes' perceived 'intelligence', 'work ethic' and 'grace under pressure' (Birrell, 1989; Sage, 1990; McCarthy and Jones, 1997).

The black athlete has been characterized by writers and commentators as having 'innate talent', while the white athlete has had to subsequently 'overcome the odds' in order to achieve athletic success. In other words, black athletes are expected to 'make it', whereas white athletes must 'pursue their dreams' with what would appear to be 'limited ability' but tremendous hard work and sweat (Wonsek, 1992). Dewar (1993) argues that, in effect, these differential assumptions are an insidious way of explaining the lack of success many white athletes have experienced while minimizing the achievements of black athletes. Dewar's (1993) argument is similar to that of Edwards (1969) – made more than 40 years ago – arguing that white broadcasters did not adequately credit black athletes for their hard work, due, in part, to perceptions of 'race'. The premise that because they are black they are naturally physically gifted is clearly based on racist assumptions and 'race' thinking.

Harris (1998, pp158–159) summarizes this as follows:

> The Media often reinforce the stereotype that African-Americans are 'natural athletes'. This stereotype poses white athletes as clearly disadvantaged relative to black athletes, who are seen as having superior physiology ... Media treatment is more likely to give European-American athletes credit for being mentally astute, whereas African-American athletes are seldom credited for their intellect.

Other media stereotypes painted African-American athletes as self-centred, selfish and arrogant, whereas white athletes were described as hardworking team players. Some studies show that, still in the 1990s, the media sometimes applied an even more negative stereotype: the depicting of male

African-American athletes as uncontrolled, oversexed or violent (Davis and Harris, 1998, pp160–164). Likewise Denham et al (2002) have addressed the issue of stereotyping of 'race' in basketball commentary. The authors suggested that: '(a) white athletes are frequently praised for their perceived "intellect" and "leadership capacity", while (b) black athletes are often praised for being naturally talented'.

Hall (1990a) argues that these stereotypes are the product of institutional racism inherent in Western society that at times erupts in open, overt hostile racism. This overt racism can be evidenced in much of the early media coverage of black sportsmen (Gordon and Rosenberg, 1989). At times it still resurfaces under the guise of national identity and culture (Hylton, 2009).

As we have already suggested, it is possible to possess more than one identity. Therefore, Brookes (2002, p88) notes the 'visibility of "hybrid" or "diasporic" identities – sport has a major role to play in the production of both of these'. Thus, crucially, although national identity is presented as fixed and eternal, we must remember that it is continually reinvented: it is a matter of becoming, not being. Within sport, golfing superstar Tiger Woods is a perfect example of how identity is duplicitous. Woods states that he is 'Cablinasian', meaning that he is 'one-fourth Thai, one-fourth Chinese, one-fourth African American, one-eighth Native American, and one-eighth white European' (Coakley, 1998, p251, cited in Brookes, 2002, pp117–118). Hence, if the US media attempt to present an 'inclusive vision' of the nation that appeals to the dominant power block, one could suggest that Tiger Woods's complex identity would not 'fit in'. Nevertheless, Brookes (2002, p118) notes that his 'mixed background means that in different media discourses different aspects of his identities are projected onto him: sometimes black, sometimes Asian'. Hence, although some athletes have dual identities, one could argue that the media still label or, in other words, 'racialize' the athlete in question for the purpose of the story (Miles, 1989; Cashmore, 2005).

Brookes (2002) highlights the difference between the English and German media's representation of nationalism within a sporting context. The English press is characterized by a 'wilful nostalgia' with 'persistent reference to its military and imperial past', whereas the German press almost disregards its past and instead favours assertions of 'contemporary economic and political superiority' (Brookes, 2002, p95). As a result, one could suggest that the German notion of national identity, which may factor in modernity, will perhaps embrace 'Others' more so than English nationalism. Arguably, English or British nationalism may exclude 'Others' because its notions fail to account for a multicultural nation. Problematically, then, the dominant representation of English nationalism 'through media coverage of sport is one that contrasts English national identity with other national identities, and is characterised by a nostalgic discourse comparing the sporting performance of its current team with an imagined golden age' (Brookes, 2002, p101). Thus, it is no surprise that non-whites or other ethnic minority groups may feel excluded from participating and watching some sports.

Blain et al (1993) highlighted the difference in reporting between African and European teams at the Italia '90 World Cup. They found that the Cameroon players, for example, were presented as 'joyful' and 'enthusiastic' (Blain et al, 1993, p71); but following their defeat to England in the quarter finals, the media concocted explanations which suggested that their style of football had not yet 'grown up', reinforcing the time-worn notions of biological and, ultimately, African inferiority (Blain et al, 1993, p76). Thus, one could articulate that the media can make issues seem unrelated to 'race', although, in reality; 'race' is the central theme and driving force behind the story.

In terms of the sports media, then, notions of 'race' and national identity have overlapped. Racial stereotypes are constructed to explain a nation's national character. Studies have highlighted that the 'efficient German', 'fiery Latino', 'naturally gifted African' and 'weak South Asian' are heavily cited within sports commentary (Blain et al, 1993; Wenner, 1998). National character is used as a metaphor for 'race', which indicates that 'race' has shifted from biological to cultural and social connotations. Hence, nations (or 'races') become racialized, therefore reinforcing and perpetuating the existence of 'race'.

Conclusion

This chapter has tried to demonstrate that the concept of 'race' must be seen in relation to power and subordination – in other words, as an ideological construct. Hall (1996) argues that the illusion of 'race' is maintained in the media and popular culture through images of 'them' and 'us'. This representation often takes the form of binary oppositional relationships, such as good/bad and civilized/uncivilized, or within the sporting context of 'naturally gifted' or not. Furthermore, 'race' ideology continues to change in relation to religious beliefs, scientific theories, cultural theory and political and economic goals. Thus, 'race' is not just about classification; it also carries connotations and meanings. Much of these connotations or assumptions are based upon skin colour.

The process of constructing, creating and employing racial meanings and categorizations is built into the institutional structure of society. The influence of racial ideology or 'race' thinking in sport has been continuous and continues to be of paramount importance today. The idea of 'race' has had a powerful impact upon history, society and contemporary culture; but it has little to do with real biological diversity among human beings. That is because the idea of 'race' assumes categories and classification that people employ to understand or explain social differences, diversity and inequalities in the world. In short, 'race' is a myth based on socially constructed ideas about variations in human experience, skills, potential and abilities that are assumed to be biological.

'Race' is based on social meanings rather than an innate biological difference, and for many this is a difficult argument to understand.

The influence of this thinking in sport, and its representation in the media, has been, and continues to be, significant in contemporary society. The following chapters will explore the character and wider significance of these representations across a variety of sports.

Chapter 3

A level playing field?

Diversity and sports journalism

> I think it [a lack of diversity] is a particular problem within the whole media. There is little to no black representation in the newsroom. The visibility of a few masks the fact that so few are working in newsrooms in TV, radio and newspapers.
>
> Lord Herman Ouseley (Interview, 18 April 2011)

Introduction

This chapter examines the make-up of the sports journalism profession and discusses the causes and consequences of this. Who are the journalists who cover sport? To what extent does the profession reflect the ethnic diversity of sport and the wider community? If there is a lack of black and minority ethnic journalists, why is this? And what can be done about it?

The issue of diversity within sports journalism is important for a number of reasons. First, it could be argued to be of significance in itself. If we want to claim to live in a society that offers opportunity and meritocracy, then there should be no barriers to people succeeding in different walks of life. If black athletes can achieve on the pitch, then black writers should be able to achieve off it.

Second, diversity can be considered significant because of the consequences that stem from it or, perhaps more pertinently, from a lack of it. Later chapters in this book will analyse some of the subtle forms of racist discourse and stereotyping that can be found in sports coverage. A lack of diversity among sports writers can only serve to perpetuate these characteristics. As Boyle (2006a, p156) has commented: 'There is no doubt that the perpetuation of particular stereotypes around race that can find articulation in the discourses produced by sports journalism is, in part, enhanced by a relative lack of diversity among the collective body of sports journalists.'

In his international overview of research into media coverage, van Dijk (2009, p199) argues that the composition of the journalism profession is a recurring factor in the production of racist discourses:

> Many forms of ethnic bias ... are crucially influenced by the fact that in all white-dominated societies, ethnic journalists are discriminated against

in hiring, so that most newsrooms are predominantly white. And those (few) minorities being hired will tend to be recruited not only for their outstanding professionalism, but also because their ethnic ideologies (and especially their moderate antiracism) do not clash with those of the editors.

The following section provides some context for the discussion by examining previous research into the diversity of the journalism profession as a whole. Subsequent sections then analyse sports journalism, in particular, drawing on interviews with journalists to explore various barriers to succeeding in the profession and what can be done to overcome these.

Context: Journalism and diversity

Current figures suggest that journalism is a 'white'-dominated profession, particularly in the case of print journalism. Taking membership of the National Union of Journalists (NUJ) as a barometer, just 2.2 per cent of the NUJ's members from regional newspapers are black or minority ethnic (BME) journalists. This figure rises slightly to 3.7 per cent in terms of national newspapers. Broadcast journalism presents a slightly different picture, with 13.7 per cent of the NUJ's membership classed as BME.

The issue of diversity within the journalism profession has been a long-standing concern. In 2002, the Journalism Forum produced research showing that 96 per cent of journalists in the UK were white. In response, the Society of Editors conducted further research and found that levels of employment of minority ethnic journalists were 'very low' across the industry. Furthermore, even newspapers published in areas of high minority ethnic population were found to be performing poorly, with many having one or no such members of staff (Society of Editors, 2004).

The report concluded that: 'Progress will not be made until senior management and editors make minority ethnic recruitment to editorial one of their top priorities and keep it there' (Society of Editors, 2004, p11). However, many of the explanations for the poor performance were laid largely outside of the newsroom. Many editors complained that the crux of the problem was that they received a lack of applications from minority ethnic communities. Blame was also directed at journalism courses at colleges and universities for failing to recruit from these communities. In response, the report recommended measures, such as school visits by journalists, new work experience schemes and training bursaries targeted at increasing diversity (Society of Editors, 2004).

More recent statistics suggest support for the idea that there is a relative lack of BME students studying journalism and media-related subjects. For example, BME students now comprise 23 per cent of the university population – in line with their proportion of the population for that age range (Equality and Human Rights Commission, 2010). Yet, figures provided to us by the Higher

Education Statistics Agency for 2010 show that just 12 per cent of those studying journalism degrees were BME students. While more and more ethnic minorities are attending university, they tend not to see journalism as a subject for them. Similarly, figures from the National Council for the Training of Journalists (NCTJ, the professional training body of the journalism profession) show that 12 per cent of their registrations in 2010/2011 were BME students. However, there must be some caution over the reliability of these statistics as there was only a 41 per cent completion rate of the NCTJ's equality survey.

But while there is clearly an issue with the number of BME students pursuing journalism as a potential career, this does not supply a complete explanation of the problem. We need to look at other factors to paint a fuller picture of the situation. For example, the Society of Editors' report does not account for the fact that diversity reduces towards the higher end of the journalism profession. Barriers exist not only in gaining entry to journalism, but also within the profession once entry has been gained. As Temple (2008, p209) has observed: 'There is a lack of diversity in newsrooms, especially in positions of power.'

Research by the Sutton Trust (2006) found that the majority of leading journalists came from a very narrow, privileged section of society. Just 14 per cent of these editors, broadcasters and columnists were educated in comprehensive schools, despite these institutions accounting for 90 per cent of the school population as a whole. Furthermore, 45 per cent of the journalists were Oxbridge graduated, while nearly three-quarters of them had attended one of the country's 13 'Sutton Trust' leading universities. Perhaps surprisingly, the report found that levels of diversity at the top of the profession had decreased in the previous 20 years. Explanations for this lack of diversity included the low levels of pay and job security at junior levels; the high costs of living in London; and a job network and informal recruitment process that showed 'bias towards those with family or personal connections within the industry' (Sutton Trust, 2006).

There is something of a consensus that, although their situation is not ideal, the broadcast media are outperforming print outlets in terms of diversity (Society of Editors, 2004). This view is shared by Boyle (2006a, p156), who says: 'In some aspects television sports broadcasters ... have led their print colleagues, in the sense that television's on-screen sports presenters and reporters are more likely to reflect the diversity in terms of gender and ethnicity of the sporting audience they both speak to and also represent.' At first glance, this analysis seems to be supported by the fact that, currently, black and minority ethnic staff comprise 12.4 per cent of the BBC's workforce. However, if these statistics are limited to journalism roles, this figure drops to 7.2 per cent (Foster, 2010). In response, the BBC recently set up a Journalism Talent Pool aimed at increasing ethnic and social diversity within the corporation. The scheme combines carefully targeted job adverts with specially trained selection panels to create a talented, and diverse, group of potential recruits. As Carol Foster, a research officer for *Equal Opportunities Review*, explains:

'The aim of the JTP is to speed up the recruitment of journalists by finding and assessing talented people from a diverse range of backgrounds in advance of vacancies becoming available' (Foster, 2010).

But some of the responses to the BBC's approach show the potentially controversial and sensitive nature of this subject. *The Telegraph* criticized the corporation after obtaining figures through a Freedom of Information request showing that between 2007 and 2010, 24 out of 51 places on the BBC Journalism Training Scheme had gone to a black or minority ethnic student. Its article said:

> Almost half of the places on a coveted BBC journalism trainee scheme have gone to candidates from ethnic minorities, a Freedom of Information Act request has shown.
>
> It comes despite the fact that non-white people make up about a tenth of the population, and deliberately favouring one race over another for jobs is illegal.
>
> (Beckford and Midgley, 2010)

Despite these criticisms, evidence suggests that attempts to increase diversity have achieved patchy and localized success. For example, the latest employment census by Skillset identified huge variations in employment diversity across the country. Their figures, which apply to employment across all of the creative media industries – show that 17 per cent of the workforce in west London is from BME populations. This compares to just 0.4 per cent in north-east England (Skillset, 2009).

Of course, attempts to increase the diversity of newsrooms are not isolated to the UK. In fact, the issue is even more significant and sensitive in countries with higher ethnic minority populations. More than one third of the US population is from BME groups, yet people from these backgrounds comprise just 12.79 per cent of newsroom staff in US newspapers. While this figure is a drastic improvement from previous generations (3.95 per cent in 1978), it is actually a small decline (0.49 per cent) from the previous year (ASNE, 2011). These figures are worrying for those who wish to see greater and more representative levels of diversity within the journalism profession. Ronnie Agnew, co-chair of ASNE's Diversity Committee, said:

> The slight decline in minority newsroom representation may be small, but is part of a disturbing trend that we need to reverse. The US Census numbers clearly tell us that people of colour populations are growing, while our newsrooms aren't reflecting that growth. This should be a concern to all who see diversity as an accurate way of telling the story of a new America.

This section has provided an overview of issues relating to diversity within the journalism profession and journalism training. The following sections will focus on these issues in the context of sports journalism. The remainder of the chapter will outline the present situation within the profession, identify some of the current barriers to greater diversity, and look at the prospects for change.

Diversity and the sports journalism profession

If the journalism profession, as a whole, is limping along in its attempts to achieve meaningful diversity, then sports journalism is crawling on all fours. Lena Calvert, equalities officer for the NUJ, summed up the problem as follows: 'I would say that sports journalism until fairly recently has been a "white" preserve – unless the journalist was working for a Black newspaper or similar, such as *The Voice*. To a greater extent this is still the case for written media.'

Exceptions to this are noticeable for their rarity value in the UK national media. Black broadcasters include sports news presenter Sean Fletcher and Leon Mann at the BBC, and Mike Wedderburn and Roger Clarke at Sky Sports. In terms of print, there is sports writer Darren Lewis and cricket correspondent Dean Wilson at *The Mirror*, and, until recently, sports writer Greg Gobere at the *News of the World*. Clive Petty, night sports editor at *The Times*, is now the only black journalist in a senior editorial position in the national media following the departure of Hepburn Harrison-Graham from BBC radio sport. The situation, according to Leon Mann, is a 'damning' indictment of the profession.

The situation is poor across the profession of sports journalism, yet is particularly noticeable in some sporting contexts due to the contrast between participants and their counterparts in the media. For example, athletics is a sport with many black and Asian competitors, yet the press boxes are populated almost exclusively by white journalists.

Simon Turnbull, athletics correspondent for *The Independent* and chairman of the British Athletics Writers Association (BAWA), said:

> At the moment, there are only two black faces you see on the British athletics circuit, in terms of journalists, and when you compare that to what you see on the track ... I don't think we have a black member of the BAWA. We had a dinner recently for the BAWA awards and I had to give a speech and I looked around the room and there was one black face and that was a coach ... and I thought as a reflection of our sport that is just not on really. It's the same with the Americans – it's a case of white journalists covering a black team.
>
> (Interview, 24 February 2011)

The Sports Journalists' Association (SJA), the voluntary membership body that seeks to represent the profession, has very few ethnic minority members in its 800-plus membership. At a recent Sports Journalism awards ceremony,

Stan Collymore, now of TalkSport, tweeted that he was the only black face in the room. Steven Downes, secretary of the SJA, acknowledged: 'He may have been wrong, but if he was, he was out by maybe one' (Interview, 15 August 2011).

Even media organizations with a reputation for their liberal social values appear to be struggling to achieve genuine diversity in their sports journalism workforce. Anna Kessel, athletics correspondent for *The Guardian*, said she was dismayed when she looked around at the lack of diversity of her paper's newsroom. Rob Steen, sports writer and now senior lecturer in journalism, takes a similar view:

> You look at *The Guardian* as being foremost in offering opportunities to minorities. But if we're talking specifically about cricket, which is the sport that is ripest for better representation of British Asian journalists, I don't see a big change happening for a very long time. All *The Guardian*'s up-and-coming writers that I'm familiar with are white, and all the opportunities are going to come to those guys who are in the paper's pecking order right now.
>
> (Interview, 6 July 2011)

As is the case across the journalism profession, there is greater diversity in broadcast sports journalism than in the written press. For example, the 'whiteness' of the press room at athletics meetings is not mirrored in the composition of the broadcast tribune. As Steve Cram, former world record holder and BBC athletics commentator, recognizes, this is in large part due to the numbers of ex-athletes moving into broadcasting as a career:

> When I look around the broadcast tribune it's a real mix – probably because there are so many past performers who end up in commentary boxes. Maybe on the journalist side there's a different mix if you go into the press room and athletics has struggled to maintain the specialist, dedicated writers. The broadcasting side tends to have more of a follow-through from the participation field, so is bound to have a better mix of representation.
>
> (Interview, 5 April 2011)

A similar tendency can be observed in other sports. In football, a number of black ex-players now perform as high-profile commentators and pundits – people such as Garth Crooks and Mark Bright on the BBC, Chris Kamara on Sky Sports and Jason Roberts on Five Live. The Professional Footballers Association (PFA) has a training scheme aimed at helping BME players who want to make a career in the media. Lena Calvert, equalities officer for the NUJ, argues that such appointments have given broadcasting the edge in terms of diversity. She said: 'Broadcasters have been trying to improve matters and e BBC have looked to former stars from various sports to become presenters – Colin Jackson for example. Sky also have a number of ex-footballers doing media reports, but overall it's still small numbers even though the position is improving.'

However, there is a question mark over whether such presenters can be classed as journalists – hence their omission from the list above. Certainly, some are sceptical whether the appointment of these ex-players really does much to address the lack of diversity in sports journalism. There is a sense in which this is just a case of papering over the cracks. Steven Downes, secretary of the SJA, says:

> There's a degree of window dressing that goes on with this issue in the broadcast media. There are people working in the media because of what they did in their sporting careers rather than because of their journalistic and media abilities. And if you asked whether the on-screen situation reflects what's really going on in the journalistic profession, then the answer would be that it doesn't.
>
> (Interview, 15 August 2011)

If the high-profile broadcast careers of some former athletes can be seen as window dressing, then what about the few black sports journalists who are progressing in other parts of the media? What can their experiences tell us about diversity within the profession?

Darren Lewis is perhaps the most prominent example of a black sports journalist succeeding in the national print media. He has been football writer for *The Mirror* since 1999 and a regular contributor on Sky Sports and Talk-Sport. His break came when he impressed while doing part-time shifts at *The Mirror* during his day off from his job at the *Enfield Gazette*.

Dean Morse, head of sport at *Mirror* Newspapers, was the man who appointed Darren Lewis. He said:

> I think he'd been coming in on a Sunday with us and I thought he was a good lad. I knew he was going into *The Sun* during the week as well, and he just struck me as a really good, capable bloke and he had a rare talent among young sports journalists, in that he had very good people skills. People sort of radiated towards him – if he was in an office, people would come up and chat to him. That's a good skill to have as a reporter. I just sort of said to him one day: 'Do you want to get onto national newspapers – do you want to do football?' He was very keen, so I think I offered him a six-month contract and he hasn't looked back since really. He's great – a top-class operator. He's tried to leave a couple of times and I've fought to keep him. That's because he does have a great skill. People love Darren.
>
> (Interview, 20 August 2011)

This route up the professional ladder will be familiar to many journalists – get in to an organization on a part-time, and often voluntary, basis – show them what you can do – make contacts and get your face known – and then be in the right place when an opportunity arises.

The Mirror is also home for another prominent black sports writer – cricket correspondent Dean Wilson. Dean Morse explains how this appointment came about:

> Our cricket writer before Dean was Mike Walters, who was very highly regarded. But cricket writing is a tough job in that you're away from home a lot and it's tough on your family – you're gone for three or four months at a time and you're never at home at Christmas. Mike had a young family and said: 'I can't do this anymore.' So I needed someone for the 2006–2007 Ashes tour over that Christmas period. Dean was working on the Hayters agency and he was very good. He kept pestering me for the job and it was getting really near the time when we had to send someone to Australia. So I took the plunge on him, we parachuted him into the cricket press pack at the Ashes, and he thrived from day one. We were all very fortunate with that. Dean can tell people his first ever newspaper job was covering the Ashes in Australia after we'd won it in 2005, and it was front page stuff, never mind back page.
>
> (Interview, 20 August 2011)

Our third example of black sports journalistic success is Greg Gobere, who until recently, when his employer was closed due to the phone-hacking scandal, was sports writer at the *News of the World*. He originally got a job as a features writer thanks to the fact that he knew someone on the paper. He says he was one of only two black employees in the office – the other being his ex-girlfriend who worked as a secretary. For one of his first assignments, Greg was sent to St Lucia to find Amy Winehouse. The rationale in the office was that 'because he was black, people wouldn't think he was a journalist'. After serving his time on features, and thanks to his persistence and pestering, Greg eventually got his chance on the sports desk. His experience was frequently one of being the only black face in a press room. He said: 'Every single press room I've been in abroad, I've been the only black or Asian face – that's France, Spain, Germany or wherever.' On occasion, he was even mistaken for being a player, rather than a journalist.

But despite being one of the few, Greg struggled to find rarity value in his position. In fact, he felt that black players and agents often shunned him because he was black, and they felt they needed to develop a rapport with white journalists to get on in the game:

> I thought that with the black players it would be easier for me as there's no one else out there. Socially I get on with them fine, but in a work sense

they'd rather go to a white guy who's 20 years older than me. And to a certain extent there's an element of racism among the players themselves.

(Interview, 18 January 2011)

However, Greg's experience has not been shared by all of his colleagues. Rodney Hinds, sports editor of *The Voice*, has often found being the only black journalist in the room as giving him an edge over his colleagues. He said:

> I've often been and remain the only black journalist in the place, but it's normally worked to my advantage. I've sat down at a press conference: Viera and Henry were at Arsenal at the time, and there's this thing in our community that if you see another 'brother' you do a nod of appreciation, and they both attended the press conference and I was the only other black person in the room and they gave me that nod. I was then comfortable going up to them, extending an arm to these legends and we dovetailed straightaway. So I think the trust levels have been there for me ... I sit down with certain sports people in certain circles and they say: 'What a relief it is to talk to someone like you', because they can relate to me rather than the guy from *The Times* who has lived out in the sticks and can't relate to a black person, and that in my time here has been one of my plus points.
>
> (Interview, 18 January 2011)

The examples discussed above show that, although not the norm, it is possible for black writers to make progress within the sports journalism profession. The stories of their progress share a mixture of talent, persistence, contacts and, to a degree, good fortune. But why are these examples such exceptions to the rule? What factors are holding others back? What barriers are preventing the employment of more black and minority ethnic sports journalists?

Sports journalism is a difficult profession for anyone to break into. It is highly competitive and this competition will only increase with the growing number of sports journalism degrees attracting hundreds of students across the country. Furthermore, as sports journalism is a job that many aspire to, once achieved, it is a job many hold on to. Sports desks are often populated with frustrated footballers or cricketers who, as they could not make it as a player, see writing about the sport as the next best thing. Once people get their feet under the table, they are often hard to shift.

Dean Wilson, cricket correspondent for *The Mirror*, recognizes this when he says: 'National sports writing jobs don't come up too often; it's a small window of opportunity and it's difficult for anyone to break into' (Interview, 2011). Steven Downes, secretary of the SJA, shares this view, acknowledging the situation is particularly difficult in sports which have seen job cuts in recent times. For example, he said: 'There has been around a 50 per cent reduction in the number of athletics correspondents in recent years. It's therefore tough for everybody to get on in the profession' (Interview, 15 August 2011).

However, this general competitiveness does not explain why the few people who do get on in the profession tend to be white. Instead, a potential explanation lies, at least in part, in a clash of cultures between the sports journalism profession and its potential recruits.

Rodney Hinds, as the experienced sports editor of *The Voice*, has seen a number of talented black sports writers pass through his editorial offices. However, none of these recruits has gone on to a career in the mainstream sports media. The reason, he believes, is a feeling that they do not belong in that world. He said: 'Why are there so few black sports journalists? I think it's because of a sense that they don't belong. I think from the black community, there's the perception that they don't fit in. That it's not a job for us' (Interview, 18 January 2011).

A similar view is put forward by Simon Turnbull, chairman of the BAWA, who believes potential athletics writers are put off by a sense of not belonging:

> I've spoken to some of the (black) lads who do cover athletics and they feel that people aren't friendly and they don't feel part of the crowd. It's a very cliquey sort of pack mentality-driven profession. In terms of athletics, the national writers would knock around together and these lads don't feel a part of that.
>
> (Interview, 24 February 2011)

Leon Mann, sports reporter and founder of the Black Collective of Media in Sport (BCOMS), believes part of the problem is that members of the black community do not see the content as being relevant to them. He said: 'I don't see a channel such as MTV struggling to recruit black presenters, but the problem is that potential black journalists just don't see themselves reflected and represented by sports media organizations' (Interview, 19 August 2011).

Such factors may also offer some explanation for why there is a relative shortage of BME students choosing to study journalism degrees or training courses. We have already discussed how the Society of Editors (2004) identified education and a lack of BME recruits as being a problem across the journalism profession. There is evidence to suggest that the problem is even more significant within the specialist field of sports journalism. For instance, the University of Sunderland is one of an increasing number of universities now offering sports journalism as a degree. The course recruits around three-quarters of its students from outside the north-east of England and has proved incredibly popular. In fact, within three years the new degree has become the biggest in its Faculty of Art, Design and Media. Yet, despite this success, only 2 of its 130 cohort were BME students.

While a sense of alienation among potential recruits is clearly a causal factor of lack of diversity, the situation is also exacerbated by a culture of cronyism within parts of the sports journalism profession. As stated above, research by the Sutton Trust (2006) found that one of the barriers to diversity within journalism was that it was who you knew that often got you on in the profession. A number of interviewees have identified such tendencies within the world of sports journalism. For example, Greg Gobere said:

> Our (the *News of the World*) back bench is run by guys who are old school and you are going to employ people you are comfortable with or people you know, not necessarily someone like me. I would never have got this job if I didn't know somebody there, and worked my way from the inside. There's not a chance in hell I would have been where I am now. Sports journalism is based on the status quo and what has come before. Football and sport has changed massively, but in terms of the reporting of it, it's very much the same. It's an old boys club and you wouldn't look to recruit from outside that.
>
> (Interview, 18 January 2011)

Similarly, sports journalist and senior lecturer Rob Steen believes many sports editors are very closed minded in how they look for future talent. He said:

> Journalism is very slow to embrace certain changes and very quick to embrace others, and I think sports journalism has been very resistant to anybody who's not white, football loving, served their time in the provinces and then came up to Fleet Street. Anyone who's outside that profile – whether you're a woman, whether you're black or brown, it doesn't matter – faces the same issues. I think it's a very, very difficult job for non-white British people to ascend the journalistic ladder in sporting terms.
>
> (Interview, 6 July 2011)

One sports journalist recalled being 'staggered' on joining the BBC to find that the majority of jobs, and senior jobs in particular, were only advertised internally within the corporation. They said: 'How are you going to increase diversity when all you're doing is keeping jobs within the organization and recycling the talent you have?' As outlined above, there is some evidence to suggest the BBC is slowly changing its practices with the introduction of diversity recruitment policies such as the Journalism Talent Pool.

Another clear barrier to black and minority ethnic recruitment is the lack of role models within the profession. One of the major reasons cited for the increased number of black footballers in the professional game has been the emergence of trailblazers who acted as inspiration for future generations. The same has not happened in sports journalism. Greg Gobere explains this in the context of print journalism:

> On the field it's fine in terms of black players. But there's a glass ceiling in terms of sports journalism and you can't see how you can change that.

There are no obvious pioneers and that's discouraging. There's Da
Lewis and me and that's about it, and that's the main reason why.

(Interview, 18 January 201 .

The situation is slightly better in the broadcast media and the visibility of
some black talent on our screens may be one factor in explaining why there is
higher representation of black and minority ethnic journalists in broadcast
organizations than in the print media. The use of ex-players as pundits and
presenters, as discussed above, while questionable in journalistic terms, may at
least act as motivation for potential recruits. As Leon Mann says:

It is about role models. The more black people you have on screen, the
more you are likely to see other black talent entering the industry. For me,
as a 14-year-old, I always wanted to be a sports journalist once I realized
I wasn't going to play for Spurs. But where were the role models for me?
There weren't any.

(Interview, 19 August 2011)

However, while the move from player to media expert may be a progressive
force in some contexts, in others, it may actually be impeding attempts to
increase diversity. For example, many newspapers are now appointing former
high-profile stars as their cricket correspondents. As Rob Steen observes:
'Newspapers want people doing the job who they believe are immediately
respected by the readers. The identity of a paper's cricket correspondent still
carries a lot of clout, and 9 times out of 10 now these guys are ex-players'
(Interview, 6 July 2011). But when it comes to cricket, these ex-players are
overwhelmingly white, middle-class university-educated men such as Mike
Atherton, cricket writer for *The Times*. Steven Downes, secretary of the SJA,
says: 'Journalism is more now than ever before a middle-class profession. And
that creates a filter into the profession' (Interview, 15 August 2011).

Having outlined the nature and some of the causes of the problem, what are
the prospects for change? Despite a general frustration about the way things
are now, there is a sense that things will slowly get better in terms of the
diversity of sports media. Just as the increase in the number and prominence of
black footballers proved to be a slow but relentless force, so there is confidence
that the same will happen in the journalism profession. Changes on the football
pitch, athletics track or cricket field will eventually be mirrored in the press
box. This is the analysis of experienced journalist Rob Steen:

Looking five years down the track, I would expect, say, four members of
the England regular Test team to be British Asians; the greater that
representation becomes, the more emphasis, I think, is going to be
on younger British Asians – you know, guys coming out of Cambridge or
Oxford – who write well, know the game and want to be journalists.

I think we will see people coming through there – but not in a hurry. Journalism may come to reflect the composition of the national team. In ten years, it may well be that the majority of the England first XI are non-white – and I think that will help things. But only eventually.

(Interview, 6 July 2011)

A similar view is expressed by Rodney Hinds, who says:

It is changing because the world is changing. We live in a world where opportunity is greater than ever and the established order is changing all the time. But it is a trickle rather than a flood. We don't have black sports editors and decision-makers, but we do have people coming in at junior level and we are seeing progress being made. I think what really has pushed it over the years is that at Arsenal or Chelsea or wherever, you've now got eight or nine black players who are not making up the numbers but who are actually pivotal to what they do. What's happened is the black community have got hold of that and said: why not? If we can do it there, then why can't we do it somewhere else?

(Interview, 18 January 2011)

But for some, the black community needs to be more confident and vocal in its calls for change. In this spirit, Leon Mann set up BCOMS in 2009. It aims to 'improve the representation of Africans and Caribbeans within the sports media through networking, campaigning and training'. At its first meeting, in a pub, the group was attended by eight people. It now has a contacts list of nearly 60 – many of whom are students and young people with aspirations of a career in the sports media. Leon Mann, a former campaigner with *Kick It Out*, acknowledges that some people are nervous about being associated with the group for fear of being seen as troublemakers. Mann himself receives tweets and emails accusing him of being a racist. But, despite this, he believes that positive action needs to be taken if change is to be achieved. He said:

People only really care about this issue once they have a real understanding of it. But most bosses are so busy with other things, how are they going to get that understanding? Our job is to knock on doors and make them understand. The situation has changed for women in the industry because they did knock on doors and were relentless in that. The problem in the black community is that many people lack confidence and don't feel we have the right to do that.

(Interview, 19 August 2011)

In Mann's experience, bosses are willing to listen when he knocks on their door. He argues that there is a strong business case for increasing staff diversity as this has the potential to appeal to a wider and younger audience. Such arguments are aimed at making diversity a priority for senior management in the way that it has not been in the past. While there is evidence of the BBC and some other broadcasters responding to this challenge, he is less optimistic about change in the press and private sectors.

Ultimately, though, there is a sense in which the black community could and should do more to improve their standing within the profession. It is a case of making change rather than simply waiting for it. This is a view shared by *Kick It Out* Chairperson Lord Herman Ouseley:

> You have to consider what people of colour have to do to overcome the perception, among TV bosses, that the country does not particularly want to see black or Asian presenters. How do they themselves deal with the consequent assumption that there is a glass ceiling above them? By contrast, when we began strongly challenging racism in football we had black players in numbers. But even they wanted to keep their head down. Until people wanted to put their head above the parapet, our task was very difficult. I think similar now applies to the sports media.
>
> (Interview, 18 April 2011)

But while many people want change, they do not want change for change's sake. There is a consensus against positive discrimination or the idea of promoting black recruits simply to have more black representation. Black and minority ethnic talent needs to succeed by having barriers to progress removed, but it needs to succeed, ultimately, because of its talent. This view is summed up in the following comments by Dean Wilson:

> I'm not militant – I don't buy into positive discrimination. I buy into a meritocracy. I have worked bloody hard to get here. Would I like to see more black faces in the press box based on them having worked bloody hard and done well? Absolutely. I want to see the Afro-Caribbean community filling top jobs for that reason right across the board. What I want to see is people from ethnic minorities, and particularly Afro-Caribbean backgrounds being given – and taking – the maximum opportunity to progress through education, learning the journalistic trade and then hammering on the door of national newspapers, magazines, TV and radio stations.
>
> (Interview, 19 July 2011)

Conclusion

Greg Dyke once described the BBC as being 'hideously white' – he could have been talking about the sports journalism profession. While the participants of many professional sports have become increasingly diverse, the press boxes have remained stubbornly white.

Ultimately, the lack of diversity within the sports journalism profession cannot be understood in isolation. The phenomenon is apparent in many other areas of sport and wider society. As Carrington (2010, p172) observes: 'Britain's sports structures, from senior coaching positions, to the membership of governing bodies, to the mainstream media outlets (including broadcast and print media) remain, with notable exceptions … largely all-white affairs with precious little acknowledgement that a problem exists.' Its media structures, particularly the top echelons, are also dominated by white wealthy men, educated at public or independent schools and a narrow range of universities (Sutton Trust, 2006). Sports journalism's lack of diversity must therefore be seen in this bigger social and professional context.

That said, this chapter has identified some factors that are particular to sports journalism and can add to our understanding of why there are so few black and minority ethnic people working within the profession.

For many a sport-lover, once they realize that they will never play professionally, a career writing about the game is their next ambition. Sports journalism becomes a dream profession. But it is clear that many potential black and minority ethnic recruits do not share this dream – not for a lack of love of sport, but because they feel the profession is not the place for them. They would not belong. Such perceptions deter recruitment at an educational and professional level.

Another barrier to diversity lies in the way in which many journalism jobs are recruited and appointed. At best, much of the profession works on informal networks; at worst, it is a case of cronyism and 'jobs for the boys'. The BBC is beginning to show that the implementation of diversity recruitment procedures, with carefully targeted recruitment campaigns and trained appointment panels, has the potential to succeed. If the wider profession is serious about addressing these issues, more organizations need to follow this lead.

For once some improvements are made, others will surely follow. Role models are crucial in inspiring greater diversity in recruitment and progression. There is evidence of these role models having some effect in the broadcast sector; but, at present, the print media is lagging far behind.

While a lack of diversity in journalism can be seen as inherently bad, van Dijk (2009) has observed how it can be a causal factor in the production of racist discourses within the media. Subsequent chapters will explore this by analysing and discussing issues of 'race' and racism, and their reporting, across a variety of sports.

Chapter 4

Athletics

The fastest 'race'?

Mechanically speaking, a black athlete with legs identical to those of a white athlete would have a lighter, shorter and trimmer mass to propel. This implies a greater power-to-total-weight ratio at any given size. Such a ratio would be advantageous in events in which the body is propelled – the sprints and jumps, for example.

Martin Kane (1971)

Athletics is the one area where prejudice is impossible in as much as you can't stop people running fast or jumping high.

Lord Herman Ouseley (Interview, 18 April 2011)

Introduction

Athletics is open to very different interpretations when it comes to issues of 'race' and racism. For some, it is perhaps the most obvious manifestation of the theory that black athletes are just naturally superior in power events such as sprinting and jumping. For others, it offers the ultimate level playing field in which issues of ethnicity, colour and background become irrelevant as one athlete simply competes against another.

Steve Cram, athletics commentator for the BBC, takes the latter perspective:

We all come across racism in different aspects of our lives, but oddly enough athletics is probably one of the most integrated sports you could find. Even at a very early stage the first black people I came into contact with were through my sport. Athletics to me was an environment with very little racial barriers in place or prejudice or anything like that. What helps is that athletics is an objective environment. People finish first, second or third or whatever and people can't not pick someone because they don't like them.

(Interview, 5 April 2011)

This chapter seeks to explore the extent to which athletics does offer a level playing field or whether, in fact, issues of 'race' or racism are a significant factor within the sport. In particular, the chapter focuses on the role of the media and how athletics and athletes are represented in sports reporting.

The chapter begins with a discussion of the history and character of some of the dominant racial stereotypes that relate to athletics and its coverage in the media. This provides context for subsequent case studies examining how the stories of three athletes have been reported by sports journalists. These case studies are Caster Semenya, Christophe Lemaitre and Christine Ohuruogu.

Semenya is the South African athlete who underwent gender tests following her success in the 800m final of the World Championships. Her case, and its coverage, sparked claims of racism from some of her fellow South Africans. It is also significant in terms of gender stereotyping and the media representations of black female athletes.

Christophe Lemaitre was dubbed the first white man to break 10 seconds for the 100m. His case is interesting as it highlights some of the dilemmas facing journalists over the use of language and the circumstances in which 'race' and skin colour can be justifiably referred to in reporting.

Christine Ohuruogu was the British 400m runner who was dropped as the 'face of London 2012' following a one-year drug-related ban. Her case raises questions about the relationships between 'race' and national identity.

Context

'It was not long ago that his [a black's] ability to sprint and jump was a life-and-death matter to him in the jungle. His muscles are pliable, and his easy-going disposition is a valuable aid to the mental and physical relaxation that a runner and a jumper must have' (Cromwell and Wesson, 1941, cited in Wiggins, 1989, p161). The words of Dean Cromwell, a US Olympic athletics coach in the mid twentieth century, may seem laughable now, but they reflect some strongly held views of the time. As far back as the late 1800s, scientists were attempting to provide racial explanations for the success of black athletes. These attempts, and the debates that they provoked, intensified following the record-breaking success of Jesse Owens during the 1930s (Wiggins, 1989).

At the core of these arguments was the notion that black athletes were physically and mentally different from their white counterparts and that these innate genetic differences gave them an advantage in certain sporting events. For example, physical educator Eleanor Metheny, during the 1930s, argued that blacks' longer arms and hands made them better suited to jumping and throwing, while their longer legs helped them in sprints (Wiggins, 1989). Kane (1971) argued that black people as a 'race' have innate differences to white people, such as wider calf bones, narrower hips and denser bone structure, which give them a sporting advantage. These arguments were later refined by Entine (2000), who argued that cultural factors are crucial in shaping athletic success, but maintained that genetic differences between populations set the parameters of this success, giving black athletes a natural 'edge'. More recently, attention has focused on certain types of muscle fibres giving athletes an advantage in power events and the notion that these fibres tend to be prevalent in some 'races' more than others.

The idea that genetic factors play some part in athletic success appears a common-sense one. The danger comes when these factors are afforded too much significance and are falsely attributed to entire 'races' of people, often on the basis of skin colour. As Turner and Jones (2007, p156) have commented: 'Actual evidence for black genetic athletic superiority is scant and often flawed and the supposed superiority of black sprinters appears geographically isolated and inconsistent over time.' Cashmore (2005, p112) is more stark in his dismissal of the notion, branding the claims of Kane and others as 'absurd'. However, although there is no convincing scientific evidence to support the notion of black natural athletic superiority, it is a stereotype that still has some potency today (Hylton, 2009; Carrington, 2010).

At first glance, the notion of natural athletic superiority may seem an empowering one for black sports people. However, the stereotype helps to reinforce and perpetuate a number of damaging social myths. For a start, it serves to negate much of the hard work, commitment and sacrifice behind the sporting success of black athletes. As Hylton (2009, p90) comments: 'this stereotype devalues black sporting achievement, and consoles the white athlete because they have to work harder to overcome this genetic deficiency'. Also, while promoting the notion of black physical superiority, the stereotype undermines their intellectual capacities. This, in turn, helps to perpetuate the idea that black athletes may be good at displays of strength, but lack the mental abilities to hold pivotal positions of influence, both on or off the field. As Sailes (1998, p190) has argued:

> The stereotype that African Americans were naturally physically superior to white precluded the racist notion that they are intellectually inferior and cannot compete with whites in American corporate boardrooms. This stereotype facilitates the maintaining of white superiority and the white status quo.

The natural ability stereotype therefore contains, implicit within it, two damaging images of black athletes. Lombardo (1978) has termed these the *sambo* and the *brute*. The sambo myth portrays athletes as lazy, immature and, ultimately, inferior. The brute myth portrays them as primitive, violent, explosive and lacking in rational capacity.

While it may be tempting to think of these stereotypes as belonging to a previous age, it is argued that they remain a pervasive force both within sport and wider society. For example, Azzarito and Harrison (2008) argue that the idea of natural athletic superiority is so prevalent in society, it affects not only opinions but performance and behaviour. They argue: 'The racialized discourse of natural black superiority and/or "white men can't jump" promoted by the media, coaches, physical education teachers, parents and young people themselves is institutionalized in schools, sport contexts, and embedded in society, shaping youth's identities, racial perceptions, and athletic performances' (Azzarito and Harrison, 2008, p349). In other words, the 'success' of the stereotype is that it can become a self-fulfilling prophecy. If enough people accept the myth, it has the potential to assemble some grains of truth.

In 2006, British sprinter Alan Wells was quoted in *The Observer* as saying: 'Given a good black guy and a good white one, the black guy will always come out in front because, basically, black athletes have an inherent natural ability, even if they're not all equal in that sense.' As Hylton (2009, p99) has observed: 'When ex-athletes make such statements as insiders they bring a validity or spurious truth that adds to the myth of difference and stereotypes that reinforce racial processes and formations.'

What is missing from the above discussion, and tends to be missing from much discussion on this subject, is a consideration of how the natural athlete stereotype affects the portrayal of female athletes. Mayeda (2001) argues that black female athletes have traditionally struggled for acceptance, particularly when succeeding in what some see as 'non-feminine' sports, such as sprinting. As well as being portrayed as naturally gifted, with similar connotations to their male counterparts, black female athletes were also represented as being masculine. Therefore, as Carrington (2010, p80) has suggested, it could be argued that the pervasive stereotype has been more damaging for black female athletes as it 'simply heightened the centuries old discourse that black females were already "mannish amazons" and hence potential if not actual hermaphrodites. Put another way, whereas black male athletes came to be seen as *hyper*-masculine, black female athletes were seen as not female at all.'

The case of Caster Semenya

Timeline, 2009

31 July: Semenya runs the fastest 800m of the year at the Africa Junior Championships.

7 August: Secret gender tests are carried out on the athlete by Athletics South Africa (ASA).

19 August: Semenya wins gold in the 800m World Championship Final in Berlin in a time of 1:55.45. It emerges that the International Association of Athletics Federations (IAAF) had asked for gender tests to be carried out. Semenya gets backing from various South African bodies, including the ANC, claiming her treatment is racist.

24 August: Reports claim that Semenya had three times the normal female level of testosterone in her body in tests carried out before the

World Championships. ASA President Leonard Chuene denies the tests took place.

7 September: ASA head coach, Wilfred Daniels, resigns, stating that Semenya had not been advised properly.

10 September: The *Sydney Morning Herald* claims that Semenya has male and female sexual organs and is technically a hermaphrodite.

16 September: Daniels claims that the athlete was subjected to almost two hours of gender tests before the World Championships.

19 September: Chuene admits that Semenya underwent tests before the World Championships, and that she did not know their purpose.

5 November: Chuene is suspended and the ASA issue a public apology to Semenya for their handling of the matter.

2010

July: The IAAF announces that Semenya can return to athletics with immediate effect; but the results of her gender tests are to be kept private. Semenya returns to competition, winning two races in Finland.

October: Semenya misses the Commonwealth Games due to injury.

Almost as soon as it emerged into the public arena, the case of Caster Semenya was linked with notions of 'race' and racism. Many of the first claims of racism emerged from South Africa following the initial news that the IAAF had carried out gender tests in the wake of Semenya's 800m victory. For example, a statement from the African National Congress, in August 2009, stated:

> We condemn the motives of those who have made it their business to question her [Semenya's] gender due to her physique and running style. Such comments can only serve to portray women as being weak. Caster is not the only woman athlete with a masculine build and the International Association of Athletics Federation should know better.
>
> (*Mail and Guardian Online*, 20 August 2009)

Around this time similar claims were made by Leonard Chuene, then president of ASA, who said:

> I say this is racism, pure and simple. In Africa, as in any other country, parents look at new babies and can see straightaway whether to raise them as boy or a girl. We are now being told it is not so simple … It is outrageous for people from other countries to tell us 'We want to take her to a laboratory because we don't like her nose or her figure.'
>
> (Clayton, 2009)

Others were even more explicit in their claims that the IAAF's actions were part of a wider racist agenda against South Africa and the African continent. A statement from the South African Football Players Union said:

> Why does IAAF only choose Semenya out of all the ladies at the Championships? It shows that these imperialist countries can't afford to accept the talent that Africa as a continent has. The athletics federation must not allow countries like Australia to push their racist agenda against South Africa.
>
> (*Mail and Guardian Online*, 20 August 2009)

Here, the claims of racism go beyond the treatment of one individual. They tap into longstanding discourses of Empire and colonialism and the perceived exploitation and persecution of a continent.

However, many of these claims must be viewed with a high degree of scepticism. The comments from Leonard Chuene, in particular, and with hindsight, read like the desperate attempts of a man trying to cover his tracks and deflect attention from his own errors. Chuene himself had overseen secret gender tests on Caster Semenya before the World Championships. It is highly hypocritical of him to then brand the IAAF as racist for conducting similar tests. In fact, once the full story of those secret tests became known, Chuene was removed from his position as president of ASA.

It must also be pointed out that claims of racism at this time were largely directed at the IAAF rather than the media. But what of the media? To what extent can reporting of this case be read as containing racist discourses and ideology?

In an overview of international research, van Dijk (2009, p199) identifies a number of characteristics of news-making which, in his view, tend to make it 'part of the problem of racism, rather than its solution'. Three key characteristics can be summarized as follows:

- sources – a tendency to quote and rely on white elite sources;
- description – a tendency for ethnic news actors to be described in negative terms;
- perspective – a tendency to take a 'white' ethnocentric perspective on events.

These characteristics will now be used to assess the reporting of the Caster Semenya case in the UK national press. In particular, we will focus on coverage at the height of the story in August and September 2009.

In terms of sources, it might be expected for reports to rely heavily on familiar 'expert' and official voices, such as current and former British athletes. However, while these voices are certainly present in coverage, sources are consistently drawn from a much wider pool. South African officials are repeatedly given a prominent say in reports. Furthermore, many journalists go beyond this to quote 'ordinary' non-official sources such as friends and associates of Semenya. There is certainly evidence of journalism exceeding the lazy desk-bound image with which it is sometimes painted. For example, a report in *The Observer*, on 23 August 2009, quotes two former school friends of Semenya, her mother and father, an ex-teammate and the principal of her former secondary school. Similarly, a report in *The Telegraph* quotes a former teacher, her father, three South African politicians and a South African athletics official. While there is much greater range and diversity of sources to be found in the reporting of the quality press, even the tabloids provide voices for South African politicians and officials to voice their concerns.

Turning to the description of news actors, more of a mixed picture emerges. These descriptions are sometimes called referential strategies (Richardson, 2006) and are important in that they can be used to undermine or condone the behaviour and character of participants in a story. Strategies used to define and describe Semenya in reports in the quality press include the following:

- South African athlete;
- young athlete;
- 18-year-old world champion;
- running hero;
- gold medallist.

The descriptions are typically reserved and conservative in nature, and handle a potentially difficult subject matter with sensitivity. However, perhaps not surprisingly, the same cannot be said of some tabloid coverage of the case. Descriptions of Semenya in tabloid reporting include:

- sex-riddle runner;
- gender row runner;
- manly athlete;
- butch 800m runner;
- drag racer.

Semenya is held up to ridicule in some of the tabloid coverage, with cruel and juvenile jokes made at her expense. For example, *The Sun* reported:

> Sex-row runner 'has bit of both'.
> Gender-row runner Caster Semenya is a HERMAPHRODITE, it was claimed yesterday.
>
> (Wheeler, 2009)

The *Daily Star* reported:

> BET SHE'S GOT ONE.
> Athlete Caster Semenya has sparked a betting frenzy over whether she's really a man. Punters are gambling on the true gender of the butch 800m champion.
>
> (Wall, 2009)

These are examples of a typically tabloid reporting style – conversational, crude, sometimes funny and often insensitive banter. As Harcup (2004, p90) says: 'Telling entertaining stories is part of a journalist's job, as is telling stories in entertaining ways.' Of course, some will criticize the style for being immature, inappropriate, simplistic or even offensive. But is it racist?

This leads us on to a third potentially racist characteristic of reporting – the idea of a case or event being reported from a white ethnocentric perspective. There is a strong case to say that this is just an example of tabloids being tabloids and that the treatment they have given Caster Semenya is the treatment they give most people regardless of skin colour, ethnicity or gender. The tension here is not a racial one, but a clash between a complex issue and the straightforward bar-room view of the world expressed in much tabloid reporting. However, because Semenya is a black African athlete, the reporting of her case can also be viewed as part of a tradition of racially inflected discourse. As Carrington (2010) has observed, black female athletes have long struggled to be accepted as 'proper' females due to being stereotyped as having male characteristics. The tabloid descriptions of Semenya, particularly those of her as being 'manly' and 'butch', live up to this tradition.

From the beginning, claims were made that the investigation of Semenya, and its reporting in the media, were based on a narrow, white Western view of

Figure 4.1 Caster Semenya wins the Women's 800m Final at the 2009 IAAF World Championships (Source: Bill Frakes/*Sports Illustrated*/Getty Images)

what it is to be female. In August 2009, Gugu Ndima, spokesman for the Young Communist League of South Africa, said:

> This smacks of racism of the highest order. It represents a mentality of conforming feminine outlook within the white race, that as long as it does not fall within this race or starve and paint itself in order to look like the white race, it therefore is not feminine.

Around the same time a statement from the ANC Youth League said:

> It feeds into the commercial stereotypes of how a woman should look, their facial and physical appearance, as perpetuated by backward Eurocentric definition of beauty. It is this culture which has forced many African women to starve themselves with the objective of reaching the model ramps of Paris and Milan.
>
> (Clayton, 2009)

In the following month, September 2009, Semenya appeared on the front cover of South Africa's *YOU* magazine, which ran a makeover feature on the athlete. The headline read:

WOW, LOOK AT CASTER NOW!
    WE TURN SA'S POWER GIRL INTO A GLAMOUR GIRL – AND SHE LOVES IT!

A photograph of Semenya dominates the magazine's front cover in which she wears a black dress, jewellery and make-up. She is smiling pleasantly and reclines in a passive posture. As Wade (2009) observes: 'The copy and the interview tells the reader that Semenya likes dressing up and looking pretty, which is an important indicator of both femininity and non-masculinity.' The headline also describes turning her from a 'power girl' to a 'glamour girl', suggesting that it is not possible to be both powerful and glamorous at the same time. Here is the athlete looking as a woman is 'supposed' to look.

But with the exception of some of the tabloid descriptions listed above, there are few such blatant examples of gender stereotyping to be found in reporting of the story in the UK press. One article described how: 'The young Semenya wore dresses and skirts and played with dolls like other girls' (Smith, 2009). Is the implication that in order to be a woman, or a girl, you need to act and behave in ways that are expected of women and girls? If someone can look like a woman and act like a woman, then maybe she could be a woman after all? The article goes on to say that at school, Semenya 'became something of a tomboy and developed a love for football, softball and wrestling. When she reached secondary school, she abandoned skirts in favour of trousers.' The report is actually suggesting that the case is a difficult one because some of the

Figure 4.2 The 'gender testing' debate prompted by Caster Semenya's victory in the Women's 800m Final at the 2009 IAAF World Championships was cast into new perspective by the ultra-'feminized' image of her, as depicted in the September 2009 edition of South Africa's *You Magazine* (Source: *You Magazine*, 10 September 2009, no 144/Media 24/www.you.co.za)

traditional signifiers of gender will not help us here. It is not as simple as saying: boys do this and girls do that. The case is more complex than a stereotypical view of gender can accommodate.

In fact, what resonates most from the whole Semenya saga are the complexities involved: the complexities of defining gender, the complexities of dealing with this in public and political arenas, the complexities created when issues of gender and 'race' combine, and the complexities of trying to report it all. The scientific perspective is that there are wide variations within traditional categories of gender that make simple and strict classifications impossible and unhelpful (Buzuvis, 2009; Camporesi and Maugeri, 2010). Partly due to this, the IAAF struggled to deal with this case in a clear and coherent manner. The ASA also handled the situation very badly and a number of people lost their jobs as a result.

The media, though, are much less culpable in the way in which they dealt with this case. A world champion winner being investigated, and potentially stripped of their gold medal, is a genuine news story. It is true that events were complex and nuanced, which always poses a problem for the space, time constraints and culture of journalism. But most of the reporting of the case was considered and sensitive, and sought to highlight and grapple with these complexities. Sources were drawn from a wide range of ethnic and social backgrounds, while the descriptions of Semenya tended to be neutral in nature. In short, most journalists and publications dealt with a tricky situation pretty well. The exceptions to this are to be found in some tabloid reporting, most notably in *The Sun* and *Daily Star*. Here, there was less of an effort to account for complexity and more an attempt to bulldozer through it. Some of their descriptions of Semenya can be viewed as part of a tradition which undermines the feminine credentials of black female athletes by taking a narrow ethnic perspective on what it means to be a woman. At best, this was some tabloids being their indiscriminating, crude but largely harmless selves. At worst, it was another chapter in a long story of racist discourse.

The case of Christophe Lemaitre

In July 2010, French sprinter Christophe Lemaitre ran a personal best time for the 100m, clocking 9.98 seconds at the French National Championships. But to what extent, and for what reason, was this a newsworthy event? The question poses some interesting issues for sports journalists and their coverage of 'race'.

The French media nicknamed Lemaitre 'White Lightning', heralding him as the first white man to break the 10 seconds barrier for the 100m. Sports paper *L'Equipe* even devoted its first three broadsheet pages to the achievement, relegating coverage of the Tour de France to later pages.

The event received less attention in the UK media, but was still deemed worthy of mention in many newspapers. Most of the UK reporting that day focused on an athletics event in Gateshead, but Lemaitre's success was mentioned as part of these reports. For example, coverage in the *Sunday Times* said:

> With a superb run, Lemaitre won the French National Championships in 9.98 seconds – becoming the first white man to smash the 10-second barrier.
>
> (Lewis, 2010)

The *Sunday Telegraph* carried similar copy:

> Meanwhile, France's Christophe Lemaitre has become the first white man in history to run the 100m in under 10 seconds after clocking 9.98sec at the French Championships in Valence. The 20 year-old now tops the European rankings ahead of Dwain Chambers before they meet in Barcelona. The previous best by a white athlete was the 10.00sec by Poland's Marian Worowin in 1984.
>
> (Hart, 2010)

In contrast, coverage in *The Observer* chose not to use the 'white man' tag, instead reporting:

> Dwain Chambers lost his ranking as the fastest man in Europe this season as France's Christophe Lemaitre ran a personal best of 9.98 seconds at the French national championships.
>
> (Kessel, 2010a)

A few days later, a report in the *Daily Mail* put 'race' at the heart of its headline and story in a preview of a clash between Lemaitre and 100m world record holder Usain Bolt:

> White lightning shock awaits Bolt in the Stade de France.
> Usain Bolt may take a 40,000 French crowd's breath away in the Stade de France tonight but they will have given their hearts to a rival.
> And he is not Asafa Powell, but the fastest white man in history.
> To the wider world the 100 metres at the ninth of this year's Diamond League meetings might appear to be about the rivalry of two Jamaicans, the first race of the year between men who share the year's fastest time of 9.82sec.
> To the French, it is more black and white, a riddle to be resolved of how a Frenchman so new that he has never before run in the Stade de France will fare against the world's best.
>
> (Wilson, 2010)

This contrast in coverage captures a small, but potentially significant, debate about the reporting of 'race' in athletics. Was it right to mention that Lemaitre was the first white man to run under 10 seconds? Was it merely reporting a fact? Or was mentioning it adding credence to the spurious and discredited notion that there is a commonly held genetic difference between white and black athletes? Was it, in other words, perpetuating a racial myth?

Simon Turnbull, chairman of the British Athletics Writers Association, recalls having such a debate with colleagues at the time. He said:

> I remember having a discussion with some journalists about this and I said I don't wish to be naive but I've covered the sport for so long I just don't see colour at all, I just see people. But I was quite horrified that some of my colleagues almost laughed at me. But the way he was being portrayed as some kind of great white hope, it definitely is still a factor in the business and people's perceptions. I said surely we are beyond this – does it matter? And I was told by a lot of people, yes, it's a big deal. I also had the discussion with my desk and they said we had to mention it. They said it's a fact and it should be reported.
>
> (Interview, 24 February 2011)

Interestingly, the debate is not a new one. In the late 1990s, sprinter Matt Shirvington was dubbed the 'Great White Hope' by the Australian media after clocking 10.03 seconds as a 19-year-old. More recently, UK athlete Craig Pickering was tipped by some to be the first white man to break the 10-second barrier.

Shirvington, Pickering and Lemaitre have all attempted to distance themselves from the 'fastest white man' label. For example, Shirvington said:

> I remember thinking I'd rather be the fifth fastest man in the world regardless of my skin colour than the fastest white man. I wanted to be the fastest of all. I didn't want to be restricted. Wearing that title only puts a ceiling on you. Christophe (Lemaitre) would much rather be winning races than worrying about whether he's the fastest white man. It's an irrelevant title for someone who wants to be the fastest sprinter in the world. It's a tag that I don't think is relevant for this day and age.
>
> (Sygall, 2010)

Lemaitre has been particularly sensitive about the subject due to fears that his achievements could be used as propaganda by extremists in France. Following his 9.98 seconds run, far-right websites celebrated it as a victory for the white race. He said: 'Talking about white sprinters, I find this absurd. This story is too much, I don't like it. I had a good race, I broke the record, but there is not much more to say. I did what I had to do, that's it' (Kessel, 2010b).

These concerns are perhaps well founded given that athletics provides fertile ground for those wishing to portray the world as black and white. Take a look at images of the 100m final and you will see eight 'non-white' sprinters racing for the line. Such images help to perpetuate the stereotype, discussed earlier, of

Figure 4.3 Christophe Lemaitre wins the Men's 100m Final at the 2010 European
Athletics Championships (Source: Josep Lago/AFP/Getty Images)

the natural black athlete, innately gifted at strength and power events. Against
this backdrop, it is easy to see why a white man succeeding in this sport is
a tempting news story for some journalists.

But the problem for such journalists is that the stereotype is a myth, a myth
which is not only discredited, but which has the potential to create much
wider harm. As Syed (2011) argues: '[It] is not merely false – it is logically
flawed. And it has big implications not merely for athletics, but for the entire
issue of race relations in the 21st century.'

First, the stereotype places too much importance on genetic factors. At a
species level, we are genetically more similar than the myth suggests. As
Cashmore (2005, p24) points out: 'In terms of genetic profile, we humans were
found to be astonishingly similar: every human being was found to be 99.9%
the same.' Genes are just one of a number of complex and varied factors
affecting performance. These include genetic and physical characteristics, but
also resources, opportunity, culture, coaching and facilities (Wiggins, 1989).
The natural black athlete stereotype ignores these complexities to provide a
generalized, oversimplified or, in other words, false view of the world.

Second, the stereotype falsely links genetic factors to differences in 'race'. As
discussed in Chapter 2, 'race' is essentially a social construction with no analytical
value. As Cashmore (2005, p112) says: 'There is no "pure" race.' Yet, the
natural black stereotype not only affords 'race' importance, but reduces it to a

matter of skin colour. In fact, it reduces it to a contrast of two skin colours – black and white. Syed (2011) argues: 'Our tendency to generalise rests on a deeper fallacy – the idea that "black" refers to a genetic type. We put people of dark skin in a box labelled black and assume that a trait shared by some is shared by all.' The truth is that, although remarkably the same as a species, humans do have telling genetic differences. However, these differences are various and complex. We are, in other words, characterized by universal similarity and localized diversity. As Robert Scott, a researcher at the Institute of Metabolic Science in Cambridge, has said: 'Scientifically, it [the natural black athlete stereotype] is a discredited notion. There is more genetic diversity within small areas of east Africa than in most of Europe' (AFP, 2010).

The precise nature and significance of genetic factors in athletics is still open to debate. One current strand of scientific thinking is that a gene called ACTN3 may be an important factor in determining speed performance. If this gene is active, it encourages 'fast twitch' fibres which have been found in many elite sprinters (AFP, 2010). The theory is that populations which tend to carry a high proportion of the active variant of this gene are therefore more likely to produce top-level sprinters. However, even this theory is disputed as an over-simplification by some scientists who point out that genes do not work in isolation, but as part of a complex and changeable network.

These complexities are acknowledged by Steve Cram, the BBC's chief athletics commentator:

> You can't be a sprinter if you haven't got a lot of fast twitch fibre, it doesn't matter what colour you are. There's a genetic and physiological basis to why you are predisposed to be good at that event and some of that is to do with your genetics. We work from facts. To be a fast sprinter, it's about physiological make-up and genetics as much as anything else and therefore it's been proven in terms of certain populations – East African, Caribbean – those areas have generated over the years a lot of power-based athletes. But there's not many kids who say just because I'm white I can't be good at this. It reaches a point where you hit a threshold you can't get beyond. Nobody at this stage can say how good Christophe Lemaitre is going to be. I would put him in the same class as Usain Bolt – nothing to do with his colour, but his technique and leg speed.
>
> (Interview, 5 April 2011)

But where does this leave journalism and decisions about how to report Lemaitre's success? Referring to the sprinter as the first white man to break the 10-second barrier could be defended as factually correct. However, ultimately, it is a misleading and potentially damaging approach to take. The 'white man' tag gives credibility to a racial view of the world and helps perpetuate a stereotype which, as discussed earlier in this chapter, devalues the efforts and achievements of many successful athletes. It can be viewed as an example of inferential racism in that it presents accounts which have 'racist premises and propositions inscribed in them as a set of unquestioned assumptions' (Hall, 1990b, p13).

The relevant guideline in the Press Complaints Commission's (PCC's) code of conduct for journalists says that the mention of someone's 'race' 'must be avoided unless genuinely relevant to the story'. All current credible studies suggest that genetic factors provide only part of the complex story of what determines athletic success. Furthermore, these genetic factors are not correlated to skin colour, but tend to be concentrated in specific geographic areas. In light of this, the mention of skin colour is surely not 'genuinely relevant' to this story.

The fastest white man tag is a tempting one for journalists in that it provides the simplicity and interest that often makes good news. However, it cannot be justified in this case and, furthermore, is actually potentially damaging in that it presents a distorted and ill-founded picture of events. While journalism often has to simplify, it must seek to do this in a way that does not distort the reality that it aims to present.

The case of Christine Ohuruogu

Christine Ohuruogu was born in Stratford, London, one of eight children to Nigerian immigrants. She would go on to achieve a linguistics degree at University College London, while developing into one of the UK's best athletics prospects.

But in September 2006, the 400m runner was banned from athletics for a year for missing three drugs tests. Under anti-doping regulations, athletes must state where they will be at a certain time each day to be available for out-of-competition testing. Ohuruogu missed a test in 2005 and then two in 2006, blaming her lapses on poor organization and forgetfulness, and missing the third test after her regular training venue was changed for a school sports day. She also faced a lifetime ban from the Olympics due to a British Olympic Association (BOA) rule stating that anyone convicted of a doping offence was ineligible to compete for Team GB. After serving her year's ban, Ohuruogu appealed against this ruling and eventually had her Olympic ban overturned. Within a month of returning to competition, Ohuruogu won the 400m final at the World Championships in Osaka. She would go on to win an Olympic gold medal in Beijing the following year.

The athlete's success divided opinion among the public and the media. On the eve of her return to major championship running at the World Championships, *The Mirror* ran the following story:

> Why we shouldn't be cheering if Ohuruogu picks up a medal today.
> Ohuruogu had three chances and she blew them all. She deserved everything she got. Everything and more. So don't waste your sympathy

on her this afternoon. Don't cheer for her. Don't exult if she wins gold, silver or bronze.

Wait for her at least to admit that she did something wrong before you even begin to think British athletics should be celebrating the achievements of people like her.

(Holt, 2007)

Similar feelings were expressed in other coverage of the time. Before her ban, Ohuruogu had been identified as 'the face' of the UK's build-up to the London Olympics in 2012. But her face was removed from London 2012 posters after her ban and some felt her misdemeanours should now rule her out of spearheading the campaign. Following her World Championship win, *The Sun* ran the following headline next to a photo of the athlete:

Please don't make this the face of our London Olympics.

(Howard, 2007)

Journalist Steve Howard praised the runner for her success, but said she was now tainted and the UK needed to be above suspicion if it wanted credibility in questioning the honesty and integrity of other nations' athletes. The same newspaper and journalist ran a very similar headline almost exactly a year later following Ohuruogu's success in Beijing. This time the main body of the article was much more critical of the athlete, accusing her of arrogance and lack of remorse for her mistakes:

We can't let Ohuruogu be face of 2012.

SOON, no doubt, there will be a campaign to reinstate Christine Ohuruogu as the poster girl of London 2012. This should be resisted at all costs.

(Howard, 2008)

Critics (see Barnes, 2007) of this coverage point out that Christine Ohuruogu has never failed a drugs test. They argue that the hostility towards her is, at least in part, due to the colour of her skin. Would the coverage of her in the red-tops have been so negative if she was a white 'conventionally' pretty female? Is it more difficult for some sections of the press to forgive a muscular black woman with Nigerian parents?

Simon Barnes, writing in *The Times,* believes issues of 'race' have affected her coverage in the media:

This villain [Christine Ohuruogu] has served her time – now let's catch the real cheats.

We should continue to pursue the cheats with unending determination, but it does no good to make villains for the sake of it. And it is my belief that if Ohuruogu had been blonde and lipstick-comely and possessed a more traditional English name, she would have been routinely praised, with the missed tests getting a mention in maybe the third paragraph.

(Barnes, 2007)

This is a view shared by BBC commentator Steve Cram:

An element of the reporting of this case is to do with her being a black girl from a certain part of London and that there was a lot of the non-athletics press looked at her as a big strong black girl. Compare her to Becky Lyne. Becky is a pretty blonde 800m runner from the Manchester area and she had two failed tests at the same time as Christine and then Christine fell foul of the third one. We had this daft rule at the time where nobody told you if you'd missed one. It was commonplace for athletes to be told missed tests are ok. We've changed all the procedures since then. Christine fell foul of the testing but it could easily have been Becky Lyne, and I suspect, and this is just my opinion, that Becky Lyne would have had very much different treatment to Christine Ohuruogu had she been the one who had the third missed test and who'd been banned for a year. This case is one where I think the opinions of the general public have been influenced by the prejudices of the media reporting of the case.

(Interview, 5 April 2011)

Suspicions that Ohuruogu's skin colour and background have played a part in some of her more critical media coverage are difficult to prove. They are based as much on a hypothetical comparison with what might have happened if a white athlete had been in the same position as they are on the content and language of the reports themselves.

In the name of balance, some words can be said in defence of the coverage under suspicion. First, *The Mirror* and *The Sun* stories quoted above are essentially comment pieces. They are intended to be provocative, to challenge perceived wisdom and to stir the debate. They must therefore be read in this light.

Second, although the pieces use emotive language, they are based on fact and construct arguments that address alternative views, albeit in a tabloid style. The first *Sun* piece, by Steve Howard in 2007 actually goes out of its way to praise Ohuruogu and acknowledge her achievements. Despite its forceful headline, the main body of the article reaches its conclusion – that she should not be the face of the 2012 Olympics – in a measured, almost reluctant manner.

Third, the stories address issues of great concern to many people – those of cheating and drug-taking in sport. If an athlete has been banned for a drugs offence, it does not seem that unreasonable to question whether they are the right person to head a PR campaign for the nation's athletes. Issues where 'race' could be construed as being a factor will always be sensitive. But it is important that these sensitivities do not inhibit debate or restrict journalists from expressing genuine opinions. Just as it would be wrong to criticize someone based on a prejudice against their skin colour, so it would be wrong to shy away from criticizing that person for fear of being seen to be prejudiced.

Another interesting aspect of the Christine Ohuruogu case is the question of her national identity. As discussed earlier in the book, identities, including national identities, can be seen as fluid constructs which change over time through different contexts. Significantly, this means that they have the potential to be used, to varying degrees, to question the 'genuine' nature of someone's national identity. For example, Hylton (2009) has argued that sprinter Ben Johnson was portrayed more as a Jamaican, than a Canadian, after his drugs cheating. Identifying the roots or family heritage of an athlete is therefore a way of highlighting otherness. In other words: 'The significance of the roots of the Other being made clear is tantamount to stating that their identities are not redolent of the host nation but an alien one instead' (Hylton, 2009, p95).

In the period after Ohuruogu returned from her year's ban, but was still trying to overturn her lifetime exclusion from the British Olympic team, a number of stories emerged suggesting that she may change her nationality in order to compete in the Olympics. Previously, reporting had tended to focus on her Nigerian parentage as a cause for celebrating the diversity of the British make-up. Now, though, reports took on a different tone, as in these examples from the *Express* and *Mail*:

> OHURUOGU COULD GO ON THE RUN FOR NIGERIA.
> Christine Ohuruogu, running for Britain again after a year's suspension, could quit her country and compete for Nigeria if an appeal against a lifetime Olympic ban fails.
>
> (Wragg, 2007)

> Ohuruogu: I'll compete for Nigeria just to be part of the 2012 experience.
> Christine Ohuruogu would consider switching nationalities in order to compete at the Olympic Games if she fails to overturn a lifetime ban imposed by the British Olympic Association.
>
> (*Mail Online*, 2007)

Interestingly, if we look at the main text of these stories, the above headlines and introductions appear to be exaggerations of what the athlete actually said or, in other words, examples of journalistic licence. The quotes show Ohuruorgu to be much more equivocal than the headlines suggest and certainly do not justify the *Mail* lead, which, although not in direct quotes, makes it appear the athlete has said she will compete for Nigeria:

> Asked whether she would consider her future in the sport if the BOA rejected her case, Ohuruogu said: 'I would probably just run for another country. The Olympics is what you train for ... It would [change my whole outlook if the appeal failed]. Could I change countries? I don't

know. I haven't really given it any serious thought. Maybe I'll have to start thinking.'

(Mail Online, 2007)

Again, though, it is difficult to assess the extent to which this is an example of a racially motivated attempt to question the national identity of a black athlete, or whether it was a more innocent example of journalists looking for a controversial news angle. However, whether genuine or not, the notion that Ohuruogu may give up her British nationality was used against her by journalists seeking to criticize her role within the sport. In Steve Howard's *Sun* article of August 2008, one of his main complaints was that she had 'even threatened to change her allegiance to Nigeria'. The argument is clear: how can we use this person as the 'face' of British athletics when her commitment to Britain is in question?

The answer, and last word, is best provided by Ohuruogu herself:

Whether or not I'm the face of the London Olympics doesn't really bother me ... What matters most to me is that the Olympics are in my borough. It's being held in the streets where I grew up. I lived there long before we got the Games and I still live there now. That's why it doesn't matter if I'm the public face of the Games or not. It has a far more personal meaning to me.

(Kessel, 2011)

Conclusion

The quality and character of athletics journalism presents a mixed picture – based on the above evidence. Much of the reporting is well researched, balanced, informed and carefully worded. Coverage in the quality press, in particular, demonstrates a mature approach to issues of 'race' and the historic sensitivities of this issue in relation to the sport.

However, while there is little evidence of overt racism in coverage, there are examples of more overt discourses and ideological influences present in reporting. First, reports in the red-top tabloids are, at times, open to question. This was identified in some of the reporting of the Caster Semenya case and in the critical coverage of Christine Ohuruogu following her ban. In their defence, these tabloids apply similarly provocative reporting styles to other areas and issues in society. Nevertheless, there was evidence of some reports tapping into discourses which have traditionally questioned the genuine 'female-ness' of black female athletes. Similarly, the condemnation of Ohuruogu drew on her family heritage to question her 'Britishness' in the way that, perhaps, a white British athlete may not have been subjected to.

Second, it is evident from the reporting of Christophe Lemaitre that many athletics journalists still view 'race' as being a significant factor in the sport. The majority of reports focused on his 'whiteness' and the rarity of white success against a tradition of black dominance. Although the nature of this reporting dismayed a minority of journalists and, to an extent, the athlete himself, it demonstrates that 'race' is still a live issue for many and provided evidence of inferential racism in reporting.

Finally, to balance some of the above criticism, mention needs to be made of the capacity for sports journalism to reflect on and improve itself. Reports by Kessel (2011) and others used Lemaitre's success to challenge assumptions about the significance of 'race' in athletics and the way in which it is reported in the media. Such reflexive journalism perhaps offers some hope for those who wish to see 'race' further diminish as a factor in athletics – not just in the headlines, but as an ideological factor underpinning the sport.

Chapter 5

Boxing

'Race' on the ropes

.

Introduction

As Sugden (1996) notes, if defined in simple terms as people fighting with fists, then boxing, along with running, could be thought of as one of the oldest sports in the world. Boxing is still perhaps one of the most widely known sports in the world. It has transcended the globe and is practised in various guises, such as gypsy bare-knuckle boxing in Europe, the various styles of kick boxing in the Far East and even what has been termed 'dirty' boxing in the US. Hence, it can be seen that boxing can carry social meaning and economic cultural value for people. As a result, it has an impact upon people's identity and their understanding of the world that surrounds them.

Early (1994) argues that the reason for boxing's enduring popularity is that it can be understood as a metaphor for the human condition in wider society. Boxing can provide discipline, respect and some level of personal control that can lead to the development of a positive social identity. More than this, boxing can be discussed as a subculture where individuals create, sustain and develop identities in a world that is, at times, closed to the general public. Wacquant's (1992, 2004) ethnographic study of a boxing gym in Chicago showed how the boxers employed the social world of the boxing gym as a refuge from the intense social pressures of outside life. Within the gym, the men followed a strict regime of discipline, both dietary and cultural, that empowered them to survive and navigate the socio-economic oppressive conditions in which they lived. Wacquant called the development of this identity a socialized lived body.

This identity is, however, a complex interplay associated with 'race', class, ethnicity and gender (Early, 1994; Sugden, 1996). Therefore, before a discussion of 'race' and boxing, it is worth briefly noting the connection between class and boxing. Control of the sport has always been in the hands of the upper class or elite, from the plantation owners who authorized slaves to box to the contemporary commercial world. It could easily be suggested that the poor fight and the rich spectate and accumulate the wealth. Wacquant's (1995, p521) analysis shows that deciding to dedicate oneself to boxing is related to class and 'race' in America: '"Don't nobody be out there fighting with an MBA ... if you want to know who's at the bottom of society, all you gotta to do is look at who's boxing", observed a trainer coach at the gym.' While boxers themselves said: 'I wish I was born taller, I wish I was born in a rich family, I ... wish I was smart, an' I had the brains to go to school an really become somebody important ... I never had nobody helping me. If it was not for boxing I don't know where I'd be' (cited in Wacquant, 1995, p523).

These contradictory and mixed feelings about the sport that they practised may seem odd. Wacquant (1995) uses the term 'coerced affection' to comprehend this feeling, but he further notes that these opinions are connected to the dynamic of class and 'race'. In short, they excelled at the sport because being a young poor black man in America 'was no bed of roses' (Wacquant, 2004, p38).

In the process of identity construction, individuals can reproduce or resist dominant ideologies. These acts can be seen in boxing and its relationship with racism in wider society. Drawing on research from the US, authors have noted that boxing is associated with 'violence' and 'backward almost primitive sport' (Sammons, 1988; Davis, 1994). Ironically, these traits have been ascribed to blacks in the US (DeGaris, 2000; Mason, 2000). Sammons (1988, p235) argues that boxing gyms 'open a window to a simpler, more human-oriented past when muscle ... allowed us to control our own destiny'. The emphasis on physiology again can be linked to biological notions of 'race'.

In describing the sport of prize-fighting, author John Dudley (2002, p54) writes that boxing is a contest for 'physical and strategic domination between two men, a reenactment of an instinctive, primal struggle for survival'. While Robert Edgren (1903, p343, cited in Sugden, 1996, p343), writing during the early part of the twentieth century, locates boxing in an historical practice when he notes that: 'The same combative spirit that animated the cave man can be seen at every glove fight that takes place in a modern ring.'

It could be suggested that the association of boxing with a backward primate culture can be related to Said's (1978) theory of Orientalism – that is, boxing is both native and foreign to the Western world. It is native in that authors have noted the historical development of boxing in Europe (Sugden, 1996), but also foreign in that it is practised successfully in large numbers by fighters who are perceived as the other. Boxers are in many ways 'Othered' (borrowing on Said's terminology) because they are overwhelmingly from the lower social classes and their ethnic composition reflects groups oppressed historically. Hence, 'backward' groups practise this backward sport in the main. 'Race' thinking is implicit here.

It could be argued that early black sporting stars transcended the boundaries of their profession and almost instantly became a personification of a black cultural currency that opened up the possibility of social and economic success. The history of heavyweight boxing is just one further example of this. However, even the success of black boxers was debated and discussed within debates of 'race' thinking and, at times, national identity discourse.

The rest of this chapter examines how three boxers have been represented and debated within popular culture and sporting media. The examination of these fighters also displays how racism has evolved. These boxers are:

- *Jack Johnson:* Johnson, the first black heavyweight champion, was represented in stark racial metaphors that seemed to signify the fear that the white population had for the black male. Two fights would bring Johnson to the fore of racial politics: his 1908 heavyweight championship bout with Tommy Burns and his win over former champion James Jeffries two years later. A review of media coverage of Jack Johnson indicates that racism was a dominant motive that animated all facets of this social drama. As such, 'race' was implicit in all media coverage of Jack Johnson.
- *Muhammad Ali:* Ali's complex identity has been much discussed and his reception by the mainstream media was a product of the social and economic climate of the civil rights/Black Power movement.
- *Amir Khan:* the global popularity of Ali helped to make boxing popular with a variety of immigrant groups in Europe. Within the UK, boxing become popular with South Asian groups, and recently the emergence of Amir Khan has been seen as a product of multicultural Britain.

Jack Johnson

In 1895, Charles A. Dana, editor of the *New York Sun*, wrote:

> We are in the midst of a growing menace. The black man is rapidly forging to the front ranks in athletics, especially in the field of fistacuffs. We are in the midst of a black rise against white supremacy. If the Negro is capable of developing such prowess in those [lighter] divisions of boxing, what is going to stop him from making the same progress in the heavyweight ranks?
>
> (cited in Ward, 2004, p14)

Figure 5.1 Jack Johnson cartoon, *The Philadelphia Evening Star*, 2 November 1909

In many respects, Jack Johnson was as Marqusee (1999, p36) notes: 'the white man's nightmare come alive'. He appeared invincible and, more importantly, arrogant in the ring. He was represented as the archetypical 'bad boy' of sports (Brookes, 2002) or, as a controversial biography noted, a 'bad nigger' (Gilmore, 1975). Johnson was further deemed controversial because of his well-publicized relationships with white women. In an era of Jim Crow where black males were routinely lynched for even talking to white women, this was deemed a major insult and affront to white society (Roberts, 1983). Johnson encapsulated the white man's fear of superior sexuality and physicality, and was finally forced into exile to escape a conviction, invented by white federal law, which ruled that Johnson transported women over state lines for 'immoral purposes'. Eugene Genovese notes how stereotyped images and myths were created from times of slavery, which were adopted into the fears of white society: 'Europeans and Americans were hearing lurid tales of giant penises, intercourse with apes, and assorted unspeakable transgressions against God and nature' (cited in Miller and Wiggins, 2004, p292).

Historically, white boxers refused to fight black counterparts. Tommy Burns (a white Canadian boxer) became the first heavyweight champion to lift the colour line, allowing him to be matched against coloured boxers with the championship on the line:

> I will defend my title as heavyweight champion of the world against all comers, none barred. By this I mean black, Mexican, Indian or any other nationality without regard to color, size or nativity. I propose to be the champion of the world, not the white or the Canadian or the American or any other limited degree of champion.
>
> (cited in Chung, 2006, p17)

To black Americans, the match was about much more than one man's shot at the heavyweight title: it was an opportunity to challenge the myths of biological inferiority that worked to oppress the entire black community (Morgan, 2003). This allowed Jack Johnson (the son of a slave) who had previously not been allowed to fight for the title an opportunity. Chung (2006) notes that Jack Johnson became heavyweight champion in 1908, beating Canadian Burns in the 14th round when police jumped into the ring to prevent Johnson from knocking out Burns. The fight film also stopped recording the final moments of the bout to save the white 'race' the embarrassment of being knocked down by a member of the black race. Jack Johnson thus became the first black to ever hold the claim of heavyweight champion (he won the title in Sydney, Australia, because no American city would stage the bout).

The response by sports journalists and commentators was scathing towards Johnson. Novelist Jack London, who covered the fight for the *New York Herald*, was one of Burns's most vocal critics. He belittled Burns for losing and Johnson for nothing more than being black: 'The fight, if fight it could be called,' he wrote, 'was like that between a pygmy and colossus ... Burns was a toy in his hands' (cited in McCaffery, 2000, p212).

London ironically switches the racially charged 'pygmy' to refer to 5 foot 7¼ inch Burns. Johnson, at 6 foot 1¾ inch, was the 'colossus', both in size and now in status. London continues: 'But one thing now remains. Jim Jeffries must emerge from his alfalfa farm and remove the golden smile from Jack Johnson's face. Jeff, it's up to you! The White Man must be rescued' (cited in McCaffery, 2000, p213). The story ran in newspapers worldwide. Jeffries became the first lauded 'Great White Hope' (in boxing circles), the one who would deliver the title back to the 'proper race'.

Hutchinson (2002) notes that *Current Literature*, a leading publication of the time, published an article prior to the Johnson–Jeffries fight that concluded that Jeffries could not lose because 'the brain of a white man is unquestionably superior' to that of a black man. The article argued that Jeffries would win if the fight were prolonged because blacks were genetically more emotional than whites; thus, the length of the bout would increase Jeffries's innate intellectual advantage and guarantee his victory. Furthermore, some commentators noted that blacks were not physically conditioned for low blows. In boxing, it was widely accepted that black men made poor fighters because they were cowardly and had weak stomachs, causing them to be susceptible to body blows. In addition, it was believed that 'only athletes from the colder Northern latitudes had enough stamina to remain strong during the course of a long boxing match' (Roberts, 1983, p62). The day prior to the Jeffries fight, the *Omaha Daily News* noted:

> The huge white man, the California grizzly, [could] beat down the wonderful black and restore to the Caucasians the crown of elemental greatness as measured by strength of brow, power of heart and lung, and withal, that cunning of keenness that denotes mental as well as physical superiority.
>
> (cited in Hutchinson, 2002, p47)

In covering the Johnson training camp for the *San Francisco Examiner*, Alfred Lewis (cited in Hutchinson, 2002, p59) alluded again to innate racial limited intellectual capacity. This piece makes references to physical biological appearance; the acknowledgement of lynching still assumes blacks to be mentally inferior:

> Johnson is essentially African ... he feels no deeper than the moment, sees no farther than his nose – which is flat and in the present. The same cheerful indifference to coming events have marked others of the race even while standing in the very shadow of the gallows. Their stolid unconcern baffled all who beheld it. They were to be hanged; they knew it. But having no fancy, no imagination – they could not anticipate.

The Johnson–Jeffries fight took place in 1910. Johnson again emerged triumphant. Considering the tremendous pre-fight excitement, the fight itself was anticlimactic. Morgan (2003, p32) notes that *The New York Times* reported:

Perhaps never before was a championship so easily won as Johnson's victory to-day. He never showed the slightest concern during the fifteen rounds and from the fourth round on his confidence was the most glaring thing I ever saw in any fighter … Jeffries didn't miss so many blows, because he hardly started any. Johnson was on top of him all the time, and he scarcely attempted a blow that didn't land.

London's 'Great White Hope' had been defeated. His 5 July *New York Herald* article began: 'Once again has Jack Johnson sent down to defeat the chosen representative of the white race, this time the greatest of them' (London, 1907, cited in McCaffery, 2000). London made Johnson out to be a buffoon, a 'smiling negro' who was 'never serious for more than a moment at a time'.

His victory was received with the worst racial violence of that decade, as white Americans avenged his triumph. Riots and lynching occurred all across the US in the days after the fight. In Little Rock, two blacks were killed by a group of whites after an argument about the fight on a streetcar; in Roanoke, Virginia, six blacks were critically beaten by a white mob; in Norfolk, Virginia, a gang of white sailors injured scores of blacks; in Washington, DC, two whites were fatally stabbed by blacks; in New York City, one black was beaten to death and scores were injured; in Shreveport, Louisiana, three blacks were killed by white assailants (Roberts, 1983; Ward, 2004).

Johnson eventually lost the title in 1915. He was forced into exile by the white establishment and it was 25 years later before another black fighter was allowed a shot at the heavyweight championship. A team of sponsors and managers, who in many ways set the motions of a slick, efficient public relations exercise, handled Joe Louis's professional career to make Joe Louis acceptable to white America. In many ways he became a mediatized celebrity (Marqusee, 1999).

In order to further endear himself to the American public (white America), Louis enlisted in the army and fought promotional bouts for various army departments (which were in racially segregated units). His reward for this public show of patriotism was being hounded by the federal government for taxes on these 'promotional bouts' that left him emotionally and financially broke.

In many respects, Jack Johnson and Joe Louis were to become the bench-marks for black fighters who followed them. Of course, these benchmarks were created and sustained by the white media who failed to understand or even attempt to comprehend the complexities of both men and of how they were received in black communities. Marqusee (1999, p29) notes:

There seemed to be only these two stereotypes for black sportsmen in America: the 'bad nigger' and the 'Uncle Tom'. Both Johnson and Louis, of course, were subjected to critical scrutiny never lavished on white champions, and both were defined by white perceptions.

Muhammad Ali

Johnson was the most famous black person at the time and even the black community were divided in their reception of his lifestyle. In many ways, Johnson's defilement by the white media echoed the treatment that Ali received over 60 years later. Ironically, Ali himself, after seeing a play of Jack Johnson, remarked: 'So that's Jack Johnson … That was a bad nigger! … This

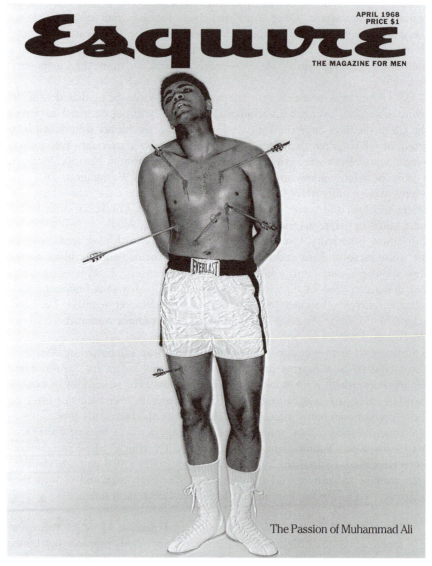

Figure 5.2 Muhammad Ali as Saint Sebastian, *Esquire*, April 1968 (Source: George Lois)

play is about me. Take out the interracial love stuff and Jack Johnson is the original *me*' (cited in Bingham and Wallace, 2000, p27).

The complex figure of Muhammad Ali offers an interesting way of thinking about the relationships between rebel heroes and those who identify with them. Ali was an iconic figure in the struggle for black civil rights during the 1960s, while simultaneously retaining extensive popular support, including within large parts of the media, because of his larger-than-life personality, entertainment value and outstanding skill as a boxer. When he was persecuted by the establishment during the mid 1960s after refusing to be drafted into the US army, this only increased his heroic status for many. By 1996, he was back in the bosom of the establishment and given the honour of lighting the Olympic flame in Atlanta. His career has been celebrated in a number of documentaries and in the 2001 biopic starring Will Smith, while his 1996 film *When We Were Kings* was widely acclaimed. Because of the 'war on terror', his identity as a Muslim is now in higher profile, and he has intervened as a peace broker between Islam and the West on a number of occasions. The cover of *The Muhammad Ali Reader* (Early, 1998) notes: 'Fighter, celebrity, draft dodger, activist, poet, victim, inspiration, champion – pick a year and choose a label. Muhammad Ali has been them all.'

When the 18-year-old Muhammad Ali, then known as Cassius Clay, returned from the Rome Olympics in 1960, he was very much received as an 'all-American hero'. Quickly turning professional, Clay endeared himself to the American nation. Mainstream publications such as *Life* and *Time* covered him in some detail with glowing articles, commending him for reinventing boxing with his repartee, boastfulness and endearing personality.

While many fight fans were unsure of his unorthodox fighting style and considered his clowning a disguise to hide his lack of boxing skills, they nevertheless welcomed him into the boxing world. When asked by a Russian reporter about the condition of blacks in the US, Clay responded that qualified people were working on those problems and retorted that, 'to me, the USA is still the best country in the world, counting yours' (Marqusee, 1999, p47). In many ways he was the personification of American patriotism and typified this on his return to his home town in Louisville, which celebrated his triumph over his Cold War adversaries:

> To make America the Greatest is my goal
> So I beat the Russian and the Pole
> And for the USA won the medal of Gold
>
> (cited in Marqusee, 1999, p48)

Time magazine, in an article entitled 'Cassius Clay: The dream', adopted a tone bordering on sycophancy:

> Cassius Clay is Hercules, struggling through the twelve labours. He is Jason chasing the Golden Fleece ... When he scowls, strong men shudder,

and when he smiles, women swoon. The mysteries of the universe are his tinker toys. He rattles the thunder and looses the lightning.

(cited in Bingham and Wallace, 2000, p53)

This reference to (possible) inter-racial intimate affection, in the above quote, coupled with the references to Greek mythological metaphors, illustrates how endearing Clay had made himself to the white American public. Despite the often violent and controversial history of black–white sexual relations in the US, this quote, during the era of Jim Crow, shows how Clay became a sporting celebrity. In many respects, the media helped to celebrate this celebrity persona and create an 'all-American hero'.

Despite the US not being used to *arrogant* blacks, and especially not tolerating acts of self-centred conceit from them, *white America* appeared to accept Clay for his endearing personality. It could be suggested that the main reason for this was not increased tolerance on the part of the US establishment, but the simple fact that Cassius Clay was not regarded as a social threat. Indeed, it could be argued that in a perverse sort of way Cassius Clay was the twin embodiment of another racist stereotype of blacks: that of the happy-go-lucky but ultimately dumb Negro and the muscle-bound but brainless athlete. Certainly, his apparent clowning around covered some subtle political thinking:

Where do you think I'd be next week, if I didn't know how to shout and holler and make the public take notice? I'd be poor and I'd probably be down in my home-town, washing windows or running an elevator and saying 'yes suh' and 'no suh' and knowing my place. Instead I'm one of the highest paid athletes in the world. Think about that. A southern coloured has made one million dollars.

(cited in Marqusee, 1995, p18)

Cassius Clay's seemingly apolitical stance, however, disguised a growing interest in civil rights and, in particular, a fascination with a small but growing organization called the Nation of Islam (NOI). The NOI grew modestly until the 1950s; however, the release of another ex-prison convert, Malcolm X, quickly changed that. Upon release from prison, Malcolm X rose quickly in the NOI hierarchy and toured the US extensively, establishing 27 mosques in different cities. Marqusee (1999) suggests that Malcolm X saw in Clay what the white sports journalists refused to acknowledge: an independent, intelligent boxer who played by his own rules and not the stereotypes laid down by white society.

On 25 February 1964, Cassius Clay became the world champion, beating Sonny Liston by a technical knockout (TKO) when Liston failed to get up for the eighth round. However, at the press conference the next day the media ignored Clay's boxing ability and wanted to know if Clay was a member of the NOI. The vilification had begun. Cassius Clay was no longer. Muhammad

Ali was here and the new heavyweight champion of the world. When asked what his new name meant, Ali replied in the literal sense 'Muhammad means *worthy of all praises*, Ali means the *most high*'.

The mainstream media refused to call Ali by his proper name and the response by the predominately white media was swift and disparaging. Jimmy Cannon wrote in the *New York Journal*:

> The fight racket, since its rotten beginnings, has been the red-light district of sports. But this is the first time it has been turned into an instrument of mass hate. It has maimed the bodies of numerous men and ruined their minds but now, as one of Elijah Muhammad's missionaries, Clay is using it as a weapon of wickedness.
>
> (cited in Bingham and Wallace, 2000, p93)

However, worse was to follow in 1966 when Ali was reclassified as eligible for draft and called up. Ali refused, citing his religious and political objections to the war. Within hours the World Boxing Council (WBC) stripped Ali of the title and reaction was swift. Bingham and Wallace (2000, p73) give the following examples:

- *Los Angeles Times*: 'Clay is a black Benedict Arnold.'
- *New York Times*: 'Clay could have been the most popular of all champions but he attached himself to a hate organization.'
- Congressman Frank Clark: 'The heavyweight champion of the world turns my stomach. To back off from the commitment of serving his country is as unthinkable as surrendering to Adolf Hitler or Mussolini.'

In *Soul on Ice*, Eldridge Cleaver (1971, p91) gave a black perspective of the outpouring of all this negative publicity:

> Ali is the first 'free' black champion ever to confront white America ... In the context of boxing, he is a genuine revolutionary ... To the mind of 'white' white America and 'white' black America, the heavyweight crown has fallen into enemy hands. Ali is conceived as 'occupying' the heavyweight kingdom in the name of a dark, alien power.

The African-American cultural critic James Baldwin also echoed Ali's famous 'no Viet Cong ever called me nigger' quote:

> A racist society can't but fight a racist war – this is the bitter truth. The assumptions acted on at home are the assumptions acted on abroad, and every American Negro knows this, for he, after the American Indian, was the first 'Viet Cong' victim.

Ali himself grew more assertive in his new role as an NOI figurehead. He toured Africa and Asia where his popularity was such that he met with heads of state such as Abdel Nasser of Egypt. From 1964 to 1966 it appeared that the sports press were more interested in Ali's political and religious viewpoints than they were of his fighting ability. Ali's growing assertiveness also paralleled similar developments in the civil rights movement. Influenced strongly by the political philosophies of Malcolm X and the growing independence movements in ex-colonial countries, these different movements heralded the rise of the black consciousness movement popularly called the Black Power movement.

In many respects, Ali's conversion to Islam and his refusal to be drafted was seen as the impetus from which Ali transcended from being just a heavyweight boxing champion to being a *world champion*. His stance was an inspiration for many black activists in America and this inspired the black civil rights movement that was the catalyst for other human rights movements in America and around the globe. For example Van Deburg (1992, p206) notes:

> Black Power energised and educated black Americans, introducing many to the concept of political pluralism. It spurred new interest in African liberation struggles and the plight of the powerless world-wide ... These, in turn, served as often-utilised models for the various ethnic, gender and class-consciousness movements of the seventies and eighties.

The Islamic concept of the '*ummah*' and conceptualizations of political blackness draw upon similar feelings of exclusion and empowerment (Saeed et al, 1999; Saeed, 2007). The concept of the '*ummah*' – the global Islamic community which supersedes nationality – is briefly explained thus: there are two tiers to Muslim identity, one related to faith and one related to country, but faith overrides any other component of identity (Saeed, 1999). This explains why Ali was so popular to countries who previously did not follow boxing, but were either Muslim countries or newly independent nations. Ali was also aware of his popularity in Islamic countries:

> I can't name a country where they don't know me. If another fighter's going to be that big, he's going to have to be a Muslim, or else he won't get to nations like Indonesia, Lebanon, Iran, Saudi Arabia, Pakistan, Syria, Egypt and Turkey – those are countries that don't usually follow boxing.
> (cited in Early, 1998, p58)

In certain respects, Ali embodied that new black consciousness. For many British Asians, Ali – a battling Muslim – was a source of inspiration and solace considering the racist climate of the time. This led to the younger generation of immigrants during the 1960s and 1970s asserting a black politics that was more assertive and demanding. The younger generations were not willing to 'bow down to the white master', and adopted an ideology of asserting their rights and being more vocal and visible in their demands to achieve equality in society. It could be argued that Black Power created a global 'imagined community'; by relating to this community, young blacks during the 1960s were in some way displaying solidarity and gaining strength from images of black assertion embodied by Ali.

Amir Khan

Like Ali, Amir Khan, who shot to fame after winning a silver medal at the 2004 Athens Olympics, also harbours a complex identity and appeal. Khan was inspired by Ali and took up boxing. Khan, a proud British Pakistani Muslim, has become a pinnacle definer of contemporary multicultural Britain, an achievement not to be underplayed when considering the current climate of Islamophobia.

Just as Johnson needs to be understood within the era of Jim Crow, and Ali needs to be contextualized within the climate of black consciousness of the 1960s, Khan needs to be understood within the environment of Islamophobia and increased racism (in its various hybrid forms) towards Muslim minority populations in the West (Saeed, 2003, 2004, 2007).

During the 1990s, interest in the Muslim community in the UK increased significantly. Beginning with national issues, such as the Rushdie affair, and international matters, such as the 1991 Gulf War, a series of events brought Muslims into the media spotlight and adversely affected the Muslim population in the UK. New components within racist terminology appeared and were used in a manner that it could be argued was deliberately provocative in order to bait and ridicule Muslims and other ethnic minorities.

Many social commentators have noted that media language has been fashioned in such a way as to cause many to talk about a 'criminal culture' (see Wahab, 1989; Modood, 1997; Saeed, 2007). Since 11 September 2001, the loyalty of British Muslims to Britain has been further questioned with polls indicating that British Muslims should make a special effort to emphasize their Britishness (Saeed, 2003, 2004).

Pakistani and Bangladeshi communities, in particular, have been represented as separatist, insular and unwilling to integrate with wider society. Furthermore, the old stereotypical image of 'Asian passivity' has been replaced by a more militant aggressive identity that is meant to be further at odds with 'British secular society' (Modood, 1997). The concept of culture clash has been reintroduced to imply that British Muslims are at odds with mainstream society. Recent comments by a variety of senior politicians appear to substantiate these populist beliefs. Labour MPs David Blunkett and Peter Hain have both lately made comments that have suggested that British Muslims must make more of an effort to integrate within society. Blunkett has gone so far as to suggest 'oaths of allegiance' and 'not marrying spouses from the Indian subcontinent', and has spoken out in favour of the introduction of 'English language tests' for anyone with a non-Anglo British background (Saeed, 2004). If, however, they were to look at recent research conducted in the area of national identity and ethnic minority communities, many of their concerns would appear to be unsubstantiated. Saeed (2004, p14) notes in this context:

> Post September 11 polls done by the British-Asian newspaper *Eastern Eye* (23 November 2001) show overwhelmingly that British-Muslims perceived themselves as loyal citizens despite opposing US/UK bombing of Afghanistan. This right to disobey is one of the cornerstones of democracy and one should consider that white Britons who may oppose government policy are not usually questioned about their loyalty. Indeed, the most recent survey on Muslim opinion (*The Guardian*, 17 June 2002) show that the majority consider themselves British-Muslims.

Khan is a good example of this hybrid identity. His complex multiple identities can be understood in his boxing ability. Sardar (2006) notes that Khan exemplifies what it means to be British in modern multicultural Britain:

> Every component of Amir Khan's compound identity is demonstrated in his boxing. As a Muslim, he prays before each bout and again on entering the ring. He is at home in his religious identity despite all the stereotypes and suspicions of Muslims as being 'fifth columnists'. And he emphatically defies Norman Tebbit's 'cricket test' of allegiance to the home country. Khan represents Britain. His parents and his supporters wave the Union flag. But he also acknowledges his Pakistani heritage: the Pakistani flag is there in evidence as well. It represents something extra that enhances his Britishness.

Khan, nicknamed the pride of Bolton, has managed to achieve a somewhat transracial popularity, thus breaking down barriers along the way. At his fights, fans wave the Pakistani flag while others wave the Saint George's cross; but significantly, both are supporting the same person. With regards to the media, then, Khan is put forward as a positive role model for young British Muslim men (Burdsey, 2007b). Furthermore, Burdsey argues that Khan has been more readily accepted because of his more Western appearance in terms of accent and physical appearance. He further points out that Khan continually underlines his British identity:

> Being selected for Britain is a positive thing for race relations in this country ... not a lot of Asians get selected for this country at anything and I'm proud to wear the British vest. I've lived here all my life and I feel English through and through ... On the night of the [David Bailey] fight I walked out with a British flag. I wanted to show people that Asian lads like me were proud to be British. My mates in the crowd had a massive flag, half Union Jack and half Pakistani.

However, Khan still stresses his pride in his religious and ethnic background. This conditional belonging by Khan has made him a role model for British Muslims, while simultaneously more acceptable to the mainstream British public (Burdsey, 2007b). However, Burdsey (2007b, p623) does not acknowledge that the acceptance of Khan hides or even consciously conceals the increased prejudice towards British Muslims in society:

> In other words, Khan is seen as filling a lacuna in communities that are believed to lack positive role models. This serves to further position Khan as the 'acceptable' or 'desirable' face of British Islam. This stance is perhaps best epitomised by the *Daily Mail*'s Jeff Powell who, in distinguishing Khan from the 'other' Muslims that his paper continues to admonish, suggests that 'this charming son of Islam is doing the power of good for Anglo-Asian relations.

For example, Khan has been questioned about being a Muslim and asked to voice his opposition to terrorism. Less than two weeks after the London terrorist attacks of 2005, *The Sun*, commonly tagged as a more right-wing newspaper, carried a story entitled: 'I'll help beat bombers', accompanied with a picture of his multi-ethnic fan base (*The Sun*, 18 July 2005). On the same day, *The Sun* carried another story that saluted Khan, not for his latest boxing victory, but 'because he has the guts to say he's a Muslim who is proud to be British ... Khan set[s] a shining example for young British Muslims to follow' (*The Sun*, 18 July 2005). This seems like almost a requirement of any prominent British Muslim to speak out against terrorism as if silence indicates a support of Islamism. Boyle and Haynes (2009, p112) note:

> By sensationally fighting his way to the silver medal at the relatively young age of seventeen Khan secured wide media exposure in September 2004 and received a hero's welcome on returning to UK when his home town of Bolton in North West England held a civic reception in his honour. Fast forward to 9 July 2005, two days after the London bombings, and Khan fought his first processional bout. In the short interim period between the bombings and the fight, the Metropolitan Police had announced that the four London bombers were British citizens of Pakistani origin. As a second-generation British teenager of Pakistani origin, the context of Khan's fight took on new significance.

Media coverage of Khan and the bout suddenly combined discourses of 'race', nationality and belonging all within a sporting context.

The above examples show that Khan has been proclaimed in the media as some kind of role model or spokesman for British Muslims. Burdsey (2007b) acknowledges that this is at times done reluctantly and in relatively 'safe' avenues. In a similar fashion Hylton (2009, p98) notes that Khan has been represented as the good Muslim: 'the underlying message is again that "this is what you should be like to fit in" as cultural markers of Asianness are diluted for commonly accepted signifiers of Britishness.' In many respects, this echoes the media coverage of black athletes as either role models or bad boys.

However, what can also be gleaned is that, at times, Khan has had to face overt racism. Khan himself notes that some British fans have not accepted him and occasionally the abuse has been racist and Islamophobic (*Guardian*, 18 January 2010). BBC boxing journalists have noted that in several of Khan's fights a racist climate was clearly apparent (Dirs, 2009). A number of debates on the BBC boxing blog have fans considering whether the animosity by some sections of the British public and British boxing fans was based on racism or Islamophobic sentiments (*Guardian*, 18 January 2010). Indeed, one of the comments notes that no matter how hard Khan tried to emphasize his British identity, he was always faced with a considerable element of racism:

> Just before Ricky Hatton fought Mayweather in America, during the build-up, Amir Khan was introduced to the crowd in the US and there were raucous boos from British fans of Ricky Hatton. Amir Khan looked embarrassed, I remember Oscar Del Hoya looking shocked, here were British fans booing a British boxer in America. When Khan fought Barrera in Manchester he was met with booing from a few hundred British fans wearing Mexican sombreros and cheering for Barrera. This sort of thing really got to him because he was very patriotic and really proud of having won silver for Britain in the Olympics.

What is also striking from newspaper reports about Khan is that boxing commentators have routinely ignored the striking and vociferous racism that Khan has experienced during boxing matches in England. Burdsey (2007b, p626) highlights the overt racism apparent at Khan fights:

> ... forty of his supporters were forced to flee his fight at Glasgow's Braehead Arena after being subjected to a torrent of missiles and chants of 'BNP' and 'Pakis go home', whilst Khan and his family were racially abused after watching his younger brother, Haroon, box at Everton Park sports centre in Liverpool.

The vast majority of the newspaper articles on Khan are overwhelmingly positive (Burdsey, 2007b); however, they are framed within a context of the 'acceptable Muslim' and the polar opposite of the militant disloyal Muslim. It is clear that complex discourses of 'race' and nation are apparent here. Nevertheless, it could be suggested that this alludes to a form of inferential racism – that only a certain type of immigrant can be accepted as British. Given the post 11 September climate, Khan's allegiance and commitment to his faith are again likely to be highlighted as a potential signifier of 'the Other'.

Conclusion

The history of boxing illustrates how conceptions of 'race' and racism have developed with wider changes in society. The Jim Crow era of Jack Johnson invokes a biological reasoning that alluded to the fear of the black male. His actual physical blackness combines with connotations of racial blackness that suggested his physical and biological make-up were a danger to white America. The anticipation and expectation of a 'Great White Hope' created by the media is testament to the animosity that Johnson engendered in mainstream American society.

Ali's journey from Olympic champion to the face of militant Islam in the US shows how issues of national identity and racial politics combine. Ali was accepted as long as he 'played the game' and did not question the racial status quo in the US. Once Ali raised his voice in support of not just civil rights but growing black assertiveness, the media onslaught was relentless. Ali and his religion were seen as un-American.

The religious element and the post-9/11 socio-economic structure are crucial to understand Amir Khan's reception in the media. Clearly, Khan is represented as the acceptable British Muslim. However, this acceptance is based on certain conditions: that he does not question the inequalities, racism and Islamophobia apparent and inherent in British society.

It is evident that issues of 'race' and racism have been prevalent for the career of all three boxers. These boxers have reacted and responded to this in a variety of ways, from the almost ambivalence of Jack Johnson, to the militant stance of Ali, to the acceptance of Khan.

Chapter 6

Cricket

Fair play in reporting the imperial game?

What do they know of cricket who only cricket know?

C. L. R. James

Introduction

This chapter will seek to analyse how issues of 'race' and national identity affect the modern cricket media and are instructed by the game's arguably uniquely colonial history. Moreover, the chapter will examine how media coverage, in concert with that history, has contributed to cricket's exertion of a cultural and sociological influence far beyond its playing field, as recognized by C. L. R. James and many others.

The chapter will examine specific, relevant examples of how matters of 'race', racism and national identity in cricket are reported today compared with previous eras, touch upon the significance of the ethnic make-up of the cricket media itself (see also Chapter 3) and draw upon the opinion of cricket journalists, former players and anti-racism campaigners, as well as cite academic texts by the likes of Marqusee, Searle and Burdsey and statistical evidence, in measuring where issues such as Islamophobia and cultural stereotyping sit within post-colonial cricket coverage.

The chapter will also look at specific evidence of the risks run by even seemingly unimpeachable cricket publications in engaging in race-related discourse, and ultimately suggest how the next generation of cricket journalists can avoid propagating stereotypes, prejudices, myths and suspicions.

Context

Amusing to relate, all kinds of queer conceptions prevail among savages as to how the game should really be played.

(William G. Fitzgerald, 'Savage cricketers',
Strand Magazine, May 1898)

Personally, I would not select Asians or blacks. It is a particular problem with team sports.

(Henderson in Baker, 1995)

These two cricket-related quotes, separated by depressingly little in ideology but almost a century in time, hint that few, if any, professional sports are as tightly bound – and dangerously so, for journalists – by such complexly woven issues of 'race' and national identity, and as historically informed (coloured, even) by racism as cricket. For the history of few, if any, other genuinely international sports has been forged and moulded in the crucible of colonialism.

Having conquered, Britain's empire-builders brandished bat and ball as cultural tools with which (as they saw it) to civilize their new subjects. From seventeenth-century North America (Canada and the US would later contest the first-ever official international match in New York) to pre-partition India as early as 1721, the West Indies by the 1780s, Australia at the start of the nineteenth century, South Africa soon afterwards, New Zealand and Ceylon (now Sri Lanka) in the 1830s, and other far-flung Commonwealth outposts such as Kenya, Zambezia (later Rhodesia, now Zimbabwe) and Polynesia, where British root was put down, cricket sprang forth.

Sports other than cricket did survive the journey to the colonies and flourish still today. 'The British took their games with them wherever they went. Sport was their chief spiritual export, and was to prove among their more resilient memorials' (Morrison, 1968). Yet, an evangelical zeal informed the particular export of what had been regarded as a game for, and of, nobility ever since Royalist gentry took it up in rural exile during the reign of Oliver Cromwell – himself having played a form of cricket when a young student – during the 1650s. When Sir Charles Darwin, during his second anthropological expedition aboard *HMS Beagle*, witnessed a cricket match at the Bay of Islands in New Zealand in December 1835, it was being played between freed Maori slaves and a British missionary. In Polynesia, the London Missionary Society's efforts to introduce cricket resulted in an adaptation of the game – *Kilikiti* – still played today.

That said, the drive to spread the Christian gospel into the 'dark corners of the earth' (a phrase proffered by a pro-colonial Pears soap advert in 1898) also formed part of the paternalistic racism with which Britain uniformly imposed her sociocultural mores on indigenous peoples she saw as requiring rescue from themselves. In that context, cricket was squarely a means of relieving the Kipling-coined 'White Man's Burden'. We shall discuss how the notion of exporting English fair play – 'as important in imperial matters as in cricket' (Sissons and Stoddart, 1984, p34) – may still exist as a subtext to some of the contentious media coverage of issues of 'race', national identity and religion in cricket's more recent history.

Ultimately, though, while some of those involved in spreading its gospel genuinely regarded themselves, however arrogantly or perversely, as philanthropists, cricket's globalization was like all other tools of Empire: a business platform (business based largely on the elitist ideals of the old slave trade). Cricket was a peculiarly aesthetic method of financial, as well as cultural, subjugation dressed up as education. Thus, the game flourished most strongly in South Africa where Cecil Rhodes mined diamonds, on New Zealand's South Island where Australian gold-rush settlers gathered in Central Otago, and among the tea plantations in Ceylon. Perhaps most prominently, and most significantly when related to the modern game, cricket prospered under the East India Company's predominance in much of the Asian subcontinent.

Yes, that modern game itself, its heartbeat quickened by the Twenty20 format and its landscape altered beyond recognition by day–night international matches, lucrative TV contracts and iconic brand-conscious players, may seem more than a couple of centuries removed from the sport which Britain exported colonially as both a symbol of will and a cultural testament. Yet, while Gemmell (2007, p1) correctly asserts that through 'the link to the Commonwealth, cricketing discourse will always be held in the shadow of race', and few who pioneered cricket in the said Commonwealth could have foretold that India (both as a cricketing and commercial force) would bestride the twenty-first-century game, cricket's latter-day reality is directly informed by the inevitability of the game in the colonies becoming more than a byword for the fight for emancipation from the Mother Country – indeed, it is its very symbol.

As Holden (2008, p337) observes: 'the adoption of cricket in colonial societies involved a complex mixture of acceptance of and resistance to elements of British imperial culture'. More than mere resistance, indeed, according to Ashis Nandy (2000, p1): 'Cricket is an Indian game accidentally discovered by the English' – that is, having been 'reconstructed' in various colonial outposts to 'serve as a critique of capitalism, colonialism, and modernity' (Holden, 2008, p18). C. L. R. James, born in Trinidad and author of the seminal book *Beyond a Boundary* (1963), perceived that the lengthy battle to see a black player captain the West Indies – Frank Worrell, in 1960, was the first to do so – and the side's dominance of cricket for almost a quarter of a century up until the mid 1980s granted the people of the Caribbean a whole new national identity 'to fill a huge gap in their consciousness and their needs' left by colonial rule. 'There is a whole generation of us, and perhaps two generations, who have been formed by [cricket]' (James, 1963, p49). But James's argument resonated throughout the old empire. In reflecting on *Beyond a Boundary*, a quarter of a century on, Vyas (2008) said:

> Cricket offered modes of self-realisation that were simply unavailable elsewhere in the colonial culture: Social and political passions, denied normal outlets, expressed themselves so fiercely in cricket … precisely because they were games.

Moreover, given what colonial rule was built upon, it is impossible not to see cricket's role as a catalyst for social change through the prism of race. 'Race was at the heart of cricket throughout the 20th century' (Williams, 2001, p1).

So, what of today, exactly? As much as it informs its past, what role will 'race' play in cricket going forward? More pertinently to us, to what extent is the modern (multi)media coverage of the post-colonial game at risk of racial stereotyping and reversion to imperialist attitudes and outright racist misconceptions, let alone of pandering to the anti-Islamist sentiments and suspicions at work in the post-9/11 age? Simon Barnes of *The Times* presented a prescient picture of the evolution of cricket in the modern era back in 1990:

> Cricket is not an English game anymore. It has been subject to the influences of, to name but a few, Islam, Indian politics, Partition, Tamil separatism, Marxist writing, Rastafarianism, the New Zealand Prime Minister, the Bishop of Liverpool, Bob Marley, King Dyall, Benazir Bhutto, aboriginal and Maori rights, George Davis, the question of trade embargo, the question of diplomatic relations, the sin of adultery, the pleasure of drugs, the morality of liars, the morality of money, but also the matter of the importance or otherwise of the rights of mankind to freedom in the face of the forces of oppression ... a pleasant, footling pastime has become an expression of national, regional and racial pride.
>
> (Barnes, 1990)

Just eight days later, British Conservative MP Norman Tebbit introduced the concept of a 'cricket test' of British Asians' loyalty to Britain, prompted by vibrant support for India, Pakistan and Sri Lanka Test teams on tour in England. Tebbit told the *Los Angeles Times*:

> A large proportion of Britain's Asian population fail to pass the cricket test. Which side do they cheer for? It's an interesting test. Are you still harking back to where you came from or where you are?

But Barnes's words have remained resonant in the two decades since, not least in their reference to Islam. Even before 11 September 2001, as we shall discuss, much Western coverage of cricket in Pakistan bore an air of creeping mistrust or outright suspicion. But post-9/11 angst, reinforced by the London bombings of 7 July 2005, has prompted some media commentators – peering through the peculiarly cricketing prism of perceived 'fair play' – to allege links between corruption in Pakistani cricket and Islam, or even between Pakistani cricket and terrorism. While much of that discourse has been expressed implicitly, others have been more forthright, with Tebbit even suggesting in the aftermath of the 7/7 attacks:

> I do think had my comments been acted on those attacks would have been less likely. What I was saying about the so-called cricket test is that it was

a test of whether a community has integrated. If a community was looking back at where it had come from instead of looking forward with the people to whom they had come to, then there is going to be a problem sooner or later.

(cited in Davie, 2005)

In these and other examples, such as the cause and effect of the renewed sociological stereotyping and physiological mythicizing – with international cricket described by Hoberman (1997, p128) as a 'dramatic and politicized theatre of white athletic decline' – of West Indian and black cricketers, the anachronistic and often grudging treatment of India's emergence as a cricketing superpower, the struggles (wholehearted or otherwise) of the Australian media to disown its nation's racist past, the depiction of South Africa's efforts to develop a truly multicultural side almost two decades into the post-apartheid age, and the under-reported but seemingly contrary trend of young British Muslim cricketers pushing for selection by England, it is clear how 'contemporary controversies such as hostile fast bowling, umpiring, ball-tampering and match-fixing have all carried racial undertones' (Gemmell, 2007, p1). Furthermore, the media coverage of cricket more than a decade into the twenty-first century is still, to an extent, informed by the ideologies and attitudes which accompanied, and shaped, the game's spread beyond the village green.

Equally, nations across colonialism's cricketing diaspora continue to heal fissures created by issues of ethnicity, race and religion. In Sri Lanka, the exclusion of northern, mostly rural, Tamils from the national team in favour of the ruling-class Sinhalese is a still conspicuous feature today, stained as it is with blood spilled in the civil conflict and 'a history of conflictual politics' (Roberts, 2005, p133) played out between two competing post-colonial nationalisms.

In India, a game described as 'a microcosm of the fissures and tensions' (Guha, 2002, p15) of class, creed, 'race' and more within its society now bears added cultural responsibility as the popular symbol, and a vehicle in its own right, of the nation's new-found, if imbalanced, wealth. While some still seek to use its cricket team to stir India's religious stew, Indian cricket itself is 'like organised religion with all its fervour, dogma and, often, a distinct lack of logic' (Ugra, 2005, p92). Moreover, the strides made by India's international team on the pitch and their cricketing administrators within the International Cricket Council (ICC) have prompted dissent interpreted in India as racist indignation from cricket's white establishment at a shift in cricket's momentum towards a former colony.

Meanwhile, the fiscal inequality within the 'new' South Africa perpetuates a level of ethnic and racial divide manifest in the nation's cricket team, which remains predominantly white despite the more than decade-long use of a 'quota' selection process. This, after the opposition to international cricket teams touring South Africa during the 1980s and early 1990s, did much to dispatch apartheid.

The racial make-up of the Zimbabwe side under the Mugabe regime has posed dilemmas for journalists elsewhere at risk of forging Ian Smith-era Rhodesia-style 'racial alliances' (Marqusee, 2005, p252) in backing a boycott of cricket against an all-black team.

In the West Indies, where the white-only captain issue was so symbolic, there remains disquiet at the struggle of Indian-origin players, who are well represented in inter-island cricket for Guyana and Trinidad and Tobago, to break into the national team in numbers.

Then there is Australia, a now multicultural land, but whose historical culture of racism continues to be felt inside cricket grounds by the nation's indigenous peoples, and harks back to long before more recent racist episodes involving the Australia team abroad (most notably, against Sri Lanka during the late 1980s and early-mid 1990s) when, 'in a strange reversal of the history of colonialism and imperialism, the "gentlemen" are black' (Fraser, 2005, p291). During 2011, almost four decades since the abandonment of the 'White Australian Policy' (limiting non-white immigration), just one cricketer of Aborigine origin, Jason Gillespie, had played Test cricket for Australia.

Case study 1: Good blokes and black c***s

Even in making little impact upon England on his Test debut at Sydney in January 2011, Usman Khawaja struck arguably the greatest cultural blow in Australia's recent sporting history.

While the inroads made by British Asians into English cricket's mainstream are testament to a belatedly more inclusive system – and perseverance – Islamabad-born Khawaja's path, as a Muslim, was blocked by an Australian equivalent of what W. James (1993, p240) describes as the 'monolithic racism' within which Caribbean immigrants to Britain were viewed simply as black, whatever their background or skin tone.

The obstacles which faced Khawaja have a more contemporary measure. Eight years earlier, Australia's Darren Lehmann became the first cricketer to be suspended by the International Cricket Council for making racist comments – having called the opposition 'black cunts' during a one-day international against Sri Lanka. The media reaction to the incident – or at least the media presentation of Australian, and Australian cricket's, reaction – was instructive, not least because race had been a contentious issue in matches between Australia and Sri Lanka since the 1980s.

Malcolm Knox, writing in *The Age*, was one of several Australian journalists who railed against Lehmann's peers' suggestion that his words were symptomatic of the heat of battle rather than an underlying prejudice. Knox cited the 'good bloke' argument as proof of a double standard in the Australian cricket community, asking:

> How is it that in the heat of the moment, he [Lehmann] did something supposedly out of character? The answer, of course, is that he did not …

Lehmann's misfortune is that he is the man who got caught revealing the unwitting racism that infuses not only Australian cricketing culture but mainstream Australia.

(Knox, 2003)

Most notably, former Australia fast bowler Geoff Lawson was quoted as saying there had 'always been a racial divide as far as India, Pakistan and Sri Lanka are concerned' and that the ICC was using Lehmann as a scapegoat (Hurrell et al, 2003, p1) to soothe what the *Herald Sun* newspaper described as 'black–white tension in the international game'. Farquharson and Marjoribanks (2006) found the illustration of cricket as a game of black- and white-playing nations to be typical in Australia and grimly informative in its portrayal of 'people of African, Caribbean and South Asian origin as an undifferentiated racial group', and concluded:

[Australian] Media representations of the racial vilification of the Sri Lankan team are part of a larger historical discourse of white colonialism and supremacy, where the black bodies of the colonized are considered inferior to the white bodies of the colonizers.

(Farquharson and Marjoribanks, 2006)

Knox (2003) concluded: 'Australian triumphalism masks the fact we lag a generation behind England in resolving the race debate … Australian clubs fix the problem by leaving non-whites out.'

In a 2007 survey by Australia's Human Rights and Equal Opportunity Commission, race discrimination commissioner Tom Calma reported: 'The fear of racism in Australian sport is … a major barrier to participation for indigenous people and those from various ethnic and cultural groups' (Calma, 2007).

In between, another 'good bloke' – Lehmann's former Australia teammate Dean Jones – referred to South Africa's Muslim batsman Hashim Amla as 'the terrorist' on an Asian satellite TV channel.

While they have faced less legislative discrimination, New Zealand's Maoris have been far more heavily represented in rugby union than cricket, which 'remains disproportionately the domain of European New Zealanders' (Ryan, 2005, p41).

Case study 2: It's (not) all white here

The potential for problems in the presentation of race and national identity in cricket is not restricted to journalism, whether broadcast, print or digital. Nor is it restricted to deliberate acts.

In November 2008, the Otago Cricket Association (OCA) in New Zealand chose to promote its hosting of the following month's Test match between New Zealand and the West Indies with the marketing slogan 'It's all white here'.

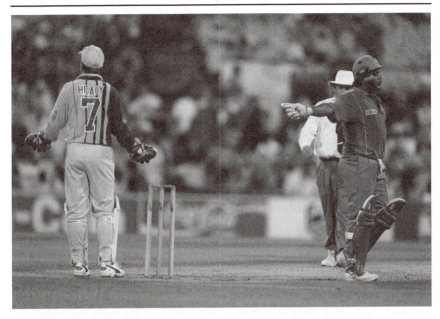

Figure 6.1 Ian Healy reacts after Arjuna Ranatunga complains, 20 January 1996
(Source: Steve Christo)

The intention was to differentiate the Test match from one-day cricket (and its multicoloured clothing) and New Zealand's all-popular rugby union national team, the All Blacks. OCA chairman Ross Dykes said: 'We just wanted a catchy phrase to help sell the game. It was all based around the association of the colour with cricket' (Seconi, 2008).

It was an act of parochial PR lost on a West Indies side well educated in colonial history, and whose players' association said the slogan 'may be reasonably perceived to be loaded with racial innuendoes' and 'comes at a time when the spectre of racial intolerance is insidiously and, at times, openly appearing in major sporting events'.

While Dykes was 'mortified' by that reaction, others suggested what could generously be described as an anachronistic – 'totally insensitive and myopic', according to the West Indies Players Association (2003) – attitude. The mayor of Dunedin said: 'If you want to make an issue of something, you find issues in anything', while former New Zealand player Glenn Turner said people could be 'too politically correct' (Seconi, 2008).

Less strongly defended were comments made by one of New Zealand's finest-ever players, Martin Crowe, to the Wisden website in January 2003. Discussing Darryl Tuffey, then the only New Zealand player of Maori lineage, Crowe said: 'Tuffey is a Maori and traditionally not many Maori make good cricketers. They don't have the patience or the temperament to play through a whole day, let alone over a Test match' (cited in Hoby, 2003).

As well as leaving another stain on the name of Wisden, Crowe's observations created a fierce backlash. He responded by first insisting his intention had been to talk up Tuffey rather than slap down Maoris, then by claiming a ghost-writing Indian sub-editor at Wisden's website had misrepresented him, before announcing he would no longer write for the website on the advice of his full-time employers, Sky TV.

The Guardian website's Lawrence Booth observed: 'At a time when racial issues and cricket are uneasy bedfellows, Sky might have made a quietly canny decision' (Booth, 2003). Booth would be appointed editor of *Wisden Cricketers' Almanack* in January 2011.

Wisden Cricket Monthly: A warning from (recent) history

Founded in 1864, the *Wisden Cricketers' Almanack* is the world's longest-running sports annual. Along with reports and/or statistical details of every significant cricket match played each year, its 1500-plus pages also contain the full exhaustive laws of the game, a thorough section on cricketing records, a full schedule for future international cricket, obituaries and more than 100 pages of opinion and comment. Not for nothing is it colloquially known as the Bible of Cricket.

However, readers of the July 1995 issue of Wisden's associated magazine *Wisden Cricket Monthly* (WCM) might have believed themselves back in cricket's colonial days. For in a prominent article under the provocative heading 'Is it in the blood?', editor David Frith allowed obscure freelance writer Robert Henderson to argue that only 'unequivocal' Englishmen should be allowed to play cricket for England, casting specific doubt on the commitment of black West Indies-born England players of the day: Phil DeFreitas and Devon Malcolm.

In the summer of 1995, the England team, following Ashes defeat in Australia the previous winter, failed to record a series win over a fading West Indies side. Meanwhile, county cricket was also in a moribund state. A nation which had given cricket to the world was wrestling with the realization that it could no longer claim paternalistic ownership of the game, particularly a one-day version in which the Empire's former subjects in the Asian subcontinent held increasing sway. Against that gloomy backdrop, the consistent failure of much-hyped overseas-born England players, such as Zimbabwe-born Graham Hick, appeared ever-more dismal, and the debate over the role – if any – played by national identity in the dynamic of a national team dressing room was ongoing. In truth, Henderson was far from alone in believing the cross of St George had become a flag of cricketing convenience.

At the same time, however, it was only a year since the final fall of apartheid. The stasis in English cricket – especially given the game's colonial provenance – appeared a mere footnote to such seismic socio-political and cultural progress. Indeed, the England side's fleeting highlights of the preceding 12 months had starred (Jamaican-born) Malcolm, whose bowling figures of 9–54 against

South Africa the previous August have only ever been bettered by one England bowler, with best support coming from DeFreitas. In the grand scheme of cricket, let alone the planet, was Henderson not obsolete?

In that context, my main focus here is not to discuss the content of Henderson's diatribe in forensic detail so much as the reasoning behind the decision to publish it, the depressingly disingenuous response of those who took that decision to the furore which followed (which saw defamation suits brought by DeFreitas and Malcolm against WCM settled out of court), and any potential for a similar error of editorial judgement today.

What was unequivocal was the counter-attack launched against Henderson by modern-day cricketers on all sides. In terms of its players, a game whose boundary ropes were marked out by imperialist racism has rarely spoken with one such strident or eloquent voice. Surely the men behind Wisden's magazine would be uncompromising in admitting the folly of promoting Henderson's claims that black England players harboured 'a generally resentful and separatist mentality' and, more sinister, that their lack of the 'desire to succeed' for England was a 'matter of biology' (Henderson, 1995b, pp9–10). The cricketing world had contributed to, and was only just benefitting from, the fall of one racially informed regime. Why entertain the notion of creating another?

In his editorial for the 1996 edition of the *Wisden Cricketers' Almanack*, editor Matthew Engel, also then a member of WCM's editorial board, did acknowledge 'the mistake' of publishing Henderson's views on 'race and cricket', while describing Henderson's 'thesis' as 'piffle' and the idea that England's team selectors should discriminate against black players as akin to apartheid and 'abhorrent and unthinkable' (Engel, 1996). What Engel did not mention was that his editorial in the 1995 *Wisden Almanack* had been quoted in Henderson's article. Engel had declared:

> It cannot be irrelevant to England's long-term failures that so many of their recent Test players were either born overseas and/or spent their formative years as citizens of other countries ... There is a vast difference between wanting to play Test cricket and wanting to play for England.
>
> (Engel, 1995, p11)

Those players included, of course, DeFreitas (born in Dominica) and Malcolm. Also missing from the 1996 *Almanack* was a real flavour of Engel's immediate response to the publication of 'Is it in the blood?' as given to *The Observer*: 'There is a problem of how you marry the wider question of race and nationality into the narrow issue of sporting patriotism. I'm not sure it helps if you scream "racist" when someone makes a contribution to that debate' (Mitchell, 1995a). Not least, perhaps, if that someone has quoted you.

Frith's tone, initially one of near indignation, also changed markedly over time, but seemingly to one of exasperated resignation rather than moral regret. Having, in cricketing parlance, gone on the front foot when speaking to

The Observer – 'Some people are scared of [this issue]. It's healthier out in the open' (Mitchell, 1995a) – the WCM editor, 'surprised' by the strength of feeling he had encountered, apologized via the Press Association to 'all whose sensibilities have been offended by the article', but complained that his wish to launch a 'beneficial debate' had fallen victim to 'distortions in certain sections of the media' (Press Association, 1995). Two days on, Frith told *The Observer*: 'I've been up there like a dart board on Henderson's behalf and I've had enough of it' (Mitchell, 1995b).

In his editorial for the following month's edition of WCM, Frith wrote of having aimed to debate a 'question-mark beside foreign-born England cricketers' in order to 'spotlight these misgivings and wherever possible to dismiss them, so that cricketers … could be cleansed of suspicion about commitment'. 'Instead', Frith added, 'a whirlwind was generated, perhaps caused almost as much by the somewhat cold nature of Mr Henderson's language as by the fact that many of his suppositions caused outrage.'

The idea that Henderson's talk of 'negro blood' and 'Interlopers' could be underplayed as 'cold language' or misinterpreted, or that Engel could provide Henderson with the succour of 'going along' with *anything* he said, prompted Marqusee (1998, p7) to bemoan the 'myopic insensitivity' of the cricket establishment on 'issues of race or nation'. Given Henderson's history, that insensitivity seems to have been not so much myopic as wilfully blind on behalf of *Wisden Cricket Monthly* – indisputably part of cricket's media 'establishment'. For 'Is it in the blood?' was not Henderson's debut work for WCM. In 1991, as an article under the heading 'A fundamental malaise', the magazine published a letter he had sent to numerous cricket writers which attributed the England team's poor form solely to 'a lack of pride' caused by 'the destruction of any real sense of national cricketing identity', and talked of how the 'inclusion of South Africans, West Indians and an Indian … offends my sense of rightness or proportion' (Henderson, 1991). Moreover, 'Is it in the blood?' was itself a response to reaction to another Henderson (1995a) missive, 'Bad selection: A case study', printed in WCM in April 1995.

In his repeated accommodation of Henderson's views, Frith clearly saw WCM as promoting a valid debate on cultural identity. After all, Henderson had produced depressing evidence that numerous older stalwarts of cricket's establishment sympathized with his crusade. Yes, perhaps also swayed by the fact that Henderson's complaints encompassed England's selection of white South African-born players such as Robin Smith (who came to be regarded as one of the most committed England players of the modern era), Frith's August 1995 editorial in WCM also bemoaned the worst of the media's aforementioned 'distortions' as its shifting of the debate from 'national identity to race'. However, that theory is exposed by the shift in ideological emphasis within the concluding paragraph of 'Is it in the blood?', in which Henderson suggested that his cultural question mark against 'foreign players' was a biological fact.

Then there was the tenor of Henderson's own defence of the article in the days following its publication. In saying he 'would not select Asians or blacks' (cited in Baker, 1995), he only further exposed a basic racist agenda he has since neglected to disguise. Nevertheless, Frith later wrote in his autobiography that the response to 'Is it in the blood?' – a title that Henderson insists was coined by Frith – was evidence of the demise of free speech in Britain.

To compare Frith's indignance with the response of, say, former England player Vic Marks – who described 'the blinkered' using 'those without Anglo-Saxon origins as convenient scapegoats for failure' as 'sinister and deeply disruptive' (Marks, 1995) – is not only to appreciate Marqusee's (1998, p4) claim that, again, the only binding element within 'Is it in the blood?' was 'the logic of racism', but to wonder whether, in the post-9/11 era, there is still the potential for misjudgements in the reporting of 'race' and national identity in cricket akin to those made by Frith.

In his optimism that a repeat racist aberration will be avoided, cricket writer and academic Rob Steen (pers comm) alludes to one happy paradox of the decade since 2001: the advancement of Asian players within English county cricket. Steen says:

> I would say I've noticed a change [in cricket's reporting of race] in the last 10 years, but particularly with Monty Panesar's emergence. He wasn't the first homegrown British Asian to play for England by any means. But he was embraced by the public, and as much because of his weaknesses as his strengths, and he became this folk hero. I think that said a lot about the public and I think in these sorts of issues the press can sometimes follow the public rather than the other way around. Monty was built up by the press to a certain extent because he was a very fine left-arm spinner and the fact he was the first Sikh to play for England. But I think the crowds took it that degree further. I think quite a lot of progress was clear from that, which is why I don't expect anyone to write or publish a piece of the Henderson nature again.

On the Panesar effect, which Carrington (2010, p158) sees as 'establishing new paradigms for what it means to be English', *Daily Mirror* cricket writer Dean Wilson says: 'There was genuine love for Monty ... but was he really adored for his cricket or as a figure of fun when he would make a mistake in the field, at least early on in his international career?' – but believes the benefit of more British Asian players, particularly those from 'traditional' Asian backgrounds such as Panesar, breaking into the England set-up will only really be felt when more of them become mainstays of the side (Wilson, pers comm). That said, Wilson adds:

> I definitely feel times have changed; that there has been a massive shift in racial attitudes in the UK in the last 15 years which certainly applies to

cricket and the way it is reported. Yes, there are issues for debate – such as guys who have learned absolutely *all* their cricket in South Africa or elsewhere playing for England – but what really concerns me now in terms of race and cricket in this country comes down to class, or rather economic issues; issues of ghettoization and some communities in which ethnic minorities are not integrating as much as we would like with cricket because it is not a cheap sport to play at club level.

Yes, at first glance, history has not been kind to Robert Henderson. Not only has he been banished from mainstream journalism, but his dismal, almost dystopian vision of an unsuccessful, multicultural England team in the grip of a treasonous but zealous liberal elite has been proved delusional. Between 1999 and 2003, the captaincy of Madras-born Muslim Nasser Hussain began the process of lifting England from their lowest ebb with an intensity which both set the tone for today's efficient England regime and lent further lie to Henderson's theories – cultural or biological – on patriotism (Henderson having marked out Hussain in 1991 as an under-committed 'Interloper').

Since then, England's rise to the number one team in Test cricket has been overseen by a captain who was born and initially bred in Johannesburg, plotted by a Zimbabwean coach and featured key contributions from several South African-born batsmen, yet all founded on a formidable team ethic. A smattering of Muslim players (and the Sikh, Panesar) have also featured, if not starred; Eoin Morgan, born and raised in Dublin and a former Ireland player, was also England's inspiration in winning the 2010 Twenty20 World Cup.

Again, a question for students of sports journalism today is not merely what someone like Henderson means by 'unequivocal' or 'true' Englishmen, but whether such a term can be safely applied in a multicultural age. Pity anyone who would have dared use Fred Trueman's Jewish grandmother to question the patriotic fervour of the frank-talking doyen of England fast bowlers. Similarly, nobody questioned the commitment of David Lawrence when the Gloucestershire bowler was stretchered off after shattering a kneecap while bowling against New Zealand in Wellington in February 1992. Born in Gloucester to Jamaican parents, Lawrence fell foul of Henderson's (2011) argument in 'A Fundamental Malaise' that: 'Where a man is born is irrelevant. What distinguishes him is his instinctive allegiance to a culture and the assumption in childhood of the manners and values of that culture.' In reality, Lawrence fell foul in Wellington of over-commitment, having felt pain in his knee before he volunteered to bowl. Henderson (1995b) may have overlooked Lawrence when he speculated in 'Is it in the blood?': 'It is even possible that part of a coloured England-qualified player feels satisfaction (perhaps subconscious) at seeing England humiliated, because of post-imperial myths of oppression and exploitation.'

Frith's reasoning for entertaining Henderson's opinions was clearly grounded in a concern for cricket and its heritage. However, it also appeared bound up in the same loose ideology of 'fair play' which informed so many English

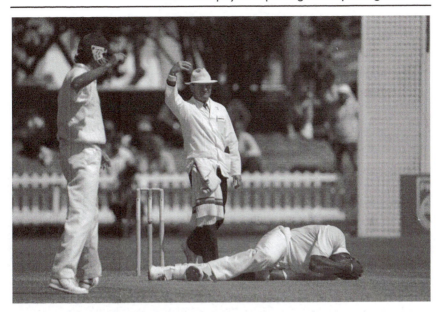

Figure 6.2 David Lawrence of England, 10 February 1992
(Source: Ben Radford/Allsport/Getty Images)

attitudes to cricket abroad, and he was at best naive in his treatment of someone who grows ever-more deserving of his dismissal, by Marqusee, as a 'rank racist crank' (Marqusee, 1998, p7). Judged more harshly, while Engel sought to be clear in separating his misgivings over the commitment of some foreign-born England players from the issue of 'race', Frith – who also once talked of (the presumably 'untrue' Englishman) Devon Malcolm acting, thinking and sounding 'like a Jamaican' – was arguably guilty of recourse to basic racial and cultural stereotyping.

All that said, Henderson may claim a measure of vindication in that his increasing preoccupation with the position of black people within UK multi-cultural society has coincided with a marked decline in the number of black youngsters engaging with cricket at English county level, let alone pressing for a place in the national team. Although this decline does not support Henderson's belief that England's selectors are hamstrung by political correctness – instead, the success of the side's current 'Interlopers' smacks of a genuine meritocracy – it suggests a dislocation between cricket and a community whose identity it once shaped.

A community lost?

In the decade after Middlesex's Roland Butcher braved the blistering pace of legendary West Indies bowlers Andy Roberts, Michael Holding, Colin Croft and Joel Garner, along with equally excoriating local newspaper headlines such as 'Our boy, their bat', to become England's first black Test cricketer at Barbados, the island of his birth, in March 1981, nine more sons of Caribbean fathers followed his lead (one of them, Mark Ramprakash, was of Guyanese Indian lineage). That total of ten is only two less than the number of black footballers who represented England in the ten years after Viv Anderson blazed a trail. If that seems surprising, it is perhaps because while the decade up to July 2011 saw 24 black footballers debut for England, just one black cricketer did so – and he played just once. In that context alone, the prospect that Hampshire's Michael Carberry's one cap will be his last (he no longer flies long haul after suffering a clot on the lung) casts its own shadow. Yet, the horizon for black English cricketers is gloomier still.

Roland Butcher was one of five black players to tour the West Indies in 1989. In 2011, excluding Carberry and the veteran Ramprakash, there were barely half a dozen black English, or English-qualified, players throughout senior county cricket: 18 teams, 2 divisions, Twenty20 razzmatazz and all. Of them, only Derbyshire's Chesney Hughes, Warwickshire's Keith Barker and Kent's Robbie Joseph were playing regular first-team cricket. That would have been unthinkable during the 1970s and 1980s, when the West Indies' grip on the game was matched only by their hold on the UK's Afro-Caribbean community, who enlivened the terraces of The Oval and other Test match grounds in paying vociferous homage to Clive Lloyd's all-conquerors. So direct was the legacy of men such as Worrell that the Middlesex team of the early 1980s featured four of England's own black pioneers. In 2011, a county able to trawl London for talent had not one black England-qualified player on its senior books (Middlesex CCC website, www.middlesexccc.com/players.asp).

In contemplating why young British black men have seemingly turned away from a game which C. L. R. James and others regarded as their birth right, much store is understandably set by a conspiracy of time and decline. The West Indies team, under the maladministration of the nation's cricket board, has grown depressingly short on class and cachet in the last decade and a half. The recent reign of Chris Gayle as captain almost invited a reinterpretation of Caribbean cricket as 'calypso' – a tag the teams of the 1970s perceived as patronizing and had fought unprecedentedly hard to escape.

'There must be a knock-on effect', said Mark Alleyne, the then Gloucestershire player-coach, in Rob Steen's pointedly titled 2004 article 'Whatever happened to the black cricketer?'. In the same lament, Gladstone Small, England's fourth black player, sang a different but not dissonant tune: 'I got my love of the game from my granddad. My cousins played, everyone I knew in Barbados played. Now we have a generation that doesn't have that history' (cited in Steen, 2004).

Fast forward to today and Steen (pers comm) admits: 'It's a very different time [in English cricket] in some ways because Asian players have pushed through in the meantime … but you still wonder where the next one [black

England player] is coming from.' Indeed, both Steen and Lord Herman Ouseley, former head of the Commission for Racial Equality and chairman of football's anti-racism campaign group *Kick It Out*, believe that cricket's relatively impoverished modern-day status of sporting poor relation on either side of the Atlantic – relative, ironically, to sports rich in black icons – both explains and perpetuates this particular malaise. Ouseley (pers comm) says:

> Young black men in the Caribbean aspire to American football and basketball, where there are a greater degree of earnings and therefore much more attraction. To an extent, it's the same situation here in the UK: it's easier for a black guy to play football.

Steen (pers comm), in a reference which also applies to Caribbean islands where football – or soccer – is now also highly aspirational, adds: 'Because black players have made such progress in football, there's almost the attitude: "Who needs cricket?" There are simply no [cricketing] role models for them.'

Steen is reluctant to attribute the problem to 'racism within cricket writing or even within county cricket'. But Ouseley (pers comm) perceives – as does Dean Wilson – an associated issue within which black cricketers are wrestling with bonds of class and culture, not simply race or national identity:

> To play cricket? Well, you've got to join a club and that often means facing up to a snotty attitude. Football is the easier – and cheaper – option. That is where much of the blame for the decline in young black cricketers is.

But while Wilson acknowledges that a lack of money and role models have undermined cricket's standing in its former Afro-Caribbean strongholds in London, Birmingham and elsewhere, he pinpoints media sociological stereotyping as another factor. 'It hurts and angers me that there is still a general perception of Afro-Caribbean men as wasteful, poorly educated and lazy.' A still chronic absence of black cricketers from coaching positions in English county cricket (Alleyne was the third and last, before former West Indies captain Jimmy Adams at Kent in 2012, to fill such a role) says as much, while also clearly linking to physiological and biological myths which have blighted black cricketers, as explored by Gilroy (1993a), Hoberman (1997), Crabbe and Wagg (2000) and others.

Efforts have been made to boost black interest in cricket through the launch of inner-city schemes such as Capital Kids Cricket and the Wisden City Cup. But both Alleyne ('They work out the sums') and former Warwickshire wicket-keeper and coach Keith Piper ('Kids' minds are geared towards the easiest way to make money') told Steen of black youngsters abandoning cricket in their teens. Along with anecdotal observations, past empirical evidence – like that provided by McDonald and Ugra (1998) – also pointed to a two-tier structure in which Asian and black teams were denied access to English club cricket's mainstream and were effectively ghettoized by the reluctance of 'white' clubs to engage with them.

Some contend that the attempt to take cricket into inner cities is itself divisive – feeding 'old myths that portray the inner cities as black, urban cricketing wastelands' (Miller, 2005, p245) and what Engel himself wrote of in 1999 as 'cricketing apartheid' and 'accepted practice' in English 'recreational cricket'. But while such concerns may have been allayed somewhat by the emergence of young British Asians almost throughout county cricket and on the England scene, has Britain's press contributed to its black community's disavowal of cricket? In 2004, Steen pre-empted Wilson in arguing:

> The reluctance to give black achievers their due has exacerbated that sense of dislocation, of un-belonging. The media reach for the stereotypes. [Alex] Tudor? Soft slacker. [Norman] Cowans? Mouthy slacker. Chris Lewis, the most gifted "New Botham" of all? Daft slacker. Lack of emotion is seized upon, inferring a concomitant shortfall in commitment.

Now, Steen (pers comm) believes the problem has evolved from within rather than without: 'Cricket just doesn't matter enough to people there [the UK's black community] now ... and I don't see it changing. But I don't think that's because of any racism that's going on on behalf of the journalistic profession, or racism in county clubs even.'

However, while the chief catalysts for this situation may lie across the Atlantic – in different, more lucrative sports or within cricket itself – why are no black former England players regulars in the Sky Sports' cricket commentary box? Why is Wilson the UK's only black or Asian national cricket writer?

In defiance of Tebbit – and of difficult times

From the all-but-disappeared to the fast-emerging: where the early 1980s appeared a landmark period – however illusory – for black English cricketers, the post-Millennium era has been a watershed for British Asian players, a stream of whom have impacted strongly enough upon the county scene to win recognition by England. Counties such as Leicestershire, Warwickshire and Worcestershire, in particular, have succeeded in connecting with local Asian communities steeped in cricket.

There were 25-plus England-qualified British Asian players in the 2011 County Championship. It is a happy but partly paradoxical situation. For while those players aspire to wear the Three Lions, they are inspired – as witnessed by the animated support within their communities for India, Pakistan and Sri Lanka Test teams touring England – by the cricketers of the Asian subcontinent.

That this marriage of heritage and birth right, in which a player such as Luton-born Panesar can do right not only by his homeland but also spiritual kinsmen such as Sikh spin bowlers Bedi or Doshi, should thrive is an obvious challenge to Norman Tebbit and co. More significantly, it should caution the Western cricket media against reporting issues of race, religion and national identity through the blinkered prism of the inarguable sociocultural tensions and creeping ignorance of the post-9/11 era, although some perspectives were skewed even before then.

Ironically, given that Robert Henderson – in 1991's 'A Fundamental Malaise' – had specifically questioned Nasser Hussain's commitment to the England side ('he thinks of himself as Indian although – how big hearted of him – for cricketing purposes he considers himself to be "English"'), Hussain himself – then England captain – said in May 2001: 'I cannot understand why those [British Asians] born here, or who came here at a very young age like me, cannot support England' (cited in Syal, 2001).

If he was ruminating on the route to better race relations, both Hussain's focus and, unfortunately for a batsman, his timing were wrong. On the same weekend, Asian youths fought with National Front members and police, most violently in Oldham, Greater Manchester, in the UK's 'worst racial violence for more than 15 years' (Bunyan and Sparrow, 2001). The contrast between glib aside and grim social reality could not have been greater. As *The Guardian*'s Vivek Chaudhary (2001) reflected: 'If Hussain cannot understand why we do not follow England, then he has obviously spent too long being pampered by the cricket establishment and become disconnected from the experience of ordinary British Asians in this country.' Assimilation? The problem on the street was alienation.

And why should British Asian kids *per se*, not just those feeling disenfranchised from 'English' society, not lean on their heritage? Does Tebbit accuse the children of English expatriates of refusing to assimilate within Australian culture if they fly the cross of St George during an Ashes series? Assimilate? Is the convenience store or the curry house, while also stereotypes, not symbols of assimilation at least as strong as Britain's adoption of the barbecue? Are Anglo-Italian football fans – whose mother country is claimed to be a genetic island – guilty of Tebbit-defined treason in cheering on the Azzurri against England? Many of India and Pakistan's British-born cricket fans support the England football team. Why? Perhaps because they enjoy no Indian or Pakistani footballing heritage to speak of or lean upon. Perhaps because they are *British Asian* and, as Chaudhary (2001) suggested, 'proud to be British' but also 'proud of our ancestry'. Less optimistically, in research into the ethnic make-up of local cricket leagues in Lancashire, Williams (2000, p52) concluded:

The rapid growth in the number of Asian clubs indicates how Asians are in many ways outside the mainstream of popular culture in England and also suggests that Asians have felt it increasingly important to emphasise their traditional loyalties and identities.

Chaudhary (2001) described the appointment of Hussain as England captain 'a wasted opportunity to reach out to Asians'. Four months later, events in New York and Washington, DC, skewed many white English people's already antagonistic view of Asians – or, for those who recognize the distinction, Asian Muslims. As well as grave sociological consequences, that retrograde ideological shift also affected UK media coverage of cricket in the Asian subcontinent.

The fixed view of Pakistan: Hypocrisy and Harry Potter

Cricket in Pakistan has long been beset by corruption, with allegations of match-fixing and player collusion with bookmakers stretching back to the 1970s, and firm proof of wrongdoing emerging in the decades since. This, among other factors, created periodic tensions between Pakistan's national side and opponents, particularly the England team, long before 9/11. Moreover, it resulted in negative representation of Muslims by sections of the UK sports press symptomatic of what we now describe as Islamophobia.

In its perceived malfeasance, however, Pakistani cricket has never been alone. Match-fixing, like cricket itself, began in England, with one of the first stars of the English game, William Lambert, found guilty of the offence in 1817 and banned for life from playing at Lord's, where bookmakers operated freely. Pycroft (1865) quotes another English player recounting how bookmakers would 'buy us up'. More recently, it is accepted that the majority of today's unscrupulous cricket bookmakers are based in India. The Indian Premier League Twenty20 competition – the richest in cricket – has faced a government-sanctioned investigation into corruption. India's former captain, Mohammed Azharuddin, was banned for life after admitting in 2000 to fixing three one-day international matches, having been implicated by Hansie Cronje when the then South Africa captain confessed to taking payments from Indian bookmakers over a four-year period. In 1998, Australia's Mark Waugh and Shane Warne admitted accepting money from a bookmaker for pitch and weather information while in Sri Lanka in September 1994 and throughout England's 1994/1995 tour of Australia. During that same winter, while not yet admitting to dealing with a bookmaker themselves, Warne and Waugh publicly accused Pakistan player Saleem Malik of offering them money to throw matches.

Malik was banned for life in 2000. But Warne and Waugh, having confessed in 1998, were only ever fined. Azharuddin, meanwhile, is now a member of the Indian parliament. In 2004, two years after his death in a plane crash, Cronje was named the 11th greatest South African. There was no Western media clamour for Warne or Waugh to be banned, just as there was no unified call for Mike Atherton to be suspended over the 'dirt in the pocket affair' at Lord's in 1994, after the England captain was caught on camera rubbing dirt on one side of the ball in a Test match against South Africa, and then failed to admit to the match referee to having had dirt in his pocket, but was merely fined £2000.

The latter instance is instructive, given that ball-tampering predated corruption as cricket's topic *du jour* in the early 1990s in examining whether its press coverage reflected a double standard – a 'them and us' mind-set. A comparison between that coverage and the reporting of two more recent events – the death of then Pakistan coach Bob Woolmer in 2007 and the spot-fixing offences committed by three Pakistan cricketers in 2010 – may also gauge whether that double standard applies ever-more strongly to Western media discourse on Pakistan cricket today.

In August 1992 in the *Daily Mirror*, England batsman Allan Lamb branded Pakistan fast bowlers Wasim Akram and Waqar Younis as cheats, claiming they had doctored the ball to achieve the then-new phenomenon of 'reverse swing'. Lamb was paid by the newspaper. The ensuing row dragged on for several years and into the civil courts. *The Mirror*'s coverage was, at best, unashamedly, unequivocally nationalistic, and informed by age-old stereotypes within what was formerly known as the 'East' as a sociological and cultural opposite – and poor relation – of the West: a 'pervasive image of Otherness' (Burdsey, 2010, p316) as also explored by Said's 'Orientalism' (1978), Saeed (2007) and others. At worst, as Searle (1993) observed, it was 'scurrilous, vicious and subliminally racist'. The message conveyed by the British tabloid headlines recorded by Searle – 'Nailed: Paki cheats' (*Daily Mirror*) and 'Pak off the cheats' (*The Sun*) – was far from subliminal.

Figure 6.3 Wasim Akram and Waqar Younis of Pakistan
(Source: Pascal Rondeau/Allsport/ Getty Images)

A small mercy, not least as reverse swing would soon be universally recognized as achievable by legal means and has become a staple feature of cricket, was that *The Mirror* did not quite win universal support within the UK press, with *The Guardian*'s Mike Selvey (1992) describing it as a witch-hunt, and even right-leaning titles such as the *Mail on Sunday*, the *Daily Mail* and the *Evening Standard* occasionally offering a more considered perspective, going so far as to describe Waqar and Wasim as blameless – perhaps in lieu of the numerous previous reports of English and Australian players applying Vaseline or lip balm to the ball, or worse.

However, Searle (1993) catalogues the general consistency with which British newspapers – tabloid and broadsheet – treated two bowlers who had been the unqualified toast of county cricket when playing for Lancashire (Wasim) and Surrey (Waqar) previously – that treatment ranging from jingoistic innuendo to socio-biological nonsense such as 'a theory that Pakistani sweat (rubbed in to provide the polish on one side) has different properties' (Johnson, 1992). While Searle (1993) observed: 'The hypocrisy between English cricket and its press guardians came teeming out', the *Glasgow Herald*'s Brian Meek claimed that 'beneath all the sporting arguments there is a nasty racist slur emerging – namely that the wogs won't play it straight. And, as ball tampering is as old as the sport itself, that is just plainly ridiculous' (Meek, 1992).

Almost two decades later, in examining the coverage of the death of Woolmer to analyse the treatment of Islam and Muslims in the UK press, Malcolm et al (2010) discerned similarly uniform use of negative cultural stereotyping in which the historical portrayal of Pakistanis as 'deviant, aggressive, volatile and ill-disciplined' (Marqusee, 1998, p189) appeared to have been crystallized by the Western paranoia at work in the post-9/11 era.

Woolmer, Pakistan's coach and former England all-rounder, was found dead in his hotel suite in Jamaica on the morning of 18 March 2007. The day before, Pakistan had been knocked out of the World Cup after a shock defeat to Ireland. The Jamaican police initially stated that Woolmer had died of natural causes; but a report by a local pathologist prompted them to announce, on 22 March, that Woolmer had been strangled. Between then and 12 June, when the police – acting on the findings of three other pathologists – reverted to their original theory, the suspicion of murder provoked reporting rooted as firmly in stereotype as it was in fantasy.

While murder was suggested, British newspapers, having evoked the paternalistic racism of the colonial era in portraying Woolmer as a figure of reason cast adrift in a culture of irrationality and instability, played judge and jury to pin the 'crime' – in a hasty stitching together of hoary prejudices and fresh paranoia – on fanaticism (fans), fundamentalism (terrorists), organized crime (illegal bookmakers) or, in their assumption that cricket, corruption, violence and terrorism are inextricably linked within Pakistan, all three. So Woolmer's death was given an 'exaggeratedly violent portrayal' (Malcolm et al, 2010) – although there had been no evidence of physical assault, the 'attack' on him was described as 'brutal' (*Daily Express*, 23 March 2007) and 'horrific' (*The Sun*, 23 March 2007) – and suspected to be the work of 'Islamic fanatics' (*Daily Star*, 30 April 2007), 'radical Muslims' or a 'Fatwa' (*Daily Mail*, 30 April 2007). Other reports made much of claimed links between match-fixing book-makers and terrorists, or entertained claims which placed the supposedly pernicious influence of Islam within cricket and right at Woolmer's door:

> Naseem Ashraf, the PCB chairman ... suggested that the heavy fundament-alism of [Pakistan captain] Inzamam[-ul-Haq] and the team's leaders was imposed counter-productively on the younger members ... Woolmer always spoke positively of the impact of religion on the team. The ques-tion being asked here, though, is whether peace of mind through Islam delivers the ideal battling mentality on a cricket pitch.
>
> (Slot, 2007)

In its own right, the 'Islamization' of a once largely secular Pakistan team under Inzamam-ul-Haq's captaincy, and several players' affiliation to the Tableeghi Jamaat preaching movement, had also bred suspicion in India. But the reluctance to distinguish between Islam and fundamentalism tapped all too casually into what Richardson (2004, p75) described as the widespread and indiscriminate post-9/11 perception in Britain of Muslim 'inferiority, negativity and threat' and the UK press's own 'reservoir of ideas, or core images about Muslims' (Richardson, 2004, p230).

However, the overarching impression left by the English media's handling of 'Woolmergate' is cultural. This was never clearer than when a rumour – apparently bandied about by some Jamaican policemen but seemingly never lent much credence by the wider authorities – that Woolmer had been poi-soned, possibly by snake venom, was seized upon by, among others, the BBC's *Panorama* programme. Yes, a seemingly classic whodunnit scenario was always likely to be pursued by the press; but the added suggestion in Britain was of a pervasive, almost medieval malevolence at work, with reference to Harry Potter and the description of an 'ancient poison' (*Sunday Mirror*, 1 April 2007; *The Sun*, 20 April 2007; *The Independent*, 21 April 2007) or 'ancient potion' (*Daily Express*, 20 April 2007), reinforcing the narrative of Pakistan as a rear-thinking sub-society in the thrall of arcane practices and dark arts, with its people – indeed, a somehow homogeneous, deviant Muslim world *per se* – barely any less savage than the Solomon Islanders depicted in *Strand Magazine* over a century earlier.

Lest we forget, the scientific and dispassionate conclusion was that Woolmer died of a heart attack. Of more lasting significance than any wild tabloid rumour sparked by this sad but personal event were the wayward suppositions that it prompted in the Western press – and their potential passive acceptance by the public. One reminder arrived in March 2009, when the purportedly inextricable link between Islam and violence was re-examined in the wake of an attack on the Sri Lanka team bus in the Pakistani city of Lahore, which killed seven people and injured two players. Pakistan has not hosted a Test series since, which is an interesting counterpoint to the refusal of any visiting teams to cancel tours of England during the height of the IRA's bombing campaign on mainland Britain during the 1970s.

However, a yet more inviting opportunity for the UK press to revert to (stereo) type came in August 2010, after the *News of the World*'s exposé of spot-fixing by Pakistan players during the fourth Test against England at Lord's. Bowlers Mohammad Amir and Mohammad Asif and batsman Salman Butt were later found guilty by the International Cricket Council (ICC) of accepting money from an agent for information on when no-balls would be bowled. The trio were banned from all cricket for five years. In November 2011, all three were jailed after being convicted of conspiring to accept corrupt payments and conspiracy to cheat.

With no lack of cold facts at hand, the coverage of the spot-fixing affair never quite lapsed into full, florid Woolmer-scale conspiracy theory or lurid rumour. The evidence against Amir and Asif was compelling enough for the affair, initially, to be widely reported without recourse to racial or religious stereotyping. Beyond the initial front-page splashes and indignant headlines, some journalists urged perspective and even a measure of sympathy for the youngest of the protagonists: 18-year-old Amir. Colin Bateman, in the *Daily Express*, wrote: 'To corrupt sport is not right but it is worth remembering that Amir does not live in the well-structured, supportive, highly rewarded world of English cricket' (Bateman, 2010). *The Mirror*'s Dean Wilson (pers comm) adds: 'You need to ask: what would you do when a bent bookie comes and says "I will do this or that to your family if you don't bowl a no-ball"? What would any of us do?' Indeed, Tariq Ali, writing in *The Guardian*, seemingly perceived the coverage to be too even-handed, denouncing the 'rotten core of Pakistani cricket' and reflecting:

> Some of the media comments on this affair are interesting, but irrelevant. Yes, W. G. Grace was a cheat on and off the field. Yes, captains of other teams – India and South Africa – have engaged in similar practices. Yes, the betting syndicates are a major part of the problem. So what? Since when has one crime justified another?
>
> (Ali, 2010)

Yet, a section of the UK press struggled to recognize more contemporaneous double standards than any to which Tariq Ali referred. The first cricketer to face criminal charges over alleged 'spot-fixing' was an Englishman, Mervyn Westfield, who was arrested in May 2010. On 16 September 2010, Westfield was charged with conspiracy to defraud. Although it came less than three weeks after the *News of the World*'s spot-fixing splash, the decision to charge Westfield commanded barely 200 words in the following morning's *Daily*

Express. Four days later, the same newspaper was one of many to give banner headlines to Sir Ian Botham's call for Pakistan to be banned from world cricket. In January 2012, Westfield admitted to accepting money to deliberately concede runs in a game in September 2009.

In that context, it is perhaps not surprising that some British newspapers ultimately remained wedded to familiar cultural generalizations in their regard of the conduct of a trio of one country's cricketers as a mirror for far graver acts committed by a much smaller minority of fanatics within a faith followed by 1.2 billion people worldwide. More than that, some journalists had already made tenuous but provocative insinuation that cricket in Pakistan is somehow complicit, or at least implicated, in Islamist terrorism. Following the attack on the Sri Lanka team in Lahore in 2009, the *Daily Mail* revisited a topic popular in the days after Bob Woolmer's death – the marriage of the son of Javed Miandad, director general of the Pakistan Cricket Board, and the daughter of underworld boss and alleged terrorist and match-fixing overlord Dawood Ibrahim. Miandad has little input into Pakistan team affairs, as witnessed by his outspoken criticism of the board's decisions on team selection; but the *Mail*'s innuendo suggested more:

> Interesting fact No 1: Javed Miandad, the Pakistani legend, now director general of the Pakistan Cricket Board, is related by marriage to one of the most wanted men in the world ... Interesting fact No 2: On the first two days of the Test match between Pakistan and Sri Lanka, the team coaches left at the same time and travelled to the match together under escort. However, on the third day, when the fateful attack occurred, the Pakistani bus left five minutes after the Sri Lankan coach. ICC match referee Chris Broad, caught up in the machine-gun assault on the Sri Lanka squad, said: 'After this happened you think, "My God, did someone know something and hold the Pakistan bus back?"' Good question.
>
> (Kelly, 2009)

Miandad's call in February 2011 for Amir, Asif and Butt to expose 'the entire mafia working behind spreading the menace of spot-fixing in our sport' (*Indian Express*, 9 February 2011) went unreported by the *Daily Mail* – not surprising, given their sports writer Martin Samuel's polemic in the days after the spot-fixing story broke, which spoke of 'no darker force in modern sport than Pakistan cricket', and asked: 'Why should we offer our hospitality (considering that terrorism has made it impossible to play international cricket in Pakistan)?', concluding: 'The fix was in. They were at it. They've been at it for years. No more. Not this time' (Samuel, 2010). Samuel's reaction to the criminal charge against Mervyn Westfield – raising as it did the prospect of 'us' being 'at it' too – went unrecorded.

The ease with which terrorism and the bowling of deliberate no-balls are presented in some quarters of the UK press as shared cultural signifiers has a parallel in what Lord Herman Ouseley believes is 'a wider reflection of the way people see Islam/Muslims in a British context following 9/11 and the 2005 bombings here' and itself further colours attitudes and behaviour towards British Asians. Perceiving a 'rich mix of Islamophobia and xenophobia', Ouseley (pers comm) adds:

> When people suggest there's a close relationship between the Pakistan sporting psyche and corruption, then other people believe it. There's always a sense of suspicion in much of the coverage of Pakistan cricket and when you look at the back pages of certain newspapers, they still carry the same message: of corruption within Pakistan. It's a case, partly, of what we're conditioned and fed to believe. The problem is how such coverage is used to reinforce so many other things.

Thus, almost two decades on, Ouseley sounds a depressing echo of Searle's (1993) condemnation of the coverage of the Waqar/Wasim affair as a 'mirror of daggers', if not explicitly his warning of 'acts of violence and malice' being committed by readers 'goaded by twisted headlines and simplistic jingoism'.

A happy paradox

All the more intriguing, then, that British Asian cricketers themselves – and, increasingly, British Asian Muslims, in particular – should provide a counter-point to the climate, whether within certain newspapers or society at large, of paranoia and prejudice. While Burdsey (2010, p315) examined how 'dominant subcultural and off-field aspects of professional cricket are perceived to be conducive to observing the obligations of Islam', Ouseley (pers comm) also applies sociocultural rationale to a seemingly paradoxical situation, saying:

> The British Asian community tend to enter into the cricket club ethos together. There's the fact that cricket, now more than ever, is all-conqueringly huge in the sub-continent. But there's also a class element to it, in which people want to be seen playing cricket, with its sense of village green decency and of generally classy people playing it. That may only be a perception, but I think it's at work in the Asian community.

As encouraging as the emergence of young British Asians in English first-class cricket has been, Rob Steen wonders if new challenges await the UK media as English cricket's accommodation of British Muslims develops in potentially awkward concert with the closed view of Islam attributed to the British public by the Commission on British Muslims and Islamophobia (1997) even before 9/11. Steen (pers comm) says:

> I do think it's still a tricky issue and that there's always potential for problems, particularly if the national team isn't doing well. Remember the context in which Robert Henderson was writing. Yes, it's very different today – we've got a good team and English cricket is generally in a good place right now. But I think over the next couple of years there are going to be some testing times for the objectivity of some of our writers.

You've got an interesting situation coming up here now I think in Moeen Ali at Worcestershire. He's the first proper homegrown Asian if you like who is captain of a county side. OK, not full-time captain [Ali deputized in the post during the 2011 county season], but he's ascended another rung in that ladder. He's obviously a little bit more religious than most Muslim players. He's got 'the beard' and he could and should be a contender for the England one-day side at the very least over the next couple of years. I think that will be an interesting little development in terms of the way he is presented.

The other interesting test for me is the guy at Yorkshire, Azeem Rafiq, who has been in trouble with his Twitter comments and got suspended, but is also as good a young Asian player as English cricket has got and is very cocky. So how people respond to him will be interesting. If he doesn't come up with the goods when playing for England, he could alienate people. These are examples of things where there could have been – or could be – issues in terms of media. I don't think there really have been but that doesn't mean that with Rafiq and Moeen Ali there isn't the potential – if the team starts losing and people start looking for scapegoats – for problems.

Potential never to be realized? In Steen's happy belief, 'at least four of the [England] team will soon be Asian', echoing Simon Barnes's prediction that 'the future of England cricket is tied up with English people of sub-continental extraction' (Barnes, 1999). Let us hope so.

Conclusion

Cricket, given its colonialist history, its origins in quintessential (some would say unequivocal, and others imagined) Englishness, the shift in its modern-day power base to the Asian subcontinent, its interfaith compass and much more besides, perhaps best epitomizes the paradox perceived by Carrington and McDonald (2001b) in which sport is both an arena where racism can be challenged and a forum for it to be expressed.

Cricket's media, never more so than in the multimedia age, can lead the fight against stereotypes old and new or reinforce them. For example, while the success of British Asian cricketers clearly promotes a positive discourse on issues of race and national identity, the concurrent rise of UK-based Islamophobia places pressures on the domestic press to properly pitch their coverage of Muslim players, no more so then when reporting negatively – albeit sometimes out of necessity – on cricket in Pakistan. The scale of the mistake made by *Wisden Cricket Monthly* as recently as 1995 underlines the danger of reverting to lazy generalizations or outright racism when discussing cricket's multiculturalism, within which the media discourse on the apparent decline of the 'black cricketer' is both essential and potentially problematic.

The relatively unicultural make-up of the Western cricket media – just one UK national newspaper cricket writer is non-white – is also, if not an outright shame, a cause for concern given the situation outlined above and accusations such as that levelled by Indian commentator Ravi Shastri amid the supposedly conciliatory events of the second Test between England and India at Trent Bridge in August 2011, when he accused English cricket – and, by insinuation, its media – of being 'jealous' of India's soon-to-be relinquished position as the world's best, as well as richest, cricketing nation (Ronay, 2011).

While cricket must try to ensure that the sport's biggest headlines are made on the field by maintaining its ethos – wherever its origins – of fair play, its media must also play fair by reporting cricket as a sport first and a cultural mirror a distant second.

Chapter 7

Football

The 'excluded Asian' representation

I think in general, football writers are waiting for more Asian lads to come through. I suppose they think it would be good for the game ... We're waiting for it to happen really and we've been waiting for such a long time. When football writers do talk about Asian footballers, they're just asking the question, 'why aren't they coming through'?

(Interview with *Leicester Mercury* sports journalist Rob Tanner, 5 May 2011)

Introduction

The exclusion of British Asian professional football players is something that has puzzled onlookers and spectators for several decades. Problematically, though, a series of common-sense rationales have been enacted in order to explain this under-representation. Sociocultural barriers are commonly highlighted, suggesting that cricket is simply more popular or that British Asian parents steer their children towards education or religion rather than football. Conversely, 'race' or physical inferiority, a colonially formed ideology or stereotype, is also one that is often utilized. Although these rationales have been witnessed within the sport media, both standpoints harbour major flaws.

This chapter aims to examine how British Asian and Anglo-Asian football players are represented within the sport media. Thus, the research will explore the interconnections between 'race', ethnicity, masculinity and national identity. The term British Asian means a British-born individual who has two parents who are of South Asian descent. Conversely, the term Anglo-Asian refers to someone who has one parent of South Asian descent and one parent who is either white English or white British.

The discussion will begin by analysing South Asian colonial stereotypes, questioning whether ideas of physical inferiority still permeate the consciousness of journalists, media consumers and those within footballing institutions today. Through using a multidisciplinary approach, the research will investigate whether the South Asian stereotype of being 'small and slight' is still prominent in the mediated public sphere (Fleming, 2001a, p114).

Next, we pay particular attention to the mediated representation of Pakistan international and former Fulham FC defender Zesh Rehman. Rehman's ethnicity, religion and 'Otherness' was questioned in 2005 following his comments on Islamic arranged marriages. His views stirred up some debate within the press and his constructed 'Otherness' will therefore be critically examined. In the broader sense, then, are British Asian players footballers first and Asian second, or vice versa? Does their ethnicity overshadow their identity as a professional footballer? And are British Asian players presented as being included within the fabric of Britain's most popular sport, or are British Asians still seen as 'Other'?

Third, role models will be analysed, particularly the media's utilization of Anglo-Asian players. It has been suggested that Anglo-Asians are perhaps not representative of wider British Asian communities, although they are commonly put forward by the media as being the next British Asian star. Thus, the analysis will highlight the potential problems of promoting Anglo-Asians as British Asian role models.

Finally, the chapter will discuss the theory of over-hyping young British Asian players to the extent that their abilities are distorted by the sport media and other organizations. The research will adopt a critical approach to this trend and examine whether this type of reporting may have, in fact, hindered the British Asian cause further. It will also contextualize this trend and offer reasons why it may or may not have decreased in recent times.

South Asians and hyper-feminization

During colonial times, the 'superior' British 'race' did not consider 'Others', particularly non-whites, as equals, but inferior peoples. For instance, Indians were considered to lack the perceived 'racial' qualities of a 'healthy race', while Bengalis were thought to be 'weak and effeminate people' (Dimeo, 2001, p61). Thus, the superior colonizers aimed to impart their 'way of life' upon the backward and inferior indigenous peoples. Burdsey (2006, p481) iterates that central to the British colonizer's mission was 'moralisation' and 'religious indoctrination' of Indian peoples. But embedded within these processes was the role of sport, and 'beliefs about physicality and representations of the body became primary agents in colonial constructions of the Indian "Other"' (Burdsey, 2006, p481).

It is worth noting that although colonized South Asians were initially considered homogeneously weak, the Indian Mutiny of 1857 managed to alter Britain's consciousness. Because the military uprising was initiated by Bengali officers, they were considered 'unreliable' and therefore 'deliberately excluded' as the British began to recruit and 'focus on soldiers from parts of India that remained loyal to the British', such as Punjabis and Gurkhas (Dimeo, 2001, p61). The media even publicized accounts of Bengalis that indicated, rather bluntly, that they were biologically inferior, as the nineteenth-century journalist

G. W. Steevens noted that: 'The Bengali's leg is either skin and bones ... with round thighs like a woman's. The Bengali's leg is the leg of a slave' (cited in Burdsey, 2007a, p22). These stereotypes were heavily influenced by the Indian Mutiny, which resulted in the Bengalis' exclusion in the post-1857 armies. Thus, because some Bengalis rebelled, they were racialized as being homogeneously untrustworthy and both physically and mentally weak.

A fitting reply to the effeminate Bengali stereotype was delivered in 1911 when a Bengali Indian football team named Mohun Bagan defeated the British military's East Yorkshire regiment in the final of the Shield competition (Dimeo and Mills, 2001; Johal, 2001; Burdsey, 2007a). Following Mohun Bagan's two goals to one win, a local Bengali newspaper, the *Nayak*, wrote that:

> Indians can hold their own against Englishmen in every walk of art and science ... It fills every Indian with joy and pride to know that rice-eating, malaria-ridden, barefooted Bengalis have got the better of beef-eating, Herculean, booted John Bull in the peculiarly English sport.
>
> (cited in Dimeo 2001, p68)

This report indicates that although Bengali Indians are at a supposed disadvantage (culturally and economically in terms of food/diet as well as equipment/boots), they can still match Englishmen biologically in the art of football. Put simply, the Shield competition allowed Bengalis to 'find a voice on the football field, and the voice echoed and re-echoed all over India' (cited in Dimeo 2001, p69). In short, this victory was not just a victory for Mohun Bagan's players; it was a victory for all Bengalis. For Dimeo (2001), the 'victory was a moment of nationalist resistance when the ideological underpinnings of colonialism, the belief in innate British superiority and in Indian physical frailty, were dramatically and publically undone'. However, despite this, the idea of South Asian (and now British Asian) physical inferiority still appears to permeate the consciousness of Western society, as one former professional British Pakistani footballer noted his experience of this stereotype:

> One time when I was younger playing for City I got knocked off the ball and a parent commented on the side saying: 'Oh, yeah, he's weak, they're weak'. At that time I didn't know what 'they're' weak meant; I didn't click on. And after that I says: 'me weak', and in the back of my head I couldn't accept that. I said, 'I'm not weak'. And I walked home that same day from the ground with my rucksack on and I thought what am I going to do when I get home? I'll try lifting some heavy stones in the garden. So, I've gone home and I've tried picking bricks up.
>
> (Interview, 19 March 2011)

As this oral testimony shows, British Asians still arguably suffer from the hyper-feminized stereotype even in contemporary times. Although stereotypes may appear innocent, they can and do have a genuine impact upon the lives of the groups whom they categorize. Despite the sport media being arguably less blatant or overt as nineteenth-century journalists with regards to biological classifications of 'race', the ideology is still upheld in popular discourse. Within modern-day journalism, codes of conduct are enacted in order to ensure ethical and responsible journalism at all times. Reports should attempt to remain objective and impartial, if possible. Although the sport media may not overtly report that British Asians are excluded from football because of biological reasons, it does not stop the media from reporting the views of institutional figures, otherwise classed as primary definers (Hall, 1978), within the game. For example, former Leicester City Manager Dave Bassett commented that 'The Asian build is not that of a footballer ... It may well be that Asian ingredients in food, or the nutrition they take, [is] not ideal for building up a physical frame' (BBC TV, 1995, cited in Fleming, 2001a, p114). Bassett is adopting a common-sense approach here, which simplifies the British Asian exclusion as being a 'racial' or genetic problem. As Burdsey (2006, p478, original emphasis) articulates, 'it is widely believed that British Asians do not or, indeed, *cannot* play football ... due to an inability to withstand the physical contact or because of inhibiting structural elements, such as diet and religion'. Therefore, one could argue that external differences such as skin colour become the first port of call when attempting to explain the under- or over-representation of certain 'races' within certain sports. There are two significant problems with Bassett's comments. First, it homogenizes all Asians as a single entity, whereas in reality, it would be more accurate to view Asians in the plural as a community of communities. Second, one has to comprehend that these views, which lack concrete scientific evidence, may influence media consumers to maintain the belief that there are real biological differences between 'races'. Furthermore, one has to question whether comments such as this which filter throughout the mediated public sphere would affect the mind-set of young British Asian footballers, let alone other managers, coaches and scouts. Although overt racism is arguably decreasing within the game, if stereotypes such as this are still upheld by elite figures, and purported throughout the sport media, is sport really a level playing field? Thus, were the media correct in broadcasting these comments which may have influenced consumers' perception regarding 'race' thinking? We are not for one moment suggesting that Bassett's views on the British Asian exclusion are in isolation; one could argue that many figures within the game today still embrace such stereotypes. It would also be difficult to prove whether Bassett and other elite figures adhere to this stereotype because of the media's dominant representation of the 'hyper-feminized' Asian, rather than their personal experiences within the game (Alexander, 2000; Goodey, 2001; Burdsey, 2004a). In short, if managers, coaches or scouts have only ever encountered one or two British Asian players during their careers and both struggled physically, they may generalize, adopting a 'common-sense' approach (Gramsci, 1971).

Nevertheless, over a decade has passed since these comments were made; however, empirical research suggests that some, though not all, white British and even British Asian players, coaches and scouts within football still embrace these archaic stereotypes:

> They don't like physical contact, I think that's their problem. Why are they good at cricket? Why are they absolutely exceptional at squash? Why do they not participate in any other sports where there is physical contact? Rugby? Football? They do participate but they don't participate to the highest level … it's just talent wise, physical contact and an understanding of the game.
>
> (Interview with white British scout, 2 June 2011)

> I do think the Asian lads struggle physically … That's not to say that every single Asian lad does, you might get one Asian lad that's stronger than a white British lad and vice versa; but generally from my experience white players are stronger and fitter as well.
>
> (Interview with British Asian scout, 27 May 2011)

Both views suggest that British Asians struggle to contend with the physical requirements of football. Again, although these arguments are littered with colonially rooted stereotypes, both opinions may have been constructed through their experiences within the game. Nevertheless, one could suggest that both of these scouts may have internalized or embraced the media's hyper-feminized Asian image. Put simply, once stereotypes are formulated and publicized within the media and society, they remain increasingly difficult to remove from popular culture and public consciousness. Although 'race' science has been thoroughly discredited from a scientific discourse, Fleming (2001a, p115) notes that the benign stereotype of 'natural' sporting ability, or in this case, lack of ability, has been 'internalized by many people'. Although the British Asian scout somewhat adheres to this stereotype, he is more 'on the fence' as he suggests that this rule does not always apply. The white British scout, on the other hand, strongly subscribes to the notion of physical inferiority. Significantly, Bains and Patel's (1996) research highlighted that such views were not uncommon as they found that 69 per cent of professional club officials believed that Asian players were physically inferior compared with those from other groups. Bains and Johal (1998, p47) rightly suggest that given clubs' 'lack of contact with Asian people generally, and footballers specifically, on what basis were they formulating such opinion?'

From a media perspective, then, this research has noted that in recent times the sport media do not overtly represent British Asians in football as different, in the biological sense anyway. Gone are the days when journalists rather overtly reported Indians as biologically inferior. Even comments such as Bassett's are very rarely witnessed within the sport media today. This could be because these dated ideologies are arguably decreasing, sports journalists may be less interested in this angle or sports journalists understand that this angle may cause offence or may be too controversial. The sport media will not explicitly state that British Asian athletes are physically inferior to any other 'race'. Nevertheless, despite Michael Chopra, who is perhaps England's most famous British Asian or, specifically, Anglo-Indian football player, holding his own at a high level of the professional game, he has not avoided comments regarding his physicality. *The Journal* ran a story with the headline 'Chopra is sent on toughen-up duty' before his 2003 loan move to Watford FC. Within the article, Sir Bobby Robson commented that: 'He will be kicked and he will be roughed up. He will have to learn about the physical side of the game. He is not the biggest of players and he has to learn to deal with that' (Edward, 2003). The tradition of sending out young players on loan to gain experience is certainly not uncommon. In Chopra's case, it appears that he needed to improve on his physical attributes to advance further. However, one could suggest that because there are so few British Asian football players, media consumers may have generalized, resulting in the British Asian physicality being seen as the obvious or common-sense barrier to their footballing exclusion. Another reference to Chopra's build can be witnessed in the *Sunday Telegraph* as Chopra 'is more of a predator, less an all-round centre-forward' because of his 'slight of build' (Barclay, 2003). These references to 'build' arguably do not help dispel the myth that the 'Asian frame' is to blame. Conversely, though, some reports have challenged such beliefs through the notion of empirical falsification, as *The Observer* commented that: 'At West Ham, centre-half Anwar Uddin is doing well in the reserve team and disproving the notion that Asians are too slightly-built to make the grade' (Campbell, 2001).

It is important to mention that we must not view sports journalism, once considered the 'toy department' of the media industry, and the news media as two separate entities as both are powerful and can utilize negative stereotypical imagery. Because there is not an abundance of articles written on British Asians in football, due to the British Asian exclusion, one has to comprehend whether the news media's representation of hyper-feminized South Asians and British Asians may have influenced media consumers' ideologies. As we have already established, the traditional stereotype was one which lacked masculinity and physicality. In comparison, black Britons, who are over-represented in professional football, have never struggled to be seen as masculine as they have routinely been represented as dangerous, hyper-sexual and naturally athletic (Back and Solomos, 1996; Hoberman, 1997; Boyle and Haynes, 2009).

During recent times, though, we have witnessed a major shift in the mediated representation of young British Asian males. There has been a repositioning concerning British Asian physicality and masculinity as Bangladeshis and Pakistanis, in particular, have shifted from being 'victims of racist violence to being viewed as hyper-masculine and prone to criminality and wanton disorder' (Burdsey, 2007a, p27). Mediated examples such as the 2001 northern riots which took place across Oldham, Burnley and Bradford highlight that British Asian communities are no longer passive receivers of racial discrimination and violence. Put simply, second- and third-generation Asian immigrants are 'unwilling to accept the second-class status foisted on their elders' (Kundnani, 2001). Hence, the British Asian male youth are attempting to resist the stereotypical connotations of 'Asianness' and what it means to be young, male and of South Asian descent in modern-day Britain (Burdsey, 2004a, p298). For Brake (1985, p142, cited in Goodey, 2001, p433), 'the stereotype of the passive, uncomplaining Asian withdrawing into his or her tight-knit community has been replaced by militancy. East London, especially the Bengali community, has long learned to defend itself physically, after hundreds of attacks.' Therefore, British-born Asians are tackling racial discrimination and are now challenging the stereotypes that have plagued their forefathers. Can this polar opposite shift from hyper-femininity to hyper-masculinity, therefore, overturn the stereotypical notions that Asian peoples are physically lacking? Can this mediated shift challenge the perceptions that British Asians are not strong enough to compete within professional football? On the other hand, one also has to acknowledge that this hyper-masculine representation, which has been fuelled by rioting and acts of religious extremism and terrorism, may in fact have an adverse effect. It may 'increase existing racial antagonisms and inequalities' (Burdsey, 2007a, p27), exacerbating the notion that ethnic minorities, or in this case British Asians, cannot 'fit into' the Western 'way of life'.

Aside from analysing newspapers, the research also examined a BBC online forum entitled 'Breaking down barriers for British Asians' which opened a lively discussion concerning the under-representation of British Asian football players. It was interesting to find that out of 58 comments that were posted while the forum was live, only one participant suggested that biology was a barrier, noting that 'An average British Asian is at a physical disadvantage' (Fletcher, 2010). Hence, has the hyper-masculine notion permeated the consciousness of contemporary media consumers? Or were these results compromised as participants may have been hesitant to note biological factors since this could be construed as racist? Arguably, the forum suggests that popular discourse does not register physicality as a significant barrier for British Asian players. The most popular view put forward attributed the exclusion to cultural barriers and, specifically, parental factors. Because scientific discourses of 'race' are becoming increasingly marginalized ideologies within media discourse, cultural barriers are now arguably seen to be more realistic, acceptable and, most importantly, less racist. As a result, skin colour is no longer the defining characteristic as 'language, dress, musical preferences, sporting identifications and religion become key cultural markers of distinguishing "insider" and "outsider" groups' (Carrington and McDonald, 2001a, p1). Thus, it is important to examine how British Asian identities, ethnicities and cultures are presented within the sport media.

The British Asian 'Other'

Although Burdsey (2007a) suggested that British Asian football players actively seek to underplay their ethnicities and adopt the 'white mask' (Fanon, 1986), there is one footballer who has arguably not played down his ethnicity, religion or identity. Former Premier League defender Zesh Rehman publicly aired his views on Islamic arranged marriages (Bhatia, 2005; Dhaliwal, 2005) and his decision to represent Pakistan, rather than England, at international level (Bassey, 2005a). Rehman has also established his own charity, the Zesh Rehman Foundation (ZRF), which aims to inspire young British Asian hopefuls and to instil a belief that football can be a likely career and no longer a pipe dream. Rehman does not shy away from his British Asian identity and is attempting to positively use it to challenge perceptions and stereotypes regarding British Asian players.

Rehman embraces his 'Asianness' and thus it is important to examine his representation within the sport media. Despite proving a positive role model, he has not escaped from criticism during his career, commenting in 2005 that he would have an arranged marriage in order to make his parents 'happy' and 'keep the tradition going' (Bhatia, 2005). Thus, his 'Other' culture, religion and identity become central to this story. Significantly, though, this case study would have been non-existent if Rehman was not a professional footballer as arranged marriage within some religions is a commonality. However, this story arguably becomes news-worthy as Rehman is a professional footballer and therefore is embedded within Britain's most popular cultural practice. Football is perceived to be ideologically 'white', Western, civilized and steeped in British national histories. Burdsey (2009, p706), who adopts a critical race theory (CRT) approach, notes that 'it remains the case that most dominant histories of the national game are "whitewashed"'. Arguably, this feeds into the notion of 'the West' and 'the rest', 'us' and 'them' (Hall, 1992a). The article, which contains the news value of surprise, suggests that being a footballer and holding strong Islamic beliefs are perceived to be conflicting identities. Nevertheless, the story is, in fact, well written in terms of objectivity and impartiality, concluding, for example, that statistics on arranged marriages suggest that this religious practice is not uncommon.

Nevertheless, in the weeks following this article, two more stories, which presented differing views, were published. The first article that followed the *Evening Standard* offered a critique of British social values compared with British Pakistani ones. *The Times* article, entitled 'Meet Zesh and Wayne and then think again' compared the lifestyles and public images of both Wayne Rooney and Zesh Rehman (Coren, 2005). The article was timely as it linked Rehman's Muslim beliefs and British Asian background within a wider context of politics and anti-immigration. Coren (2005) reported that:

> I am afraid that what we are looking at here is the difference between prevailing British social values, and Pakistani ones. And yet Michael Howard has chosen to fight this general election on immigration, on

promises to keep people like the Rehmans out, so that people like the Rooneys will vote for him.

He highlights that Rehman has worked hard to make it professionally, noting that Rehman has also acquired A-levels and does not adhere to the common

Figure 7.1 Zesh Rehman of Fulham jumps (Fulham v Celtic, 16 July 2005)
(Source: Jamie McDonald/Getty Images)

stereotype of a Premiership footballer. Coren juxtaposes the social values of Rooney and Rehman in terms of lifestyle, culture and education. Although Bhatia's story was impartial, Coren's report favours Rehman's 'way of life', suggesting that his views on arranged marriages display a 'touching respect for his family and its original culture'.

Coren's article received a stern response, entitled 'Unhappy ever after' (Dhaliwal, 2005):

> The litmus test for the assimilation of Asians into British society has long been their breaking into professional football ... don't hold your breath if you think this 21-year-old [Zesh Rehman] is going to contribute to Britain becoming a beige-coloured, race-mixed Utopia.

Dhaliwal's (2005) comments are highly hostile towards Rehman and his Islamic beliefs, suggesting that Rehman is not the ideal man to challenge stereotypes concerning British Asians because he is arguably still 'backwards' in his thinking and at odds with British values. The article, therefore, subscribes to the notion that true assimilation will occur when 'Others' fully adopt the Western 'way of life', thus downplaying their own individual ethnicity, religion and identity. Dhaliwal (2005) further cites that arranged marriages are 'racist', 'homophobic' and do not play a 'constructive role in a modern multicultural society'. Arguably, these views are not uncommon as arranged marriages have faced criticisms in recent years. Nevertheless, these stories are significant because they promote the ideology that a Premiership footballer possesses alien views, which, in turn, mark him out as 'Other' or an 'outsider' within. Dhaliwal's article indicates that English football and strong Islamic beliefs do not go hand in hand. In turn, this may arguably fuel the belief that religion can perhaps act as a barrier to British Asian players.

This idea is further upheld when the sport media publish comments of football officials that suggest: 'You hear about Asian players stopping to say their prayers. They're different from us, have a different culture' (*Independent on Sunday*, 17 September 1995, cited in Back et al, 2001, p179). Bains and Patel (1996, cited in Back et al, 2001) found that half of the English professional football clubs they interviewed noted that cultural differences – meaning religion, language and diet – were reasons behind the British Asian exclusion in football. One interviewee noted that:

> I'm born and bred a Muslim and my religion comes into it. And, obviously, I've fasted and played. You've got people like Kolo Toure, Anelka, Mido, these are all Muslims. We fast for 30 days and when you say: 'Fast, for 30 days', they just look at you and say: 'How you gonna fast for 30 days'? You just cannot eat in daylight, that's it, eat or drink in daylight. It's hard to grab this concept, but the teams that I've played for,

I've just explained it to them and, honestly, they've appreciated it ... there's a lot of players I know don't fast, there's a culture breaking off.

(Interview with former professional British Pakistani footballer, 19 March 2011)

This player suggests that religion has not affected his playing career. Significantly, he notes that 'a lot of players' refrain from fasting now as there is a 'culture breaking off'. Hence, this purports the notion that perhaps the Asian 'culture' is being diluted or that these players arguably see themselves as footballers first and Muslims second, highlighting the fact that their identity as footballers takes centre stage. These examples suggest that it is possible to be a footballer while maintaining religious beliefs and practices, thus contesting Dhaliwal's (2005) claims that British Asians face insurmountable cultural and religious barriers.

As of the 2009–2010 season: 'Premier League teams have, on average, 13 foreign-born stars within their ranks' coming from countries ranging from Togo, Iran and South Korea (Williams, 2009). Put simply, one could strongly argue that it would be easier for a second- or third-generation British Asian player to 'fit in' in comparison to a foreign-born player with limited English skills. For *Leicester Mercury*'s sports reporter Rob Tanner, cultural background or skin colour is now inconsequential to sports stories:

We don't talk about their ethnicity ... I think football has gone beyond that now. It looks at a player now and it is: is he a good player or is he not a good player, not where he comes from or what colour skin he has. It doesn't even enter my head to be fair when I write about these lads.

(Interview, 5 May 2011)

This comment certainly adheres to the colour-blind notion that footballers are reported as footballers and their ethnicities, religious beliefs and identities are simply unimportant. Therefore, British Asians' skills on the pitch should drive stories, not perceived sociocultural differences. However, there have been several news stories published which overtly highlight such differences between communities, such as the *Sunday Mercury*'s diet-related story entitled 'Red card for mum's fatty curries' that focused on Zesh Rehman's eating habits (Bassey, 2005b), while Michael Chopra was tagged as 'the kid from the corner shop' within the *News of the World*'s piece entitled 'Corner Chopra' (Beasley, 1999). Although both stories appear innocent and soft news pieces, they both utilize stereotypical notions of 'Asianness' as 'corner shop'-dwelling 'curry lovers'. Despite these players wanting to be presented as footballers first and Asian second, these stories use the 'Asian' ethnicity and 'Otherness' to carry the article. Nevertheless, one should not be surprised by these types of stories as British Asians in professional football have been largely non-existent; thus, arguably, while British Asians remain excluded, they will continue to be under the white-dominated sport media's watchful gaze. Significantly, though, sports journalists must understand that British Asian communities are not simply homogeneous and can differ across various contexts. For example, the sport media need to think carefully before promoting an Anglo-Asian as a role model for the wider British Asian community.

Role models

It has been suggested that sport offers nations and 'races' a chance to combat stereotypes, while also reifying them (Hoberman, 1997; Brookes, 2002; Bernstein and Blain, 2003; Burdsey, 2007a; Boyle and Haynes, 2009). Muhammad Ali fought inside the ring but also outside in terms of tackling the negative stereotypes concerning Afro-Americans. Within football, Back et al (2001, p34) suggest that stereotypical perceptions of black players' skills and attributes have been 'exploded by the variety of black players in the professional game'. This led former England international John Barnes to suggest that 'Gone are the days in England when a black player could only be a forward, didn't like the cold, couldn't be a goalie or a defender or a manager. Barriers are going down … so stereotypes about black players are receding' (*The Observer*, May 1998, cited in Lindsey, 2001, p197). Because there is an over-representation of black players in English professional football, this has aided in combating negative stereotypes. However, one could argue that Barnes's comments do not apply to all ethnic groups and certainly do not correspond with British Asian experiences. Due to the limited British Asian involvement in the game, elite figures may adhere to time-worn notions of physical incapabilities or alleged sociocultural differences that have been prevalent throughout media and society. Sporting icons are powerful tools to help break down barriers. Within cricket, many British Asians have excelled and been capped at international level, such as Monty Panesar, Ravi Bopara and the Anglo-Asian former skipper Nasser Hussain. These players can arguably act as positive role models for young aspiring British Asian cricketers. Conversely, British Asian footballing icons are few and far between. Historically, it is Anglo-Asians, who are of dual heritage just like Hussain, who have had more success (Burdsey, 2007a, p65). But to what extent can Anglo-Asians be considered a success story for British Asian communities?

For Burdsey (2004b, p769), there is a perception that a 'more Anglicized upbringing might equip a player with a greater degree of the specific cultural capital necessary to become involved with a professional club'. Therefore, one could suggest that those of dual ethnicity, who have one white British parent and one Asian parent, stand a better chance of 'fitting in' at 'white' professional clubs, rather than those with two Asian parents. At the time of writing there are only five British Asians with professional contracts; three of those are of dual ethnicity and therefore should be rightly classed as Anglo-Asian. Only two of the five players have definitively 'made it' and play week in, week out.

Significantly, these two players, Michael Chopra (Ipswich Town) and Anwar Uddin (Barnet FC) are both of dual ethnicity, with white British mothers and Indian and Bangladeshi fathers, respectively. Thus, is it easier for Anglo-Asians to make it professionally? Does this suggest that the British Asian 'culture' acts as a genuine barrier? For Johal (2001, p159), 'to become a foot-baller in Britain one does not necessarily have to be white, rather one must be seen as being white, seen as being British, in a cultural, and thus a perceived ideological, context'. Hence, one could suggest that players who adopt the 'white mask' will therefore increase their chances of success (Fanon, 1986). In addition then, those players of dual ethnicity are arguably born with a slight advantage as they are equipped with an understanding and experience of both 'ways of life' and cultures. Professional Anglo-Asian footballer Anwar Uddin commented that:

> I've grown up with two sorts of cultures. I'm thankful for that and I think it's made it easier for me to *fit in* because it's made me more aware of how each culture lives. But ... the Asian people see me as being sort of different and the white people saw me as different so I've never really had a race or a culture that I can really call my own; I've always been that other.
>
> (Interview, 7 April 2011)

These comments highlight the feelings of many Anglo-Asians as they appear to be 'in the middle' of cultures and struggle to gain the acceptance of both groups. It is interesting to understand how the sport media covered Uddin's rise to fame. Was Uddin presented as being Anglo-Asian or was he wrongfully labelled as British Asian, ignoring significant social, cultural and, perhaps, religious differences?

> I was the first real [Asian] player to sign a pro contract at a Premiership club and the media jumped on it like a circus, but they all labelled me Asian, it was all Asian this and that. So it was forgetting that, you know, my mum's white and as cockney as they come and I'm half white and that is who I am; but having said that, as there was no one to fly the flag, no one to be the role model, I was happy for them to use me however they felt was right to help increase the Asian interest in football. I didn't really question it. Looking back on it now, you know, I am who I am. I am Asian, yeah, but I'm also English and I'm proud of that as well.
>
> (Interview, 7 April 2011)

Uddin was used as a figurehead to 'fly the flag' for British Asian communities. However, this simply ignores the fact that he has grown up in a very different sociocultural environment. Puwar (2005, pp64–65, cited in Burdsey, 2007a, p139) notes that racialized bodies, in this case Anglo-Asians, are seen as 'visible carriers of their ethnicities' and are therefore 'marked and bounded

Figure 7.2 Anwar Uddin of Barnet in action (Barnet v Northampton Town, 20 November 2010) (Source: Pete Norton/Getty Images)

by their ethnic identities' – meaning that they are considered and permitted 'to speak on behalf of *British Asian* footballers'. Arguably, from Uddin's account, the sport media presented him as 'more Asian' than 'white' in order to drive these stories. But as Uddin recalls, he has always been 'that other', stuck between cultures. This has led some British Asians to suggest that these differences are significant enough to separate Anglo-Asians into their own specific ethnic or 'racial' group; thus, Anglo-Asians, rightly or wrongly, may not be representative of the wider British Asian community.

The experiences of Uddin are not in isolation; fellow Anglo-Asian Michael Chopra was also presented as an Asian role model. For example, the *Daily Mail*'s headline of 'Loan star looking to set a trend; Chopra hopes he inspires Asians' illustrates that he is arguably perceived as being a representative figurehead for the wider British Asian community (Hardy, 10 April 2003). It is worth mentioning, though, that most (not all) newspaper articles that discussed Chopra's ethnicity rightly noted that he has an Indian father and a Geordie mother. Although Chopra had been built up to be a British Asian hero, he was reportedly 'striving to be a Geordie hero, not just an Asian star', thus putting more emphasis on his Geordie as opposed to his Indian roots (Bird, 2003). This remark caused some discomfort amongst young aspiring British Asian players:

> No disrespect to Michael Chopra; he's a talented guy. But when I was younger I saw an interview of his where he said he didn't consider himself Indian ... For me, I took a bit of offence to that because he was supposed to be representing us and instead he's turned his back on us.
> (Interview with British Indian semi-professional footballer, 3 May 2011)

> If you look at Michael Chopra, a lot of the kids from the South Asian community didn't relate to him because they didn't see him as fully South Asian. When the media portray him as a British Asian player, he's not British Asian; he's not viewed as a British Asian player by his own community, so how can you call him British Asian because he's not. He's not fully Asian ... he's not seen as coming from the same background; he hasn't had the same upbringing.
> (Interview with British Pakistani coach, 8 June 2011)

> If he was a proper Sikh, everyone would love it. No offence to him; but, like, if he had an Asian name, like, rather than Michael, do you know what I mean? Then everyone would be proud of him. Michael Chopra, sounds like he's basically English. He doesn't look Indian, he looks English.
> (Interview with British Indian semi-professional footballer, 6 May 2011)

The latter individual references religion, name and skin colour as being important markers of 'Asianness'. Put simply, because Chopra does not speak out about his religious beliefs in the media, because he has an English first name and has a light skin tone, he is seen as being unrepresentative of the British Asian community and therefore not an 'ideal' role model. Burdsey (2004b, p770) explains that because the media do not pay enough attention to the differences between Anglo-Asian and British Asian players, it covers over the reality that very few players with two British Asian parents are reaching professional level. Therefore, the sport media, various governing bodies and anti-racist football organizations that promote Anglo-Asians as success stories for all British Asians are actively forming a 'smokescreen' which masks the lack of real progress being made (Burdsey, 2004b, p771).

'Wonderkids' and the trend of over-hyping

Not only are British Asian and Anglo-Asian players presented as being physically and culturally different at times, the sport media and anti-racist organizations are also alleged to misrepresent players' progression. Burdsey (2007a, pp135–141) highlights three major problems with regards to this trend. First, the sport media misrepresent players' development, which subsequently paints a rosy picture concerning the British Asian inclusion within football. Second, it unfairly juxtaposes players with renowned international stars, making the expectation levels too high. Lastly, it separates these players on the lines of ethnicity, which may also go against the player's wishes (Burdsey, 2007a, p135). The sport media and anti-racist organizations towards the mid to late 1990s arguably jumped on the 'British Asian exclusion' bandwagon and began to publicize any player who fitted the bill.

Two players, in particular, started to receive press attention despite not having actually played for their first teams. Michael Chopra, who made his Newcastle league debut at the beginning of the 2003–2004 season, first started to attract the media's gaze several years earlier while playing for Newcastle Reserves, as well as England under 18s. Chopra was described in *The Observer* as being 'potentially' better than Alan Shearer, reminiscent of Michael Owen with regards to his 'lethal' finishing and tagged as 'the Premiership's first home-grown British Asian Star' who had 'the world at his feet' while being 'destined for greatness' (Campbell, 2001). Chopra was commonly heralded as a 'wonder-kid ... tipped to take the football world by storm' (Fraser, 2002), a 'toon wonderboy' who can 'break down barriers for Asian youngsters' (Lloyd, 2002) and a 'whizzkid' who will be partnering Wayne Rooney up front at the 2010 World Cup Tournament (Murtagh, 2002).

Similarly, another young British Indian player named Harpal Singh, formerly of Leeds United, also began to attract interest. *Kick It Out* (1998, p4, cited in Burdsey, 2007a, p136) widely publicized the former Leeds United manager George Graham's comments that 'Liverpool may have Michael Owen but we have Harpal Singh.' In addition, Singh was also tagged as 'City's first Bradford-born Asian superstar' following his loan move to Bradford City (*Telegraph and Argus*, 6 November 2002).

Figure 7.3 Michael Chopra celebrates after his goal (Sunderland v Newcastle United, 17 April 2006) (Source: Serena Taylor/Newcastle United via Getty Images)

Neither Chopra nor Singh effectively 'made it' at their respective clubs. Chopra played a handful of first team games for Newcastle United and has since plied his trade in the Championship despite having a short spell with Sunderland AFC in the Premier League. Although Chopra was labelled as a future England international and the first 'Asian star', he failed to gain a call-up to the England national side and in 2010 signalled his desire to play for India at international level. Additionally, Singh never played for Leeds United's first team and after a succession of loan spells and an unsuccessful permanent spell at Stockport County, he now plays non-league football.

Burdsey (2004a, p285; 2007a, p135) highlights that the media and anti-racist organizations publicize British Asian success stories, which in turn enables these players to be identified as role models by British Asian communities. However, the *Asians Can Play Football* report noted that: 'The proliferation of clumsy promotional events and occasional claims that we have unearthed the next Asian "superstar", a role model for others to follow, is merely a distraction from the much more pressing need for structural change' (Asians in Football Forum, 2005, p7, cited in Burdsey, 2007a, p137). Put simply, publicizing young British Asian footballers as 'superstars' and potential role models misrepresents the real progression. Second, it arguably indicates that racism or exclusionary forces are on the decline; thus, these 'clumsy' claims act as a distraction from the institutional barriers within football, such as the scouting system (Bains and Patel, 1996; McGuire et al, 2001; Burdsey, 2004a, 2007a). Third, because these claims are made far too often and the players in question do not fulfil their high expectations, it may reify colonially rooted biological stereotypes. The report also added that professionals such as Rehman and Chopra represent a 'novelty value' in football as they are just 'token Asian players who are wheeled out to demonstrate "progress". Instead, they should be part of a production line, one which is churning out dozens of British Asian football wannabes every year' (Asians in Football Forum, 2005, p7).

Problematically, then, by singling out British Asian players as 'token Asians' and unfairly building them up as role models, they are forced to carry the 'burden of representation' (Puwar, 2005, p62, cited in Burdsey, 2007a, p137). In other words, these players become permitted to speak for 'their' community and participate on behalf of 'their' peoples. Arguably, this places undue stress and unneeded pressure on young shoulders. Not only do they become representatives of the wider community due to their ethnicity, but they also become 'objects of fascination within the world of football and beyond' (Burdsey, 2007a, p137). This led one British Asian sports journalist to comment: 'We need to get rid of the whole "let's put them on a pedestal" scenario and just respect them for how they are doing and see how they progress' (Interview, 6 April 2011).

Aside from the media's role, it has been suggested that anti-racist organizations such as *Kick It Out*, who publicized Amrit Sidhu (formerly of Derby County) and Nevin Saroya (formerly of Brentford) during the late 1990s, as well as Chopra and Singh, may have a hidden agenda (Burdsey, 2007a). Thus, anti-racist groups need to show that 'they are achieving their objectives – both to justify their existence and to continue receiving funding – and so they need to give the impression that, as a result of their activities, British Asians have started to progress into professional football' Burdsey, 2007a, p138). Over-hyping a player and speculating that he has major potential undoubtedly looks better, from the group's point of view, than stating the plain and rather disappointing facts. Arguably, promoting such players as the stars of tomorrow indicates that 'progress' is being made, 'racisms' are receding and they are actively meeting targets to combat the British Asian exclusion. However, this continued under-representation has led some figures to criticize anti-racist organizations' efforts. One British Indian grassroots coach argued: 'It's all a front really. Are they [*Kick It*

Out] actually doing anything about it? Well, if they were ... we'd see a massive difference' (Interview, 4 April 2011). Another British Indian coach commented that: 'Even though I support *Kick It Out* and the work they're doing, what I'm finding is that not much has changed in terms of the Asian representation' (Interview, 6 April 2011). Thus, anti-racist organizations as well as football clubs that have policies and practices in place in order to combat the British Asian exclusion will be judged on the numbers that come through. Although this issue has been on the *Kick It Out* agenda for over a decade, numbers-wise, little advancement has been made. Hence, one can understand that when one British Asian professional footballer nears his first team debut, publicizing it will make the organization look like it is actively combating the exclusion, while simultaneously showing the players' football club in an anti-racist and positive light. *Kick It Out*'s media and communications officer, Danny Lynch, noted his personal experiences with regards to the over-hyping trend when attempting to gain an interview with former Walsall defender, Netan Sansara:

> Their response [Walsall FC] was 'Look, fine, but you do realize that he's only played about two games in 40 matches.' I was between a rock and a hard place as I needed that player to get an article in the *Standard* or the *Telegraph* or something; I needed that to do my job. However, I was happy that the club was taking on that responsible attitude for the wider issue. Perhaps I'm as much to blame as some of the media people that you're talking about. But our intentions I think would be slightly more honourable because I'm talking more about communities and community engagement; certainly not sensationalizing stories about the next Harpal Singh.
> (Interview, 5 April 2011)

Although it has been suggested that both the media and anti-racist organizations have over-hyped British Asian players, Lynch makes an important distinction between the content and style of their reports. Anti-racist groups attempt to tackle the 'wider issue' and promote the fact that players can be good role models for young kids, thus explicitly or implicitly highlighting the positive role that sport can play within society. Furthermore, *Kick It Out* need to raise awareness of the British Asian exclusion as it is on its agenda and championing promising players is therefore an arguable prerequisite. On the other hand, the sport media, in general, would arguably not attack such stories using the same news angle as anti-racist groups. Nevertheless, regardless of the angle or the reason, both groups are singling out British Asian players because of their ethnicity. If Chopra, Singh or Uddin were all white British, would they have received the same attention? It has also been suggested that professional clubs who publicize their British Asian players may also harbour an ulterior motive:

> Was he [Uddin] a guinea-pig for the publicity? Was he just at West Ham for publicity because he didn't play first team? He was just at the academy

and played under 19s and reserves. They got their marketing out there whilst they had their Asians in football project at the same time.

(Interview with British Bangladeshi former semi-professional player, 5 April 2011)

This account indicates that not only can the media and anti-racist groups be guilty of over-hyping, but so too can professional clubs. Many clubs such as West Ham, Leicester City and Bradford City have a large British Asian community on their doorstep. Thus, if these teams harbour a British Asian player within their ranks, it has been suggested that this would increase British Asian spectatorship levels and bring in more money for these clubs. In short, the sport media, anti-racist organizations and football clubs may all have their own specific reasons with regards to highlighting British Asian success stories in football.

Despite Chopra and Singh being particularly over-hyped, it was commonly suggested during the interview process that this trend is not specific to only British Asian players:

It happens all the time. Look at Gareth Bale, he has two good games and he's tagged as the second best player in the world, what's all that about? It goes on all the time; someone scores a couple of goals, the national papers jump on it and everyone calls them a superstar.

(Interview with *Telegraph and Argus* sports journalist Simon Parker, 27 April 2011)

You can blame the media for all sorts of things; but if you look at players from any background, players get built up to be shot down in flames very soon after, so I don't think that's a phenomenon exclusive to the Asian community at all.

(Interview with *Kick It Out*'s Danny Lynch, 5 April 2011)

All of those interviewed indicated that over-hyping players' reputations was just a facet of the media, regardless of colour, creed or 'race'. In recent years, aside from the British Asian community, we have witnessed a number of teenage players who have been built up within the media, such as Arsenal's Jack Wilshere and Theo Walcott. Walcott was tagged as a 'future world great' (Armitage, 2006), the 'new Messi' (Irwin, 2006) and the 'next Ronaldo' (Jiggins, 2006). The first two of these accolades were delivered just months after his Arsenal debut at the beginning of the 2006–2007 season, while the latter headline was utilized before his Premiership debut, having only ever had Championship experience. Significantly, before his move to Arsenal from Southampton in January 2006, he was described as a 'wonderkid' 41 times in the regional press, 5 times in broadsheets and 101 times in tabloids. In comparison, Chopra was only labelled a 'wonderkid' six times during his entire time at Newcastle United. Hence, to suggest that over-hyping is a phenomenon that only attaches itself to British Asian players is simply incorrect. In short, the empirical evidence indicates that any player from any background is susceptible to this trend. But with hindsight, how many white British or black British players have been unfairly over-hyped who did not make the grade at Newcastle United (Chopra), who never played a first team game for Leeds United (Singh), who never played a first team game for Derby County (Sidhu), or who never played a first team game for West Ham (Uddin). All of these players were championed as future Asian stars by various organizations; but with respect and due to various reasons, none managed to fulfil their unfairly high mediated expectations. A player should build their own reputations rather than have them built for them by the media and other organizations. One could suggest that British Asian players who appear to be on the fringes of making it professionally will always suffer from an increased media gaze simply because no player from a South Asian background has managed to hold their own in the top flight for a sustained period of time. However, during recent times, this trend of over-hyping British Asian players appears to have decreased.

Sidhu and Saroya prominently featured during the late 1990s; Chopra, Singh and Uddin received attention at the turn of the twenty-first century; and, more recently, Rehman and Sansara have gained some attention. But one could suggest that this trend has actually diminished during recent years. Arguably, we have not seen a British Asian or Anglo-Asian player receive unjustifiable media intrusion since Chopra and Singh over a decade ago. There could be a number of reasons for this, such as the fact that the current crop of players are not as good and therefore cannot be over-hyped; the media and other groups may have learned from their experiences with regards to past players; the new generation of players may be wary of media intrusion, drawing on past players' experiences; or perhaps the new British Asian talents are actively seeking to underplay their ethnicities in a bid to 'fit in', thus refraining from discussing their 'Asianness'. Nevertheless, there are two very promising young players, one British Indian and one British Pakistani, who have recently signed professional contracts with Premier League teams in 2009 and 2011, respectively. However, these players have received minimal media attention so far: they have not appeared on the *Kick It Out* website and their respective clubs have not publicized their Asian ethnicities. Thus, one has to question why this trend appears to have faded and why players such as Chopra and Singh were unfairly over-hyped.

Context is very important within this debate as the media increasingly began to scrutinize British Asians and Islam at the turn of the twenty-first century. The 2001 terrorist attacks on New York, as well as the urban unrest witnessed in the Northern cities during the summer of 2001 have intensified the fear of the 'Other' and, in particular, heightened the notion of Islamophobia. British Muslim, which means British Asian in the contemporary British context, has been constructed as dangerous and threatening to social cohesion (Saeed, 2003; Poole and Richardson, 2006). However, Burdsey (2007a, p62) notes an example of media hypocrisy as Muslims were 'criticised and admonished' during the aftermath of 9/11, but just one year later, 'notions of "Asianness" began to be celebrated and embraced rather than feared and rejected ... In 2001 the notion of "British Asian" was anathema; within twelve months it had become a marketing dream.' Thus, popular culture appeared to embrace all things 'Asian' as *Bend It Like Beckham* hit the cinema screens, Sanjeev Bhaskar hosted the comedy chat show *The Kumars at No. 42*, Channel Four screened a number of Bollywood films as part of its 'Indian Summer' season, while British Asian bands such as Echobelly and Babylon Zoo began to have some success through traditionally 'white music genres', such as indie (Burdsey, 2007a, pp62–63). Put simply, the mediated construction of 'British Asian' almost went full circle from enemy to friend. Conversely, although the media was awash with a constructed Asian exotica whereby British Asians were positively presented within the realms of entertainment and fashion, Poole and Richardson (2006, pp96–97) note that during 2003, the most prominently featured British Muslim in the press was Abu-Hamza al-Masri, who expressed 'hatred and violence' which had 'significant implications for the way British Muslims are perceived'. Thus, there appears to be two conflicting representations of 'Asianness' in the early twenty-first-century media reports. If we contextualize this period of time in relation to when Chopra and Singh began to emerge, 'Asian' was at the forefront of the news agenda. Significantly, the sports department does not work in isolation to 'hard news', and if 'Asian' is big news within current affairs, politics or entertainment, then it will arguably become a much more pressing news angle within the realm of sports reporting. Hence, promoting young British Asian success stories within football, a traditionally white working-class sport with a history of overt racism, perhaps highlights the advances that are being made by some British Asians and professional clubs with regards to social cohesion. Therefore, because 2001 saw 'race' riots in Bradford, Oldham and Burnley between British Asian and white British communities, Chopra and Singh thus become role models for the British Asian youth as they highlight that they can fit into a predominantly white social space. Just like Amir Khan who was championed as the acceptable face for British Muslims (Burdsey, 2007b), one could note that Chopra and Singh were also presented as 'acceptable Asians' within the post-9/11 and urban unrest era. The following anecdote indicates how important the media perceived British Asian football players and role models to be at this time:

> I felt there was a slight agenda with the Harpal Singh thing because at the time he was certainly the first Asian player involved. It was apparent to me that we would push this because he was from Pudsey, so he was like a local Asian player ... When they signed him in on loan it was the back page lead on the same day as we signed Delroy Facey from Bolton. I'd spoken to Facey the day before and he'd said about how he's just got over a bout of a very serious illness and he feared that he might have died in the summer, so I did this piece with him where I thought: 'That's a good

piece.' I wrote that as the back page lead with Singh inside and then found that Singh was the back page with Facey inside. There was more pressure to promote him because he was a locally based Asian player, that's fair to say.

(Interview with *Telegraph and Argus* sports journalist Simon Parker, 27 April 2011)

One could suggest that from a journalist's point of view, signing a relatively well-known Premiership player who has just recovered from a critical illness would be the back page lead nine times out of ten. However, because Singh was British Asian and Yorkshire born, his newsworthiness becomes heightened. When considering that Bradford is home to a large British Asian population, it is more likely that they would find greater interest in reading about 'City's first Bradford-born Asian superstar' (*Telegraph and Argus*, 6 November 2002). Newspapers gauge the mood and publish front and back page leads on something that will sell and thus bring in more revenue for the newspaper. This is a prime example of newsroom selection policies at work. Although the Facey story may have been more newsworthy in a national sense, Singh arguably offers more relevance to the immediate target demographic, especially when considering that his loan signing occurred less than 18 months after the Bradford riots. This is yet another example where a British Asian player has been singled out on the grounds of ethnicity. Once again, then, Singh is presented as Asian first and footballer second.

Aside from 9/11 and the 2001 northern riots, another significant landmark that heightened the scrutiny and gaze over the British Asian community was the London bombings of 7 July 2005. If we contextualize this time in relation to British Asian football players, Zesh Rehman, who was with Fulham at the time, was perhaps the most high-profile and brightest talent on the scene. Thus, just like 9/11 and the urban unrest of 2001 intensified the attention on Chopra and Singh, one would expect the same to happen with Rehman. Between 1 January 2005 and 6 July 2005, the day before the attacks, Rehman featured in 15 newspaper articles where he was considered a major element to the story. During this time, most of the articles focused on his Islamic views on arranged marriage and his shifting eating habits, from unhealthy to healthy curries. From 7 July 2005 to 31 December 2005, considering that the football season finishes during this period, Rehman featured in 29 articles, with most focusing on his decision to play for Pakistan at international level. Although the number has doubled, one cannot suggest from this evidence that Rehman became 'big news' despite being the first British Pakistani footballer to ever start a Premier League match. One British Pakistani coach highlights a potential reason for this:

People don't go watch defenders, they go watch attacking players, they wanna watch the goals, they wanna watch the flair, and they wanna watch the creative players ... I believe that only an attacking player can break down the stereotypes because all the hype surrounds them, all the media interest.

(Interview, 8 June 2011)

Aside from Rehman and other footballing role models at this time, another British Asian sportsman emerged: cricketer Monty Panesar. Significantly, then, the same quantitative test was applied to Panesar and it was found that between 1 January 2005 and the day prior to the London bombings, he appeared in only five newspaper articles, with the *Sunday Telegraph* calling the spinner a 'long-shot' selection for England (James, 2005). It is worth noting that the domestic cricket season runs from April to September and all five reports featuring Panesar appeared between April and June. Significantly, between 7 July 2005 and 31 December 2005, Panesar appeared in 173 articles. Although he was mentioned in only one article in June, he was discussed in 29 reports in July, 39 in August and 83 in September. Despite the *Sunday Telegraph* phrasing Panesar as a 'long-shot' England selection six-months earlier, by December, 'the promise of the full Monty' was a 'tantalising prospect for England' (Berry, 2005). Some other important factors may have enhanced Panesar's newsworthiness, such as the fact that England spinner Ashley Giles was nearing the end of his career and Panesar was tipped as a likely replacement, among others. Conversely, though, one could suggest that because being 'Asian' again became big news during the summer of 2005, Panesar's news appeal may have been exacerbated. Thus, he became a role model and an acceptable face for British Asians, just like Chopra and Singh previously.

The research has suggested that the socio-political context determines to what extent a player may be over-hyped. Thus, because being 'Asian' was big news at the turn of the twenty-first century and also in 2005, the media and other organizations promote community representatives as role models and, significantly, sports stars appear to fit that criterion. Although the trend of over-hyping is not necessarily specific to any 'race' or ethnicity, the evidence indicates that a high number of British Asian and Anglo-Asian players have been unfairly scrutinized and unjustly over-hyped. Nevertheless, during recent times this trend appears to be on the decline, suggesting that British Asian players are no longer being singled out to the same extent as they were a decade earlier. The media and society do not stay static: attitudes alter, ideologies change and what made news a decade ago may not make news today. Although the media and other groups turned the Asian exotica into big news at the turn of the twenty-first century (Burdsey, 2007a), more recently, 'Asian' may not carry the same newsworthiness as before. This may explain why the trend of over-hyping appears to have decreased in contemporary times. Nevertheless, this is not to suggest that a Chopra or Singh scenario will not happen again.

Conclusion

This chapter has critiqued the sport media, anti-racist organizations and football clubs' representations of British Asian and Anglo-Asian football players. Although the concept of 'race' has distanced itself from crude biological connotations, they still appear to exist within popular discourse to some degree. Problematically, ideas of physical inferiority still permeate the consciousness of some within the institutional sphere of football. However, as one would expect, explicit or even implicit references to physical differences are very scarcely witnessed within the contemporary mediated public sphere.

Conversely, because connotations of 'race' have attached themselves to ideas concerning national identity and ethnicities, racial markers can still be witnessed within the sport media. The utilization of role models has also been examined and it has been noted that the sport media and other organizations present Anglo-Asians as being representative of the wider community. However, British Asians are not a monolithic group as they differ across multiple factions. Hence, promoting an Anglo-Asian as just Asian simply disregards significant cultural, social and religious differences. Aside from Anglo-Asians, though, the 'ideal' role model scenario could be further complicated if broadened – for example, if a British Pakistani Muslim signed for a Premiership club, he may not actually be the 'ideal' role model for a British Indian Sikh.

Finally, the trend of over-hyping has suggested that this phenomenon is not exclusive to British Asian players; it is a feature that can apply to any player. Although Chopra and Singh are arguably the most over-hyped British Asian players whom we have seen to date, it has been noted that this trend is now on the decline. At the turn of the twenty-first century, 'Asianness' was a major news angle; now, ten years later, this news angle may arguably be less newsworthy. The fact that there are two promising professional British Asian players at Premiership clubs who have received minimal coverage may prove this. Although this research has examined the British Asian identity in a media sport context from various angles, what is clear is that British Asian and Anglo-Asian players have historically always been reported as 'Asian footballers', not footballers.

Chapter 8

Formula One racing

Non-whites in 'the world's whitest sport'

Race is both ever present and absent in the media framing of Hamilton ... He has been compared to Tiger Woods, Theo Walcott and Amir Khan – but rarely Nigel Mansell, James Hunt or David Beckham.

(Carrington, 2010, p159)

Introduction

Formula One (F1) racing has always been a multinational sport since its emergence in 1950. *The Times Online* published their '50 greatest Formula One drivers', which consisted of 33 Europeans, 4 Brazilians, 3 Americans, 2 Canadians, 2 Australians, 2 New Zealanders, 2 Argentines, 1 Columbian and 1 South African (Eason, 2009). This list of nationalities does nothing but emphasize how diverse F1 racing has traditionally been. Nevertheless, despite its much-credited diversity, non-white drivers have been invisible until now.

The Australian Grand Prix of March 2007 marked a significant landmark in F1 history as black Briton, Lewis Hamilton, donned the helmet to take to the track. Significantly, though, 'despite the efforts of his racing team McLaren to "play down" the race stuff earlier in his career by discouraging journalists from asking Hamilton questions about his colour, "race" remains a constitutive part of the many narratives about Hamilton' (Carrington, 2010, p159). Thus, with reference to two case studies, this chapter will discuss how Hamilton's 'race' has often become almost unavoidable from a journalist's perspective.

The analysis will begin with a discussion of non-white pioneers in F1 racing. Hence, the newly established team, Force India, will be examined, as well as Indian driver Narain Karthikeyan. We also explore Hamilton's emergence in F1 and analyse his somewhat non-traditional framings in comparison to other non-white sports stars. In short, we question to what extent non-whites are now embedded within F1 racing.

Following this, we look at the overt racism that Hamilton faced at the Spanish Grand Prix in 2008. We examine how Hamilton was presented, how the Spanish fans were portrayed and also attempt to gauge both British and Spanish media perspectives on the incident.

Finally, we explore Hamilton's controversial comments from May 2011 while live on the BBC. Following a disappointing race in Monaco where he was penalized by the stewards, he joked afterwards that the penalties enforced were because he was 'black', thus implying that institutional racism may be present. The discussion will focus on the somewhat problematic interlinking between 'race' and class within the subsequent media reports.

Non-white pioneers and the media

Just like the Olympics or the Football World Cup, F1 racing is an event that is closely followed worldwide. Drivers who have competed in F1 have emerged from different continents: Felipe Massa (Brazil), Kazuki Nakajima (Japan), Jody Scheckter (South Africa), Fernando Alonso (Spain). On that illustrious list it is now possible to add the first-ever black driver: Hamilton (more specifically, he is of dual ethnicity). But aside from Hamilton, further non-white participation has been witnessed in recent years.

Force India was officially launched in January 2008. The key figure behind the launch was Chairman and Team Principal Vijay Mallya, owner of India's iconic UB Group and Kingfisher Airlines. Force India's website claims that:

> With its name and patriotic logo now incorporating the colours of the Indian flag and its chakra, the team has become a sporting representation of the emerging generation of young, success-hungry, fast paced global Indians and the growing strength of India as a nation.
>
> (Force India Online, 2011)

This statement highlights the shifting ideological connotations that underpin the newly constructed Indian national identity. In short, Force India has become a 'sporting representation' or a societal mirror for the future generation of 'success-hungry' Indians in the globalization era. But to what extent does this show that Indians or non-whites, in general, are now embedded within F1 racing?

To the average spectator, one would expect a team called 'Force India' to harbour Indian drivers, employ Indians behind the scenes, have Indian owners and, most importantly, be based in India. However, Force India is based in Silverstone, England. Although Mallya masterminded the creation of Force India, it is currently co-owned by Dutch businessman Michiel Mol. None of the three employed drivers (Adrian Sutil, Nico Hulkenberg and Paul Di Resta) are Indian. Finally, none of the team's personnel listed online are from India. Hence, although the team is named 'Force India', its only real Indian link is through its founder, Mallya. Quite possibly, then, it could have been named 'Force Holland' because of Mol's co-ownership. Nevertheless, having a team called Force India promotes or symbolizes inclusion and diversity within, perhaps, the 'world's whitest sport' (Sanghera, 2011). Thus, it is arguably designed to raise awareness of the team's Indian ownership, therefore placing Mallya's 'race' and identity at centre stage. However, this does not suggest that Indians are widely included within F1 racing.

Another Indian involved in F1 is Narain Karthikeyan, who is making good progress. Karthikeyan's call-up to Team HRT also coincided with the first Indian Grand Prix, which took place in October 2011. Karthikeyan has placed India 'on the world map of motorsport' and has been tagged '"The fastest Indian in the world" by Autosport (the world's premier automotive racing magazine)' (Narain Karthikeyan Official Website, 2011). But is it right to label him as the 'fastest Indian in the world'? Clearly, Karthikeyan thinks so as the tag line is brandished on his website's homepage. Nevertheless, is this racializing his successes as being Indian first and driver second (see Chapters 4 and 7 for more information on this mediated facet)?

These two examples perhaps show that Mallya and Karthikeyan are more than happy for their 'Indianness' to be publicized. Arguably, there is a fine line between promoting one's sense of national pride and one's 'race'. Unlike the case of Christophe Lemaitre, where his skin colour was his defining characteristic within reports, Karthikeyan is tagged the fastest Indian, not 'brown-skinned' man. Hence, one could note that Karthikeyan and Mallya are not racializing their successes; they are just taking pride in their Indian roots and giving India something else to cheer about on the world stage other than cricket.

With the inclusion of Indian owners and drivers, the traditional whiteness of F1 appears to be slowly decreasing. Hamilton's emergence arguably suggests that F1 is open to anyone regardless of colour or background. But despite McLaren's attempts to steer reports away from Hamilton's 'race' (which was arguably the sensible and correct approach), it is hardly shocking that some reports have focused on this 'difference' simply because he is the first black driver in the history of the sport. Similarly, when Viv Anderson became the first black player to represent the England football team in a full international match in 1978, this would inevitably attract media attention. And, finally, when Barack Obama won the US presidential election in 2008, his 'race' was inescapable to the story simply because he is the first black president. Thus, was McLaren naive in thinking that Hamilton's 'race' would be inconsequential to reports?

Inevitably, when someone becomes 'the first' to achieve a feat, win an event or compete in a sport, it will always attract media attention. In this respect, it would appear difficult to ignore the concept of 'race'. But although Hamilton's 'race' is rarely explicitly referenced, it is often implicitly included. Thus, one could argue that this has led to Hamilton being framed in problematic ways:

> Profiles of the driver often talk in metonymic terms about him being a 'breath of fresh air', 'irresistibly different' and 'new and exciting'. Race is both ever present and absent in the media framing of Hamilton ... He has

been compared to Tiger Woods, Theo Walcott and Amir Khan – but rarely Nigel Mansell, James Hunt or David Beckham.

(Carrington, 2010, p159)

Hamilton is framed as 'new' and 'different' not because of his ability or driving style, but arguably because of the colour of his skin. Therefore, he is aligned alongside other non-whites as opposed to other white sporting icons. Quite simply, Hamilton's representation has been implicitly racialized.

Arguably, these parallels appear irresistible from a journalist's perspective as both Woods and Hamilton are non-white, from a similar socio-economic background and have emerged as champions in 'predominantly white, middle-class' sports. This link with Woods again shows that 'race' cannot remain dormant; it will always exist either explicitly or implicitly. In short, Hamilton is a black F1 driver here, not an F1 driver. The reports of his white McLaren teammate Jenson Button have not suggested that he can act as a great role model for folk in Somerset, the place of his birth, because he is presented as a dominant member of society, thus reflecting the racial status quo. Hamilton, however, is 'different', and his media coverage highlights this.

Hamilton and cricketer Monty Panesar have nevertheless 'broken the mould' and have been framed in non-traditional ways compared with most black and Asian athletes. Unlike the footballer John Barnes or the sprinter Linford Christie, whose stories were framed with 'immigrant' connotations, Hamilton and Panesar are exempt from this world:

> [Both] come from the sprawling suburbs – Panesar from Luton and Hamilton from Stevenage – and not the inner cities so beloved of the tabloids 'rags to riches', out of the ghetto sporting narratives. Both are softly spoken ... Hamilton, a model of understatement and professional respect for his rivals, is variously described as 'likeable and humble' ... they are 'mould breaking' in as much as Panesar is the first Sikh cricketer to have played for England and Hamilton the first black Formula One driver to have won the world title, they are also establishing new paradigms for what it means to be English.
>
> (Carrington, 2010, p158)

Both sports stars emerged from English middle-class suburbia and although they may be categorized as ethnic minorities, are undoubtedly English/British through and through. Similarly, British boxer Amir Khan has been described as a 'pinnacle definer' of British multiculturalism and has arguably become a positive role model for young British Asians (Sardar, 2006). But, significantly, he has gained the support of white Britons, as have Hamilton and Panesar, indicating that he has achieved a somewhat transracial popularity and identity. With regards to Hamilton, he has been accepted by the British media as 'one of us' and following his F1 championship win in 2008, former Prime Minister

Gordon Brown commented that Hamilton is 'the pride of Britain' (Cary, 8 December 2008). Carrington (2010, p160) adds that following this win, 'Our Frank had become Our Lewis'.

It has been widely noted that Frank Bruno managed to gain the acceptance of the white British nation, hence leading to the affectionate nickname of 'Our Frank'. Despite the colonial stereotypes of Afro-Caribbeans as being dangerous and 'hyper sexual' (Mercer, 1994, p174), Bruno was represented as 'loveable' and non-threatening, which was quite remarkable considering he was a boxer. Similarly, Hamilton has also managed to achieve this transracial appeal.

For Fanon (1986) and King (2004), though, the concept of 'whiteness' holds the key to acceptance. Thus, in order to achieve inclusion, one has to not necessarily be white, but must act white. Arguably, McLaren's downplaying of Hamilton's 'race' and ethnicity has perhaps aided his transition from being a role model for black Britons to being a role model for all. Despite some non-white sports stars such as John Barnes and former boxer Prince Naseem Hamed struggling to gain acceptance from the white demographic, Hamilton, Bruno and Panesar have arguably been embraced.

Hamilton conducts himself well on and off the track, and has seemingly fitted into the 'white sport' with relative ease. As Fanon (1986) would argue, the adoption of the 'white mask' is crucial for success. Thus, as the second case study indicates, it is critical for non-whites in white worlds to downplay their 'Otherness' and never 'cry racism'. But first we shall discuss the overt racism that Hamilton faced in Spain and add theoretical weight to the debate by applying van Dijk's (1993, 1998, 2001) concept of the ideological square.

The Spanish Grand Prix

It was less than a year into Hamilton's professional career when he first encountered overt racism. A small minority of Spanish fans had 'blacked' themselves up, brought along racist banners and shouted racist insults. *The Independent* (Tremayne, 2008) noted that shouts of '"*puto negro*" [black bastard] and "*negro de mierda*" [black shit] were clearly heard'. In addition, *The Mirror* (Maclean and Young, 2008) also wrote that Hamilton 'allegedly had missiles thrown at him'. So, what was the media's general consensus on these examples of overt racism?

- 'Hamilton was the *victim* of racist abuse' (Garside, 2008).
- 'British ace Lewis Hamilton was *subjected* to racist abuse' (Murray, 2008).
- '*Sick* racists *taunted* Formula One whizzkid Lewis Hamilton' (Wells, 2008).

These reports highlight the media's sympathetic tone towards Hamilton as he was the victim in the incident (this directly contrasts with the second case study). In addition, it is hardly surprising that the media make a stand against racism. However, what was noteworthy in the stories was the inclusion of

Figure 8.1 F1 fans racially abuse Lewis Hamilton at the Spanish Grand Prix, 2 February 2008 (Source: Joanne Burnett/Getty Images)

further references to problems that Spain has had with overt racism in recent years. For instance, many reports highlighted the Spanish fans' treatment of England's black footballers during the 2004 'friendly' at the Bernabeu, which saw Rio Ferdinand, Ashley Cole and Shaun Wright-Phillips being subjected to monkey noises. Another example included was of former Spanish manager Luis Aragones and his reference to Thierry Henry as a 'black shit' when talking to one of his players in a training session, also in 2004. Other reports discussed the overt racism that the Cameroon and former Barcelona striker, Samuel Eto'o, faced against Real Zaragoza in 2006. Eto'o emotionally protested on the pitch and almost refused to continue after almost half an hour of booing and monkey noises every time he touched the ball. Put simply, it has been widely publicized in the UK media that Spain has struggled to combat racist sentiments within sport during recent years.

These mediated references can be related to the social-cognitive model of van Dijk's (1993, 1998, 2001) ideological square. In short, the ideological square determines choices between referential strategies. Thus, he notes that this concept is based on positive self-presentation, while concurrently highlighting negative 'Other' presentation. Van Dijk's model can be summarized as follows:

- positive self-presentation: emphasize one's good qualities and de-emphasize one's bad qualities;
- negative Other presentation: emphasize their bad qualities and de-emphasize their good qualities.

The ideological square can be applied to the media and the ways in which they present the world to their consumers. Although this concept is evident within the realm of political reporting, it can also be applied to sports stories and, specifically, the examples of overt racism among contemporary Spanish fans.

The UK media is quick to condemn racism and to criticize the lack of acceptance of ethnic minority groups in other nations. Put simply, the media promotes a paradoxical ideology indicating that racism is rife elsewhere, but in the UK there is no problem. Is this really the case within a sporting context, though?

For Burdsey (2007a, p41), 'despite the efforts of the anti-racist football movement in challenging terrace racism, many English football stadia continue to be hostile environments for minority ethnic groups'. Relatively recent research suggests that 36 per cent of spectators at Rangers and 38 per cent at Everton recorded hearing racial abuse (Brown and Chaudhury, 2000, cited in Collins and Kay, 2003, p136). A clear example of overt racism was displayed in April 2003 when England played Turkey at Sunderland's Stadium of Light. England fans were heard singing 'I'd rather be a Paki than a Turk', which is almost a metaphorical way of stating contempt for an emblematic 'Other' identity: a Turk. In addition, Kelso (2003) notes that Islamophobic sentiments were also aired during the game as 'Die, Muslim, die' and 'Kill all Muslims' was chanted. In 2005, the Muslim former Middlesbrough striker Mido faced racial abuse as fans chanted 'Shoe bomber' and 'Your mother's a terrorist' (Burdsey, 2007a, p58). This type of overtly racist fan behaviour has even been witnessed in cricket as the former Indian test bowler, Anil Kumble, 'was pelted with bananas when he fielded on the boundary' while playing for Northamptonshire against Yorkshire in 1996 (Gardiner and Welch, 2001, p140). Despite there being countless examples of overt racism within English sport, Gardiner and Welch (2001, p138) suggest that there is a 'dominant discourse within the Football Association that the problem is decreasing, if not completely eradicated'. This mind-set is worrying as the problem has not yet been solved; overt racism within UK sport continues to occur (Back et al, 2001; Crabbe and Brown, 2004; Burdsey, 2007a).

Significantly, from a UK media perspective, the examples noted above all received minimal attention. Nevertheless, although most reports chose to ignore mentioning the racist chanting heard during the England versus Turkey match, *The Telegraph* writer Henry Winter adopted a marginalized, but critical, approach, stating that:

> For too long, the FA have complained about the racist behaviour of other countries, notably Albania, Bulgaria and Slovakia, while ignoring the 10 or so per cent of England supporters who denigrate opponents ... the FA's smug spell on the moral high ground is about to end.
>
> (Winter, 2003)

Just as Winter suggests, organizational sporting bodies, as well as the UK media, have a tendency to act as the voices of morality when it comes to cases of racism in foreign lands. The mediated portrayal of Hamilton in Barcelona indicated that Spain is battling against racial discourses within modern-day society. The utilization of other examples of overt racism simply adds to the 'racist Spain' picture, which thus feeds into the notion of negative Other presentation, while the UK's media simultaneously promote positive self-presentation, indicating that 'racism here' is a thing of the past.

In response to the UK's negative representation of Spanish sports fans, some journalists responded angrily, claiming that the UK media's hypocrisy is actually worse than the racist incident itself. What was noted in these reports relies heavily on contextualizing contemporary Spanish society, something that was largely absent from many of the UK's reports. There are significant social and political differences between Spain and the UK in relation to 'race' and immigration, which has thus affected contemporary ideologies. However, and most importantly, these differences categorically do not condone racist behaviour.

John Carlin (2008) illustrates how the British media have exacerbated Spanish racism following the Hamilton incident:

> What a load of *mierda*! Really, it's hard to judge what is more ridiculous: the imbecility of four politically retarded Spanish F1 hooligans who insulted Hamilton in curly-wigged, black-boot-polish fancy dress or the frothings of the massed ranks of the British media, whose indignant ravings granted an unintended peep into the island nation's very own entrenched and ancient prejudices, in this case regarding the racial inferiority of the benighted cultures of Mediterranean Europe – the hot-tempered Latins; the primitive-minded, passionate dagos. How wonderful to be able to cloak bigotry in virtue. How satisfying to trumpet one's faith in Britain's essential superiority without seeming impolite.

Carlin's (2008) analysis conflicts with stories put forward by the British media. Carlin is quick to point out that racism was displayed by only 'four politically retarded … hooligans', not the thousands of other fans. He also rather sarcastically notes that the UK media's anger over the incident indicates a sense of 'superiority' over other nations in terms of the acceptance of ethnic minorities. In short, Britain acts as the moral voice while emphasizing negative Other presentation. However, as we have suggested, England is not 'whiter than white': recent examples suggest that racism is still apparent in domestic sport.

Nevertheless, racism among football spectators is decreasing following widespread anti-racist campaigns such as *Kick It Out* and *Show Racism the Red Card*. But during the 1950s and 1960s, overt racism was a major problem within British society following mass migration from former colonies. Importantly, though, half a century after mass migration, second- and third-generation immigrants are born and bred in Britain and cannot be labelled migrants in any meaningful way (Anwar, 1998). Britain had several decades of widespread overt racism before it started to decline, and now the British media decide to adopt the moral voice: the voice of 'superiority'. It is at this point that the Spanish context becomes highly noteworthy.

During the last 500 years, or specifically since the Jews and Moors were expelled in 1492, Spain has had racial and religious homogeneity. It was not until the late 1990s that immigration first began to arise within Spain. Today, nearly 10 per cent of Spain's 45 million inhabitants are foreign born; not even Britain has encountered migration on such a mass scale.

Recent figures, however, show that rising unemployment, which is touching 2 million for the first time in three years, has hit the immigrant population hardest. There are now more than 400,000 unemployed foreigners in Spain – a cause of concern to those who fear ghettoization (Hamilos, 2008). Thus, Spain's immigrant population is arguably fast becoming an ethnic underclass, and tensions between 'insiders' and 'outsiders' have arguably arisen. Conversely, Carlin (2008) points out two facts: 'there is no far right, racially fixed political party in Spain' as witnessed in France, Austria and Britain; and following the Madrid train bombings in 2004, 'there was no spate of revenge assaults on Muslims or on mosques'. Thus, although the British media are quick to accuse Spain, Russia or other Eastern European countries of racism in sport, one has to first acknowledge the context of the incident or the country in question and, second, not promote one's own country as being flawless and a model for others to follow.

Nevertheless, despite Carlin's critical response to the British media, the photographs taken indicate that there were more than 'four politically retarded' racists in the stands. And although Carlin (2008) notes that the 'Spanish racism' examples were over-hyped by the British press, one could argue that England has not witnessed examples of overt racism to the same degree for a number of years. It is also important to highlight Carlin's use of referential strategies as he labels the racist fans as 'hooligans'. Van Dijk (1993, p250) highlights a facet of media discourse within sport and racism stories as the racist sentiments are 'condemned', but then 'conveniently associated with social out-groups, such as football hooligans or skinheads'. For Carlin, this referential strategy connotes that majority society is non-racist while a minority of 'hooligans' (the social out-group) are guilty of racism. The UK press most commonly referred to the Spanish racists as 'fans' rather than thugs or hooligans. Arguably, this normalizes the racism as being a problem within the social in-group as opposed to Carlin's reference to the out-group: the 'hooligans'.

This case study has not only suggested how Hamilton's 'race' will inevitably be the focus of some stories, but has also examined how journalists should report stories concerning 'race' and racism abroad. Van Dijk's concept of the ideological square has been positioned alongside these reports, and it can be argued that the British media are almost critiquing other nations' intolerance of ethnic minorities, thus ignoring decades of overt racism on its shores. But the media is a business, first and foremost; would back-page leads on racism in sport every other day sell? Although the media should adopt a critical approach to all racism, journalists should not promote the ideology that racism on its shores has been defeated, in this way promoting a false sense of reality.

The following debate indicates that Hamilton's 'good guy' image is not untouchable from the media's wrath (Brookes, 2002). Despite Hamilton being the victim in Spain, he became the aggressor in Monaco when suggesting that institutional racism might be at play.

Hamilton: 'Maybe it's because I am black'?

Following a disappointing race at the 2011 Monaco Grand Prix, where Hamilton had been stopped by stewards, he stated:

> You know what? Out of six races I've been to the stewards five times. It's a joke. It's an absolute fricking joke. Maybe it's because I'm black. That's what Ali G says. I don't know.
>
> (Lewis Hamilton, cited in Sanghera, 2011)

Figure 8.2 Lewis Hamilton at the Monaco F1 Grand Prix, 28 May 2011

To suggest that the media were critical of these comments would be an understatement. The following snippets are taken from a selection of articles which discuss Hamilton's racism claim:

- 'Hamilton must learn to be a good loser … In an outburst after finishing sixth, the 2008 champion slated stewards, suggest[ing] racism was behind some of the decisions' (Young, 1 June 2011).
- 'In too many instances these days the *race card* is played for effect, excuse or to deflect attention from the real issue … The only thing more distasteful than blatant racism and guaranteed to cause anguish is being perceived to have indulged in racism yourself when you know this is simply untrue' (*Birmingham Evening Mail*, 2011).
- '[Hamilton's] quip … was a staggering misjudgement … It's almost never acceptable to play the *race card* in any situation' (*Belfast Telegraph*, 2011).

All three reports criticize Hamilton's employment of the *race card*. Although he said these comments out of frustration after a disappointing race, should somebody in his position make such comments? Was Hamilton correctly criticized for making such a remark?

The *Birmingham Evening Mail* (2011) argues that being accused of 'blatant' (overt) racism is worse than actually being racially abused – quite a bold statement to make to say the least. The article summarizes by noting that although we all emerged from 'different buckets of paint, under the skin we are all the same. Sadly Martin Luther King's "I have a dream" is still just that.' Can this article be any more of a paradox? It suggests that racism has been so heavily defeated that non-whites cannot use 'race' as a barrier any more. Is the article claiming that racism has been eradicated from sport and society? Perhaps it is; but it also argues that we cannot achieve Martin Luther King's 'dream' because non-whites still play the *race card* and have not 'moved on' following centuries of slavery and racial discrimination.

Hamilton's racial abuse in Spain indicated that racism has not yet been defeated. As we have noted, the reports showed the media's sympathetic tone towards Hamilton as he was framed as the victim. Garside (2008) articulated that 'What Hamilton's Spanish experience demonstrates is the painfully apparent present-day racism in sport and that racism needs to be fought and not swept under the carpet.' But, just three years later, the media lambast Hamilton for suggesting that racism in F1 may be at work. Arguably, if it is 'hooligans' who are displaying overt racism whereby the story can be told through pictures, the media will be quick to condemn it. However, accusations of institutional racism are a different ball game – it is a lengthy process and very difficult to prove. In response to Hamilton's 'jokey' claims, former F1 driver David Coulthard (2011) wrote:

> As for whether Formula One has any institutional racism, let's not even go there. Teams and drivers come from every walk of life. The FIA is a

world governing body, not a bunch of rich, white men. The stewards change race by race and come from all sorts of countries and backgrounds.

These reports lead to the assumption that sport is an egalitarian premise. For Marqusee (1999, pp4–5), 'the major cliché about race in sport is that sport offers black people opportunities denied to them in other spheres'. But access to the 'level playing field' is anything but equal. Academics who have adopted a critical race theory (CRT) approach would suggest that race relations are more nuanced than the traditional approach indicated (Delgado and Stefancic, 1995, 2001; Hylton, 2005, 2009). Thus, through the use of micro-aggressions, for example, 'race' and racism is everywhere and is still deep rooted within sport and society. The National Football League (NFL) established the Rooney Rule in 2003. This rule requires NFL clubs to interview at least one black or minority ethnic (BME) candidate per managerial or coaching position that arises. The regulation was named after Dan Rooney, owner of the Pittsburgh Steelers and chairman of the league's diversity committee, because of his longstanding tradition of providing opportunities for Afro-Americans within leadership roles. For some, this rule might be seen as affirmative action. Nevertheless, what this does indicate is that sport is not egalitarian and that institutional racism has prevented BME communities from having the chance to succeed in coaching. It could be argued that this rule should be applied within other sports, such as English football, which is a sport where non-white managers remain largely excluded. In sum, was Hamilton really wide of the mark when he made these accusations of institutional racism? And was he really 'joking'?

'Racisms' have not been eradicated and, from a sceptical point of view, some pockets of society will always harbour racist views. From a mediated perspective, though, as we have seen with Hamilton's hostile reception in Spain, overt racism will quickly and correctly be denounced. But in a case of institutional or 'invisible' racism, the media have criticized Hamilton, although many would argue that racism in all forms still lingers within sport at some level. The analysis is not, however, making bold claims and suggesting that F1 racing is institutionally racist; but this incident is noteworthy because of the media's reaction to Hamilton. Put simply, the reports indicate that a black man is now the aggressor and that sport is the victim – quite the paradox. It is at this point that Hamilton's mediated construction needs to be further scrutinized: the coupling of 'race' and class may reveal why Hamilton was so fiercely criticized by the predominantly white British media.

One could articulate that 'race' and class had problematically become infused within the scathing reports. But 'race', racism and class are three very different concepts. Significantly, then, the reports almost implicitly suggest that Hamilton cannot 'cry racism' or utilize the *race card* because of his privileged upbringing, background, and more specifically, his middle-class status. Thus, this indicates that only the poor non-white lower classes encounter racism. Put simply, Hamilton is exempt from racism because of his socio-economic status, and class becomes a central theme of Hamilton's condemnation. Arguably, if Hamilton 'rose out of the ghetto' and his mediated construction was more in line with the outspoken and politically active Muhammad Ali of the 1960s, then the reports would have utilized a different news angle.

Despite the majority of articles criticizing Hamilton's 'joke', the black British *Guardian* journalist Joseph Harker offered a different position. Harker's (2011) article notes quite simply that 'social status and relative wealth do not protect black people' from racism. Harker, who is obviously adopting a black perspective and talking from personal experience, discusses the notion of class:

> For me, middle class is a racially exclusive term in Britain: because it's not about wealth, or educational achievement, but about certain values that one has to adhere to. About living in the 'right' area; attending the 'right' theatres; sending your children to the 'right' schools. And in all of these, the 'right' is white.

Harker suggests that middle class is almost a metaphor for being white. As a result, those who are non-white will struggle to gain inclusion within the dominant power block. Put simply, skin colour will inevitably always be an exclusive social marker regardless of one's class. Although Hamilton quickly fired back, suggesting that his comments were a 'joke', for Harker, 'his sentiment was clear' and not out of line.

Problematically, then, Lawton's (2011) article is a prime example of how 'race' and class have become wrongly entwined:

> Not only was his remark unfunny, as he had the grace to admit so quickly, it was also surely offensive to all those millions of young people who, with infinitely *greater legitimacy*, might claim that racism, either institutionalized or implicit, still presents a barrier to their progress in life ... Hamilton surely *cannot begin to make such a claim*. He has, in a complete sense, been fasttracked to the most enviable of lifestyles.

In short, the article concludes that Hamilton cannot make a *legitimate claim* of racism because of his social status. In other words, it almost suggests that his class outweighs his 'race'; in effect, it neutralizes his 'blackness' and therefore his *legitimacy* to play the *race card*. As a result, *Independent* journalist James Lawton (2011) then indicates that Hamilton's illegitimate *claim* is 'offensive' to millions of other non-whites (most likely from poorer backgrounds) who can genuinely *claim* racism. Because Hamilton has an 'enviable' lifestyle and has made it to the top, he categorically cannot 'cry racism'. However, one could argue that if Hamilton came from a background similar to 'those millions' in question, his accusations may have been treated with more seriousness by media writers. In summary, journalists must never discredit somebody's accusations of racism simply because of their socio-economic status. 'Race' and class are two completely different concepts and racism can affect non-whites of any social stature. A move up the social ladder does not mean a move towards a greater sense of racial equality. In short, journalists must always attempt to take the class out of 'race'.

What this analysis has shown is that 'race' and class are problematically interconnected within media discourses. Hamilton is not seen as a *legitimate* source to 'cry racism' because of his socio-economic position. Arguably, Hamilton's mediated representation has been similar to the traditional embodiments of Jesse Owens, Arthur Ashe, Carl Lewis and Michael Jordan: 'All come from predominantly non-contact sports, all were portrayed as having based success on hard work, all mastered the art of delivering to the (white) media an appropriately bland and respectful performance' (Whannel, 2002, pp177–178). Hence, in order to succeed, non-whites should remain 'respectful' within the white world and not highlight their colour or 'race' as a barrier (Fanon, 1986). In short, it almost appears to be social and professional suicide if the *race card* is employed. As *The Mirror* concludes: 'Time to keep your head down, Lewis' (Young, 2011). Or time to suppress your thoughts, Lewis, because white society wants to keep believing that those dark days are finally behind us.

Conclusion

Hamilton's framing has marked a new chapter within sports journalism. He is unanimously regarded as being British/English despite being black. Hence, sports journalism has moved with the times as other stars, such as Monty Panesar and Amir Khan, have been portrayed as also being British/English rather than being framed within the traditional 'immigrant' paradigm.

With reference to the Spanish Grand Prix reports, the application of van Dijk's (1993, 1998, 2001) model proved a perfect fit. Importantly, one of the principle rules of journalism is to report matters fairly and accurately; one must not fall into the trap of sensationalizing incidents (negative Other presentation). Thus, this chapter suggests that context remains an important factor when reporting 'racisms' on other shores.

For some, Hamilton achieved his transracial popularity by playing the 'good guy' (Brookes, 2002), keeping his head down and de-emphasizing his 'blackness' (Fanon, 1986; Back et al, 2001; Whannel, 2002). But Hamilton's comments on institutional racism highlighted that he is not untouchable from the media's fury. Arguably, athletes who do play the *race card*, rightly or wrongly, will inevitably face criticism within media discourse. Journalists must always view such accusations with fairness and objectivity. What we should understand, then, is that although some sports stars have an elevated social status, it does not make them impervious to any form of racism.

Chapter 9

Conclusion

It is possible, tempting even, to think of 'race' as being in decline, as an issue of diminishing prevalence and importance in sport and the sports media. On the pitch, teams that were once exclusively 'white' are now filled with 'black' athletes, cheered rather than abused by fans. Off the pitch, the situation is so good that regulators, such as the Press Complaints Commission (PCC), feel no need to chastise journalists on the grounds of racial discrimination.

But appearances can be deceiving. 'Race' is a social construction (Malik, 1996; Pilkington, 2003) and racisms are fluid and in flux (Mason, 2000). Therefore, as Carrington (2010, p174) observes: 'We need to avoid adopting theoretically naive and empirically suspect positions, however widely held they may be, that suggest the significance of "race" has diminished merely because formal segregation no longer exists and white fans now sing the names of black players.' Throughout our analysis we have found evidence of a variety of these racisms appearing across sports coverage of a range of sports. There is evidence of racisms ranging from the institutional or structural, to the inferential (Hall, 1996), in the form of the stereotyping, 'Othering' and racial labelling of athletes.

It could be argued that there is evidence of institutional, or structural, racism in the character and composition of the sports media. Long and Spracklen (2010, p5) claim that 'The multiplicity of racisms is one reason for the apparent paradoxes we continually observe: on the one hand, public commitment to tackling racism in various sports governing bodies; on the other, the continued cultural and structural dominance of those governing bodies by white people.' This conclusion, in our assessment, could equally be applied to the sports media.

Sports journalism and whiteness in the UK press have traditionally gone hand in hand. We have shown that there are very few black or minority ethnic (BME) journalists working within the sports field despite recent efforts being made by the BBC. In general, though, this phenomenon appears to have received little acknowledgement. This book has importantly managed to raise this issue, and relevant groups and organizations arguably need to look at themselves and pay close attention to this facet. One could suggest that ethnic diversity within sports journalism is necessary, and that employing more BME writers will allow contemporary British society to receive another viewpoint or ideology as opposed to the traditional white-centric, well-educated, middle-class discourse. For example, within the F1 chapter we highlighted how notions of 'race' and class had become problematically entwined within UK media reports following the aftermath of Lewis Hamilton's comment concerning institutional racism. Conversely, one of the few non-white writers, *The Guardian's* Joseph Harker (2011), correctly disentangled these concepts and suggested that class does not diminish the threat of racism. Thus, using this as an example, one could note that having more BME journalists would offer UK society a view that is largely absent at present. Diversity would arguably create better and more accurate reports; after all, Britain is a multicultural nation but has a predominantly mono-cultural mainstream media. Change is needed in the sports media to mirror the transformations that we have seen within contemporary British society.

However, as Chapter 3 suggested, attracting more BME sports journalists may prove difficult as there is the perception of not belonging. Nevertheless, just like footballing and cricketing pioneers such as Cyrille Regis and Devon Malcolm, one could articulate that trailblazers are needed within sports journalism. Perhaps a role model is needed to raise awareness and challenge the status quo, notions of whiteness and feelings of not belonging.

There are two schools of thought in relation to this. First, more BME writers simply equals a much-needed diversity in reporting which would help to benefit how sports and sporting icons are represented. But one could note that due to 'racisms', BME writers would become socialized or institutionalized within the existing norms of media production. To use Fanon's (1986) argument, the adoption of the 'white mask' is crucial for non-whites to succeed in white worlds. Hence, BME sports journalists may not feel comfortable challenging 'racisms', especially covert and institutional racism, which is seen to be almost invisible and difficult to prove, when, after all, they are working in a white-dominated space. As we witnessed with the Hamilton case study in Chapter 8, non-whites can face a backlash or exclusion for 'crying racism' or employing the *race card*. In short, would more BME sports writers mean that we receive a more accurate representation of reports concerning 'race' and racism? Or is assimilation the only way to achieve diversity within sports journalism?

The second school of thought is to train our journalists better and to pay more attention to the power that 'race' and racism can have. Despite sports journalism being a popular degree within British universities, one should note that issues of 'race' are being underplayed within modules. The University of Sunderland, however, incorporates a mix of theory teaching ('race', 'racisms', ethnicity, national identity) within modules, and rightly so. Future and present sports journalists must understand that there is influence and power within every stroke of the keyboard, and if one is uneducated on issues of 'race' and racism, then stereotypes may persist. Therefore, it is crucial for sports journalists to avoid falling into traps when writing about certain sports or sports stars.

As we have seen, racialization is a commonality within the present-day sport media.

The case studies in this book have examined sports journalism in great depth. What we have found is that 'race' and ethnicity become central to the story, although they should often be insignificant. Christophe Lemaitre became a 'white' sprinter; Zesh Rehman was framed as an 'Asian' footballer and Lewis Hamilton was presented as a 'black' driver. Put simply, their ethnicities override their profession. Sometimes this facet can go a step further and other racial or ethnic labels can be attached. Muhammad Ali is not just 'black', he is 'militant black'; Jack Johnson is not just 'black', he is 'negro black'; Amir Khan is not just 'Asian', he is an 'acceptable Muslim'. Cricket is somewhat different as it is not so much the players who are racialized, it is more the teams and nations. Arguably, cricket is represented as a sport first and a cultural mirror second.

Despite the PCC stating that journalists must first avoid 'prejudicial reference to race' and, second, avoid referring to a person's 'race' unless it is 'genuinely relevant to the story', this book has highlighted that 'race' is often included although it may be totally irrelevant. It is also noteworthy to again highlight that throughout the PCC's history, it has never upheld a single complaint based on racial discrimination. Is it time to update these rules and regulations? A particular rule appears to be in need of attention as journalists are allowed to racialize a nation but cannot racialize an individual. Why is one legitimate but not the other? Nevertheless, as this book has shown, racializing individuals, although deemed unacceptable, is a commonality within sports reporting. In a cricketing context, nations are often racialized and England's imperial and colonial legacy continues to thrive, which, according to the PCC, is perfectly acceptable. As long as this 'individual' and 'nation' clause remains, we will arguably continue to receive homogenizing stereotypes of 'Other' nations. And despite a rule which states that mention of an individual's 'race' must be 'genuinely relevant', the countless examples throughout the book make a mockery of this clause.

However, is one's 'race' unavoidable? Christophe Lemaitre breaks the 10-second barrier; but is his 'race' noteworthy? Lewis Hamilton becomes F1's first black driver; but is his skin colour important? Differences will always continue to attract attention and generally what is 'new' makes news. Thus, one has to accept that certain nations and sporting icons will inevitably be racialized. However, it is how these nations and individuals are framed and represented that is important. The framing of Zesh Rehman was arguably unnecessary. Examining his religious beliefs and diet is not good journalism and, ultimately, 'Others' him. Lewis Hamilton's obvious difference, his skin colour, has to attract coverage due to the sport he participates in. If he was a basketball player, his 'race' would be insignificant. But it was how he was framed that raises problems: compared with other non-white athletes as opposed to other white British F1 drivers. As a result, he becomes implicitly racialized.

In addition, he was framed as a role model and hero for the black community although, rather importantly, he is of dual ethnicity. The book has further highlighted how non-whites can be assigned with colonially rooted 'racial' characteristics, such as laziness, as in the case of cricketer Devon Malcolm.

It would be naive to suggest that notions of 'race' will disappear from the media and sport media's attention any time soon. Nevertheless, as long as the term is employed and nations and individuals are racialized, its usage will continue to live on in contemporary discourses. The book has therefore raised some important findings: 'race' is often unnecessary within reports but still commonly utilized; non-white sporting icons are sometimes 'Othered' along the lines of ethnicity and religion. Furthermore, a shift from biological to cultural connotations of 'race' has been witnessed within the framing of sports stars; non-whites are commonly presented as role models for 'their community'. Finally, the PCC's regulations on 'race' have been found wanting and in need of attention.

Journalists need to break the cycle of racializing the successes and failures of white and non-white sports stars within the sport media. In short, we need to stop 'Othering' individuals and nations. We need to achieve greater diversity in the media while simultaneously training journalists on 'race' reporting. We need to break away from the questioning of which is better: black or white?

Why does it matter? It matters because although 'race' is a biological myth, it is a social construction which has real consequences for society. It is an ideological force that can reinforce and perpetuate real inequalities. As Long and Spracklen (2010, p5) argue: 'The continuing salience of "race" suggests that it is one of the forces sustaining a particular world order.'

Did you read the article arguing that the composition of the European Ryder Cup team demonstrated the 'white race's' innate ability to swing a stick in pendulum motion? Or did you read the quote from the biologist claiming to have identified a golf gene in some of the whiter tribes of deepest Surrey? No, neither did we. But we did find repeated use of the 'natural black' athlete stereotype across a range of sports coverage.

'Race', the myth that will not die, is alive and kicking on our back pages – in the language, mind-set, cultures and structures of the sports media.

What is black and white and read all over?

Sports journalism today.

Bibliography

AFP (2010) 'French sprinter breaks 10s barrier in 100m dash', http://www.france24. com/en/20100709-valence-france-christophe-lemaitre-100-metre-dash-under-ten-seconds

Ahmed, A. (1993) *Living Islam*, BBC Books, London

Alexander, C. (2000) *The Asian Gang: Ethnicity, Identity, Masculinity*, Berg, Oxford

Alexander, C. and Knowles, C. (2005) *Making Race Matter: Bodies, Space and Identity*, Palgrave Macmillan, Basingstoke, UK

Ali, T. (2010) 'There's only one Imran', *The Guardian*, 31 August

Allison, L. (1998) *Taking Sport Seriously*, vol 6, Meyer and Meyer, London

Anderson, B. (1991) *Imagined Communities: Reflections on the Origin and Spread of Nationalism*, Verso, London

Andrews, P. (2005) *Sports Journalism: A Practical Introduction*, Sage, London

Anwar, M. (1998) *Between Cultures: Continuity and Change in the Lives of Young Asians*, Routledge, London

Armitage, D. (2006) 'Theo's worth GBP 50m now; Walcott is hailed as a future world great', *Daily Star*, 23 November

Asians in Football Forum (2005) 'Asians can play football', Asians in Football Forum, London

ASNE (American Society of News Editors) (2011) *Newsroom Census*, http://asne.org/key_initiatives/diversity/newsroom_census.aspx

Azzarito, L. and Harrison, L. (2008) 'White men can't jump: Race, gender and natural athleticism', *International Review for the Sociology of Sport*, vol 43, no 4, pp347–364

Azzarito, L. and Solomon, M. A. (2006) 'A poststructural analysis of high school students: Gender and racialized bodily meanings', *Journal of Teaching in Physical Education*, vol 25, pp75–98

Back, L. and Solomos, J. (1996) *Race and Racism in Contemporary Britain*, MacMillan, Basingstoke, UK

Back, L., Crabbe, T. and Solomos, J. (2001) *The Changing Face of Football: Racism, Identity and Multiculture in the English Game*, Berg, Oxford, UK

Bagdikian, B. (1997) *The Media Monopoly*, Beacon Press, Boston, MA

Bains, J. and Johal, S. (1998) *Corner Flags and Corner Shops: The Asian Football Experience*, Gollancz, London

Bains, J. and Patel, R. (1996) *Asians Can't Play Football*, D-Zine, Birmingham, UK

Baker, M. (1995) 'Author obsessed by questions of race', *Evening Standard*, 6 July

Balibar, E. (1991) *Race, Nation and Class*, Verso Press, London

Barclay, P. (2003) 'Chopra wary of becoming an Asian role model', *Sunday Telegraph*, 13 April

Barker, C. (1999) *Television, Globalization and Cultural Identities*, Open University Press, Milton Keynes, UK

Barker, C. (2000) *Cultural Studies: Theory and Practice*, Sage, London

Barker, M. (1981) *The New Racism: Conservatives and the Ideology of the Tribe*, Junction Books, London

Barker, M. (1982) *The New Racism: Conservatives and the Ideology of the Tribe*, Alethia Books, London

Barnes, S. (1990) 'The importance of being too earnest', *The Times*, 12 April

Barnes, S. (1999) 'Fragile talents prove forever intoxicating', *The Times*, 21 June

Barnes, S. (2007) 'This villain (Christine Ohuruogu) has served her time – now let's catch the real cheats', *The Times*, 28 November

Bassey, A. (2005a) 'Home goal: England miss out as Asian football star joins Pakistan team', *Sunday Mercury*, 23 October

Bassey, A. (2005b) 'Red card for my mum's fatty curries: How Brummie became first Asian Premier League star', *Sunday Mercury*, 23 January

Bateman, C. (2010) 'But they all say the tour must go on', *Daily Express*, 31 August

Beasley, R. (1999) 'Corner Chopra', *The News of the World*, 18 July

Beckford, M. and Midgley, N. (2010) 'Half of recruits to BBC's training scheme are from ethnic minorities', *The Telegraph*, 3 June, http://www.telegraph.co.uk/culture/tvan dradio/7798083/Half-of-recruits-to-BBCs-trainee-scheme-are-from-ethnic-minorities.html

Belfast Telegraph (2011) 'Hamilton's race claim staggering', *Belfast Telegraph*, 1 June

Benedict, R. (1983) *Race and Racism*, Routledge and Kegan Paul, London (originally published in 1942)

Bernstein, A. and Blain, N. (2003) 'Sport and the media: The emergence of a major research field', in A. Bernstein and N. Blain (eds) *Sport, Media, Culture: Global and Local Dimensions*, Frank Cass, London

Berry, S. (2005) 'Realising the promise of the full Monty: Young spinner is a tantalising prospect for England', *Sunday Telegraph*, 18 December

Best, C. (1987) 'Experience and career length in professional football: The effect of positional segregation', *Sociology of Sport*, vol 4, pp410–420

Bhatia, S. (2005) 'I'll let my parents pick me a footballer's wife and they just might have a girl in mind', *The Evening Standard*, 12 April

Billig, M. (1995) *Banal Nationalism*, Sage, London

Billings, A. C. and Hundley, H. L. (2010) 'Examining identity in sports media', in H. L. Hundley and A. C. Billings (eds) *Examining Identity in Sports Media*, Sage, London

Bingham, H. and Wallace, M. (2000) *Muhammad Ali's Greatest Fight: Cassius Clay vs the United States of America*, Evans and Co, New York, NY

Bird, S. (2003) 'Chop idol', *The Mirror*, 29 November

Birmingham Evening Mail (2011) 'Playing the race card not funny, Lewis', *Birmingham Evening Mail*, 2 June

Birrell, S. (1989) 'Racial relations theories and sport: Suggestions for a more critical analysis', *Sociology of Sport*, vol 6, pp221–227

Blain, N., Boyle, R. and O'Donnell, H. (1993) *Sport and National Identity in the European Media*, Leicester University Press, Leicester, UK

Blalock, H. (1962) 'Occupational discrimination: Some theoretical propositions', *Social Problems*, vol 9, pp240–247

Booth, L. (2003) 'Great cricket, bad timing, Jekyll and Hyde; and Martin Crowe and the Maori', *The Guardian*, 18 February, http://www.guardian.co.uk/sport/2003/feb/18/thespin.cricket

Boyle, R. (2006a) *Sports Journalism: Context and Issues*, Sage, London

Boyle, R. (2006b) 'Running away from the circus', *British Journalism Review*, vol 17, no 3, pp12–17

Boyle, R. and Haynes, R. (2009) *Power Play: Sport, the Media and Popular Culture* (revised edition), Edinburgh University Press, Edinburgh

Brah, A. (1996) *Cartographies of Diaspora: Contesting Identities*, Routledge, London

Brooke, C. and Merrick, J. (2007) 'Did Muslim radicals order the murder of Woolmer?', *Daily Mail*, 30 April

Brookes, R. (2002) *Representing Sport*, Arnold, London

Bunyan, N. and Sparrow, A. (2001) 'Race riot town on a knife-edge', *Daily Telegraph*, 28 May

Burdsey, D. (2004a) 'Obstacle race? "Race", racism and the recruitment of British Asian professional footballer', *Patterns of Prejudice*, vol 38, no 3, pp279–299

Burdsey, D. (2004b) 'One of the lads? Dual ethnicity and assimilated ethnicities in the careers of British Asian professional footballer', *Ethnic and Racial Studies*, vol 27, no 5, pp757–779

Burdsey, D. (2006) 'No ball games allowed? A socio-historical examination of the development and social roles of British Asian football clubs', *Journal of Ethnic and Migration Studies*, vol 32, no 3, pp477–496

Burdsey, D. (2007a) *British Asians and Football: Culture, Identity, Exclusion*, Routledge, Oxon, UK

Burdsey, D. (2007b) 'Role with the punches: The construction and representation of Amir Khan as a role model for multiethnic Britain', *The Sociological Review*, vol 55, no 3, pp611–631

Burdsey, D. (2009) 'Forgotten fields? Centralising the experiences of minority ethnic men's football clubs in England', *Soccer and Society*, vol 10, no 6, pp704–721

Burdsey, D. (2010) 'British Muslim experiences in English first-class cricket', *International Review for the Sociology of Sport*, vol 45, no 3, pp315–334

Buzuvis, E. E. (2009) 'Caster Semenya and the myth of the level playing field', Paper presented to University of Baltimore School of Law Amateur Sports Law Symposium, Baltimore, 29 October

Calma, T. (2007) *What's the Score? A Survey of Cultural Diversity and Racism in Australian Sport*, http://www.hreoc.gov.au/about/media/media_releases/2007/84_07.html

Campbell, D. (2001) 'Football's new star rises from the East', *The Observer*, 9 September

Camporesi, S. and Maugeri, P. (2010) 'Caster Semenya: Sport, categories and the creative role of ethics', *Journal of Medical Ethics*, vol 36, pp378–379

Carlin, J. (2008) 'Who's worse ... these fans or the frothing British media?', *Sunday Times*, 10 February

Carmichael, S. and Hamilton, C. (1967) *Black Power: The Politics of Liberation in America*, Vintage Books, New York, NY

Carrington, B. (1998) 'Sport, masculinity and black cultural resistance', *Journal of Sport and Social Issues*, August, vol 22, no 3, pp275–298

Carrington, B. (2010) *Race, Sport and Politics: The Sporting Black Diaspora*, Sage Publications, London

Carrington, B. and McDonald, I. (2001a) 'Introduction', in B. Carrington and I. McDonald (eds) *'Race', Sport and British Society*, Routledge, London

Carrington, B. and McDonald, I. (2001b) *'Race', Sport and British Society*, Routledge, London

Cary, T. (2008) 'Gordon Brown hails F1 world champion Lewis Hamilton as "pride of Britain"', *The Telegraph*, 8 December

Cashmore, E. (1982) *Black Sportsmen*, Routledge, London

Cashmore, E. (1996) *Dictionary of Race and Ethnic Relations*, Routledge, London

Cashmore, E. (1997) *The Black Culture Industry*, Routledge, London

Cashmore, E. (2005) *Making Sense of Sports*, Routledge, Abingdon, UK

Cashmore, E. and Troyna, B. (1990) *Introduction to Race Relations*, 2nd edition, Falmer, London

Chaudhary, V. (2001) 'A question of support', *The Guardian*, 29 May 2001

Chung, T. (2006) *Jack Johnson: Public Enemy Number One*, MA thesis, California State University, Sacramento, CA

Clayton, J. (2009) 'Racism protests surface amid storm', *The Times*, 21 August

Cleaver, E. (1971) *Soul on Ice*, Pan Books, New York, NY

Coakley, J. (2009) *Sports in Society: Issues and Controversies*, McGraw-Hill, New York, NY

Coakley, J. and Donnelly, P. (eds) (1999) *Inside Sports*, Routledge, London

Collins, M. and Kay, T. (2003) *Sport and Social Exclusion*, Routledge, London

Commission on British Muslims and Islamophobia (1997) *Islamophobia: A Challenge for Us All*, Runnymede Trust, UK

Coren, G. (2005) 'Meet Zesh and Wayne and then think again', *The Times*, 16 April

Cottle, S. (2000a) 'Media research and ethnic minorities: Mapping the field', in S. Cottle (ed) *Ethnic Minorities and the Media*, Open University Press, Buckingham, UK

Cottle, S. (ed) (2000b) *Ethnic Minorities and the Media*, Open University Press, Buckingham, UK

Cottle, S. (2002) '"Race", racialization and the media: A review and update of research', *Sage Race Relations Abstracts*, vol 17, pp3–57

Cottle, S. (2004) *The Racist Murder of Stephen Lawrence: Media Performance and Public Transformation*, Praeger, Westport, CT, and London

Cottle, S. (2006) *Mediatized Conflict*, Open University Press, Buckingham, UK

Coulthard, D. (2011) 'A little sympathy is needed', *Daily Telegraph*, 31 May

Crabbe, T. and Brown, A. (2004) '"You're not welcome anymore": The football crowd, class and social exclusion', in S. Wagg (ed) *British Football and Social Exclusion*, Routledge, London

Crabbe, T. and Wagg, S. (2000) '"A carnival of cricket?": The cricket World Cup, "race" and the politics of carnival', *Culture, Sport, Society*, vol 3, no 2, pp70–88

Creedon, P. (1994) *Women, Media and Sport: Challenging Gender Values*, Sage, London

Crikey.com (2009) 'Muslim = Al Qaeda … Penbo's Punch in top comic form', 14 July, http://www.crikey.com.au/2009/07/14/penberthy-hits-wicket-over-the-12th-man-from-al-qaeda/

Davie, E. (2005) 'Tebbit: "Cricket test could have stopped bombings"', 19 August, http://www.epolitix.com/latestnews/article-detail/newsarticle/tebbit-cricket-test-could-have-stopped-bombings/

Davis, L. R. (1991) 'The articulation of difference: White preoccupation with the question of racially linked genetic differences among athletes', *Sociology of Sport Journal*, vol 7, no 2, pp179–187

Davis, L. and Harris, O. (1998) 'Race and ethnicity in US sports media', in L. A. Wenner (ed) *MediaSport*, Routledge, New York, NY, pp154–169

Davis, R. (1994) *America's Obsession: Sports and Society Since 1945*, Harcourt Brace College Publishers, Fort Worth, TX

Davis, T. (1995) 'The myth of the Superspade: The persistence of racism in college athletics', *Fordham Urban Law Journal*, vol 22, pp615–698

DeGaris, L. (2000) 'Be a buddy to your buddy: Male identity, aggression, and intimacy in a boxing gym', in J. McKay, M. A. Messner and D. F. Sabo (eds) *Masculinities, Gender Relations, and Sport*, Sage Publications, Thousand Oaks, CA

Delgado, R. and Stefancic, J. (1995) *Critical Race Theory: The Cutting Edge*, Temple University Press, Philadelphia, PA

Delgado, R. and Stefancic, J. (2001) *Critical Race Theory: An Introduction*, NYU Press, New York, NY

Denham, B., Billings, A. and Halone, K. (2002) 'Differential accounts of race in broadcast commentary of the 2000 NCAA men's and women's final four basketball tournaments', *Sociology of Sport*, vol 19, no 3, http://hk.humankinetics.com.proxy1.cl.msu. edu/eJournalMedia/pdfs/5163.pdf

Dewar, A. (1993) 'Sexual oppression in sport: Past, present and future alternatives', in A. G. Ingram and J. W. Loy (eds) *Sport in Social Development*, Human Kinetics, Champaign, IL, pp147–165

Dhaliwal, N. (2005) 'Unhappy ever after', *The Times*, 30 April

Dimeo, P. (2001) 'Football and politics in Bengal: Colonialism, nationalism, communalism', in P. Dimeo and J. Mills (eds) *Soccer in South Asia: Empire, Nation, Diaspora*, Frank Cass, London

Dimeo, P. and Mills, J. (2001) 'Introduction: Empire, nation and diaspora', in P. Dimeo and J. Mills (eds) *Soccer in South Asia: Empire, Nation, Diaspora*, Frank Cass, London

Dirs, B. (2009) 'Khan fighting a losing battle?', http://www.bbc.co.uk/blogs/bendirs/ 2009/07/khan.html, last accessed 17 November 2010

Dudley, J. (2002) 'Inside and outside the ring: Manhood, race, and art in American literary naturalism', *College Literature*, vol 29, no 1, winter, pp53–82

Dyson, M. (1993) *Reflecting Black: African-American Cultural Criticism*, University of Minnesota Press, Minneapolis, MN

Early, G. (1994) *The Culture of Bruising: Essays on Prizefighting, Literature, and Modern American Culture*, Eccro, New York, NY

Early, G. (1998) *The Muhammad Ali Reader*, Yellow Jersey Press, London

Eason, K. (2009) 'The fifty greatest Formula One drivers', *The Times Online*, http:// www.timesonline.co.uk/tol/sport/formula_1/article5986660.ece, accessed 18 August 2011

Edward, L. (2003) 'Chopra is sent on toughen up duty', *The Journal*, 5 April

Edwards, H. (1969) *The Revolt of the Black Athlete*, The Free Press, New York, NY

Edwards, H. (1973) *Sociology of Sport*, Dorsey Press, Homewood, IL

Engel, M. (1995) 'Notes by the editor', in *Wisden Cricketers' Almanack*, John Wisden and Co Ltd, London

Entine, J. (2000) *Taboo: Why Black Athletes Dominate and Why We're Afraid to Talk about It*, Public Affairs, New York, NY

Equality and Human Rights Commission (2010) *How Fair Is Britain?* http://www.equality humanrights.com/key-projects/how-fair-is-britain/full-report-and-evidence-downloads/

European Race Bulletin (2007) no 60, summer 2007 edition

Fanon, F. (1986) *Black Skin, White Masks*, Pluto Press, London

Farquharson, K. and Marjoribanks, T. (2006) 'Representing Australia: Race, the media and cricket', *Journal of Sociology*, vol 42, no 1, pp25–41

Fitzgerald, W. G. (1898) 'Savage cricketers', *Strand Magazine*, London, May 1898, reprinted in D. R. Allen (ed) (1987) *Cricket's Silver Lining: 1864–1914*, Willow, London

Fleming, S. (2001a) 'Racial science and South Asian and black physicality', in B. Carrington and I. McDonald (eds) *'Race', Sport and British Society*, Routledge, London

Fleming, S. (2001b) 'Sport, schooling and Asian male culture', in *Sport, Racism and Ethnicity*, Falmer Press, London

Fletcher, P. (2010) 'Breaking down barriers for British Asians', BBC Sport, http://www.bbc.co.uk/blogs/paulfletcher/2010/05/breaking_down_barriers_for_bri.html, accessed 28 June 2011

Force India Online (2011) 'The Force', http://www.forceindiaf1.com/index/page_id/173, accessed 19 August 2011

Foster, C. (2010) *The BBC: Attracting Black and Minority Ethnic Journalists*, http://www.eortrial.co.uk/default.aspx?id=1134706

Franklin, B. (1997) *Newszak and News Media*, Hodder Arnold: London

Fraser, D. (2005) *Cricket and the Law: The Man in White is Always Right*, Routledge, London

Fraser, P. (2002) 'Chopra can go all the way, says his England coach', *Northern Echo*, 29 November

Frith, D. (1995) *Wisden Cricket Monthly*, August

Frost, C. (2004) 'The press complaints commission: A study of ten years of adjudications on press complaints', *Journalism Studies*, vol 5, no 1, pp101–114

Gardiner, S. and Welch, R. (2001) 'Sport, racism and the limits of "colour blind" law', in B. Carrington and I. McDonald (eds) *'Race', Sport and British Society*, Routledge, Oxon, UK

Garner, A. and Hodgson, G. (2007) 'Witch's potion: Woolmer and the Potter poison', *Sunday Mirror*, 30 March

Garside, K. (2008) 'McLaren play down Spanish racism', *Daily Telegraph*, 4 February

Gellner, E. (1964) *Nations and Nationalism*, Basil Blackwell, Oxford, UK

Gemmell, J. (2007) 'Cricket, race and the 2007 World Cup', *Sport in Society*, vol 10, no 1, Routledge, London

Gilmore, A. (1975) *Bad Nigger: The National Impact of Jack Johnson*, Kenniket Press, Port Washington, NY

Gilroy, P. (1987) *There Ain't No Black in the Union Jack*, Hutchinson, London

Gilroy, P. (1993a) *Small Acts: Thoughts on the Politics of Black Cultures*, Serpent's Tail, London

Gilroy, P. (1993b) *The Black Atlantic: Modernity and Double Consciousness*, Verso, London

Goldberg, D. (1990) 'The social formation of racist discourse', in D. Goldberg (ed) *Anatomy of Racism*, University of Minnesota Press, Minneapolis, MN

Goodey, J. (2001) 'The criminalization of British Asian youth: Research from Bradford and Sheffield', *Journal of Youth Studies*, vol 4, no 4, pp429–450

Gordon, P. and Rosenberg, D. (1989) *Daily Racism: The Press and Black People in Britain*, The Runnymede Trust, London

Gramsci, A. (1971) *Selections from the Prison Notebooks* (edited by Q. Hoare and G. Nowell Smith), International Publishers, New York, NY

Guha, R. (2002) *A Corner of a Foreign Field: The Indian History of a British Sport*, Picador, London

Hall, S. (1978) *Policing the Crisis: Mugging, the State, Law and Order*, Macmillan, London

Hall, S. (1990a) 'The whites of their eyes: Racist ideologies and the media', in M. Alvarado and J. O. Thompson (eds) *The Media Reader*, British Film Institute, London, pp7–23

Hall, S. (1990b) 'Cultural identity and diaspora', in J. Rutherford (ed) *Identity*, Lawrence and Wishart, London, pp222–237

Hall, S. (1991) 'Old and new identities, old and new ethnicities', in A. D. King (ed) *Culture, Globalization, and the World System*, Macmillan, London, pp42–43

Hall, S. (1992a) 'New ethnicities', in J. Donald and A. Rattansi (eds) *'Race' Culture and Difference*, Sage, London

Hall, S. (1992b) 'The question of cultural identity', in S. Hall et al (eds) *Modernity and Its Futures*, Polity Press, Cambridge, MA

Hall, S. (1996) *Questions of Cultural Identity*, Routledge, London

Hall, S. and Jacques, M. (1983) *The Politics of Thatcherism*, Lawrence and Wishart, London

Hamilos, P. (2008) 'Racism, what racism? asks Spain', *The Guardian*, http://www.guardian.co.uk/world/2008/feb/08/spain.sport, accessed 25 August 2011

Harcup, T. (2004) *Journalism: Principles and Practice*, Sage, London

Hardy, M. (2003) 'Loan star looking to set trend; Chopra hopes he inspires Asians', *Daily Mail*, 10 April

Harker, J. (2011) 'Accepted in polite society: Social status and wealth don't protect people from prejudice. Race is not a subset of class', *The Guardian*, 6 June

Harris, K. (1998) 'Suited up and stripped down: Perspectives for sociocultural sport studies', *Sociology of Sport*, vol 6, pp335–347

Harrison, K. C. and Lawrence, S. M. (2004) 'College students' perceptions, myths, and stereotypes about African American athleticism: A qualitative investigation', *Sport, Education and Society*, vol 9, pp33–52

Hart, S. (2010) 'Gay reaffirms his class', *Sunday Telegraph*, 11 July

Hartmann, P. and Husband, C. (1974) *Racism and the Mass Media*, Davis-Poynter, London

Hayes, S. and Sugden, J. (1999) 'Winning through "naturally" still? An analysis of the perceptions held by physical education teachers toward the performance of black pupils in school sport and in the classroom', *Race Ethnicity and Education*, vol 2, pp93–107

Henderson, R. (1991) 'A fundamental malaise', *Wisden Cricket Monthly*, republished at http://englandcalling.wordpress.com/2011/02/14/a-fundamental-malaise/

Henderson, R. (1995a) 'Bad selection: A case study', *Wisden Cricket Monthly*, April

Henderson, R. (1995b) 'Is it in the blood?', *Wisden Cricket Monthly*, July, pp9–10

Henderson, R. (2006) 'In response to Wagg, S. (1996) "Racism and the English cricket party"', http://www.juliushonnor.com/catalyst/Default.aspx.LocID-0hgnew0fx.RefLoc ID-0hg01b001006009.Lang-EN.htm

Henderson, R. (2011) *A Fundamental Malaise*, http://englandcalling.wordpress.com/2011/02/14/a-fundamental-malaise

Hesse, B. (2000) *Un/settled Multiculturalisms: Diasporas, Entanglements, 'Transruptions'*, Zed Books, London

Hoberman, J. (1997) *Darwin's Athletes: How Sport Has Damaged Black America and Preserved the Myth of Race*, Mariner Books, Boston, MA

Hoby, K. (2003) 'Crowe: Cricket not the game for Maori', 18 January, http://www.nzherald.co.nz/nz/news/article.cfm?c_id=1&objectid=3052026

Holden, G. (2008) 'World cricket as a postcolonial international society: IR meets the history of sport,' *Global Society*, vol 22, no 2, Routledge, London

Holt, O. (2007) 'Why we shouldn't be cheering if Ohuruogu picks up a medal today', *The Mirror*, 29 August

Howard, S. (2007) 'Please don't make this the face of our London Olympics', *The Sun*, 30 August

Howard, S. (2008) 'We can't let Ohuruogu be face of 2012', *The Sun*, 21 August

Hundley, H. L. and Billings, A. C. (eds) (2010) *Examining Identity in Sports Media*, Sage, London

Hurrell, B., Williams, V. and Pierik, J. (2003) 'Race row boils', *Herald Sun*, 18 January

Hutchinson, P. (2002) *The Media, Motives, and Jack Johnson: A Narrative Analysis of the Search for a 'Great White Hope'*, Presented at American Journalism Historians Association (AJHA) Second Annual Rocky Mountain Regional Conference, Brigham Young University, Provo, Utah, 9 March

Huyssen, A. (1995) *Twilight Memories: Marking Time in a Culture of Amnesia*, Routledge, London

Hylton, K. (2005) '"Race", sport and leisure: Lessons from critical race theory', *Leisure Studies*, vol 24, no 1, pp81–98

Hylton, K. (2009) *Race and Sport: Critical Race Theory*, Routledge, Abingdon

Indian Express (2011) 'Miandad urges banned trio to expose people behind betting', 9 February 2011, http://www.indianexpress.com/news/miandad-urges-banned-trio-to-expose-people-b/747900/

Irwin, I. (2006) 'Theo is a new Messi', *The Sun*, 23 November

Jackson, D. Z. (1989) 'Race logic and "being like Mike": Representations of athletes in advertising, 1985–1994', *Sociological Focus*, vol 30, pp345–355

James, C. L. R. (1963) *Beyond a Boundary*, Yellow Jersey Press, London

James, S. (2005) 'Academy is a crucial aid to selection', *Sunday Telegraph*, 5 June

James, W. (1993) 'Migration, racism and identity formations: The Caribbean experience in Britain', in W. James and C. Harris (eds) *Inside Babylon: the Caribbean Diaspora in Britain*, Verso, London

Jiggins, P. (2006) 'Theo can be next Ronaldo', *The Sun*, 17 May

Johal, S. (2001) 'Playing their own game: A South Asian football experience', in B. Carrington and I. McDonald (eds) *'Race', Sport and British Society*, Routledge, London

Johnson, K. (2003) 'The legacy of Jim Crow: The enduring taboo of black–white romance', *Texas Law Review*, February 2006; UC Davis Legal Studies Research Paper no 57, http://ssrn.com/abstract=834966

Johnson, M. (1992) 'Well-kept secret of Waqar's delivery', *The Independent*, 1 July

Johnson, M. (1995) 'English onslaught changes the game', *The Independent*, 24 June

Kane, M. (1971) 'An assessment of black is best', *Sports Illustrated*, 18 January

Kellner, D. (2004) 'Sports, media culture and race: Some reflections on Michael Jordan', *Sociology of Sport Journal*, vol 13, 458–467

Kelly, D. (2009) 'Stonewall job for Pakistan?', *Daily Mail*, 7 March

Kelso, P. (2003) 'Fans facing sanctions after violence', *The Guardian*, 3 April

Kennedy, E. and Hills, L. (2009) *Sport, Media and Society*, Berg, Oxford, UK

Kessel, A. (2010a) 'Gay turns on afterburners', *The Observer*, 11 July

Kessel, A. (2010b) 'Christophe Lemaitre scorns controversy over breaking the 10s barrier', *The Guardian*, 26 July

Kessel, A. (2011) 'Christine Ohuruogu: It doesn't matter if I'm the face of the Games or not', *The Guardian*, 25 July

King, C. (2004) 'Race and cultural identity: Playing the race game inside football', *Leisure Studies*, vol 23, no 1, pp19–30

Knox, M. (2003) 'Lehmann reveals the unwitting racism that infuses Australia', 26 January, http://www.theage.com.au/articles/2003/01/26/1043533952023.html

Kundnani, A. (2001) *From Oldham to Bradford: The Violence of the Violated*, Institute of Race Relations, http://www.irr.org.uk/2001/october/ak000003.html, accessed 12 August 2011

Kundnani, A. (2007) *The End of Tolerance: Racism in 21st Century Britain*, Pluto Press, London

Lawrence, M. (2005) 'African American athletes' experiences of race in sport', *International Review for the Sociology of Sport*, vol 40, pp99–110

Lawton, J. (2011) 'Hamilton could hardly be less accurate', *The Independent*, 31 May

Lewis, P. (2001) *Constructing Public Opinion*, Columbia University Press, New York, NY

Lewis, R. (2010) 'Gay floors Powell in heavyweight scrap', *Sunday Times*, 11 July 2010

Lindsey, E. (2001) 'Notes from the sports desk: Reflections on race, class and gender in British sports journalism', in B. Carrington and I. McDonald (eds) *'Race', Sport and British Society*, Routledge, London

Lloyd, A. (2002) 'Toon's Asian star breaking barriers', *Evening Chronicle*, 7-November

Lombardo, B. (1978) 'The Harlem Globe Trotters and the perception of the black stereotype', *The Physical Educator*, vol 35, no 2, pp60–63

Long, J. and Spracklen, K. (2010) 'Positioning anti-racism in sport and sport in anti-racism', in K. Spracklen and J. Long (eds) *Sport and Challenges to Racism*, Palgrave Macmillan, London

Loy, J. and McElvogue, J. (1970) 'Racial segregation in American sport', *International Review of Sport*, vol 5, pp5–24

McCaffery, D. (2000) *Tommy Burns: Canada's Unknown World Heavyweight Champion*, James Lorimer & Company, Toronto, Ontario

McCarthy, D. and Jones, R. (1997) 'Speed, aggression, strength and tactical naiveté: The portrayal of the black soccer player on television', *Journal of Sport and Social Issues*, vol 21, pp348–362

McCrone, D. (1998) *The Sociology of Nationalism: Tomorrow's Ancestors*, Routledge, London

McDonald, I. and Ugra, S. (1998) *Anyone for Cricket? Equal Opportunities and Changing Cricket Cultures in Essex and East London*, Centre for Sport Development Research, London

McDonald, M. G. (2005) 'Mapping whiteness and sport: An introduction', *Sociology of Sport Journal*, vol 22, no 3, pp245–255

McGuire, B., Monks, K. and Halsall, R. (2001) 'Young Asian males: Social exclusion and social injustice in British professional football?', *Culture, Sport and Society*, vol 4, no 3, pp65–80

Maclean, S. and Young, B. (2008) 'In the pits', *The Mirror*, 4 February

Mail and Guardian Online (2009) 'SA lashes out at "racist" world athletics body', 20 August

Mail Online (2007) 'Ohuruogu: I'll compete for Nigeria just to be part of the 2012 experience', 18 August, http://www.dailymail.co.uk/sport/othersports/article-474121/Ohuruogu-Ill-compete-Nigeria-just-2012-experience.html

Malcolm, D., Bairner, A. and Curry, G. (2010) 'Woolmergate: Sport and the representation of Islam and Muslims in the British press', *Journal of Sport and Social Issues*, vol 34, no 2, pp215–235

Malik, K. (1996) *The Meaning of Race: Race, History and Culture in Western Society*, Macmillan, London

Margolis, B. and Pilavin, J. (1999) '"Stacking" in Major League Baseball: A multivariate analysis', *Sociology of Sport Journal*, vol 16, pp16–34

Marks, V. (1995) 'Racism in Sport: Atherton: Why I had to make a stand', *The Observer*, 9 July

Marqusee, M. (1995) 'Sport and stereotype: From role model to Muhammad Ali', *Race and Class*, vol 36, pp1–29

Marqusee, M. (1998) *In Search of the Unequivocal Englishman*, http://www.mike marqusee.com/?p=69

Marqusee, M. (1999) *Redemption Song: Muhammad Ali and the Spirit of the Sixties*, Verso, London

Marqusee, M. (2005) 'The ambush clause: Globalisation, corporate power and the governance of world cricket', in *Cricket and National Identity in the Postcolonial Age: Following On*, Routledge, London

Mason, D. (2000) *Race and Ethnicity in Modern Britain*, Oxford University Press, Oxford, UK

Mayeda, D. T. (2001) 'Characterizing gender and race in the 2000 Summer Olympics: NBC's coverage of Maurice Greene, Michael Johnson, Marion Jones, and Cathy Freeman', *Social Thought and Research*, vol 24, no 1–2, pp145–186

Meek, B. (1992) 'The racist subtext to the question that dominates the press', *Glasgow Herald*, 31 August

Memmi, A. (2009) *Racism and Difference in Theories of Race and Racism*, Routledge, London

Mercer, K. (1994) *Welcome to the Jungle: New Positions in Black Cultural Studies*, Routledge, London

Miles, R. (1982) *Racism and Migrant Labour*, Routledge and Kegan Paul, London

Miles, R. (1989) *Racism*, Open University Press, Milton Keynes, UK

Miles, R. (1993) *Racism after 'Race Relations'*, Routledge and Kegan Paul, London

Miller, D. (2002) 'Promotion and power', in A. Briggs and P. Cobley (eds) *Introduction to Media*, 2nd edition, Longman, London, pp41–52

Miller, N. (2005) 'Clean bowl racism? Inner city London and the politics of cricket development', in *Cricket and National Identity in the Postcolonial Age: Following On*, Routledge, London

Miller, P. (1998) 'The anatomy of scientific racism: Racialist responses to black athletic achievement', *Journal of Sport History*, vol 25, spring, pp119–151

Miller, P. and Wiggins, D. (2004) *Sport and the Color Line: Black Athletes and Race Relations in Twentieth-Century America*, Routledge, London

Milmo, C. (2007) 'Breakthrough as Woolmer suspect is caught on camera', *The Independent*, 21 April

Mitchell, K. (1995a) 'Cricket world divided by Negro loyalty row', *The Observer*, 2 July

Mitchell, K. (1995b) 'Racism in sport: Cricket's racism hit for six', *The Observer*, 9 July

Modood, T. (1997) *Ethnic Minorities in Britain: Diversity and Disadvantage*, Policy Studies Institute, London

Montagu, A. (1974) *Culture and Human Development*, Prentice-Hall, Englewood Cliffs, NJ

Morgan, D. (2003) 'Jack Johnson: Reluctant hero of the black community', in K. R. Johnson (eds) *Mixed Race America and the Law: A Reader*, NYU Press, New York, NY

Morrison, J. (1968) *Pax Britannica: The Climax of an Empire*, Faber and Faber, London

Murray, J. (2008) 'Lewis in race storm', *Daily Star*, 4 February

Murtagh, I. (2002) 'Young strikers clash; battle of the babes', *Daily Star*, 6 November

Nandy, A. (2000) *The Tao of Cricket*, Oxford University Press, Oxford, UK (originally published 1989)

Narain Karthikeyan Official Website (2011) 'Profile', http://www.narainracing.com/profile.html, accessed 19 August 2011

Otis, J. (1993) *Upside Your Head!: Rhythm and Blues on Central Avenue*, Wesleyan University Press, Hanover

Owusu, J. (2008) 'Institutional racism within the print media: A content analysis of *Sports Illustrated*'s media coverage of black NFL head coaches', http://library.ttu.edu/about/facility/face/entries/social_sciences/PDF/MarbleyInstitutional.pdf, accessed 15 November 2011

Pilditch, D. (2007) 'Woolmer had marks on his throat and a broken neck', *Daily Express*, 23 March

Pilkington, A. (2003) *Racial and Ethnic Diversity in Britain*, Palgrave MacMillan, Basingstoke, UK

Poole, E. and Richardson, J. (2006) *Muslims and the News Media*, I. B. Tauris, London

Pycroft, J. (1865) *Cricketana: Tales of Cricket 1743–1864*, J. W. McKenzie, London

Richardson, J. E. (2004) *(Mis)representing Islam: The Racism and Rhetoric of British Broadsheet Newspapers (Discourse Approaches to Politics, Society, and Culture)*, vol 9, John Benjamins Pub Co, Philadelphia, PA

Richardson, J. (2006) *Analysing Newspapers*, Palgrave Macmillan, London

Roberts, M. (2005) 'Sri Lanka: The power of cricket and the power in cricket', in *Cricket and National Identity in the Postcolonial Age: Following On*, Routledge, London

Roberts, R. (1983) *Papa Jack: Jack Johnson and the Era of White Hopes*, Free Press, New York, NY

Ronay, B. (2011) 'How Ravi Shastri, the big noise of cricket, called it wrong', *The Guardian*, 5 August

Ross, C. K. (2005) *Race and Sport: The Struggle for Equality On and Off the Field*, University of Mississippi, Jackson, MS

Rowe, D. (2003a) *Sport, Culture and the Media*, 2nd edition, Open University Press, Maidenhead, UK

Rowe, D. (ed) (2003b) *Critical Readings: Sport, Culture and the Media*, Open University Press, Maidenhead, UK

Rowe, D. (2004) *Sport, Culture and the Media: The Unruly Trinity*, second edition, Open University Press, Maidenhead, UK

Rowe, D. (2005) 'Fourth estate or fan club? Sports journalism engages the popular', in S. Allan (ed) *Journalism: Critical Issues*, Open University Press, Maidenhead, UK

Rowe, D. (2009) 'Media and sport: The cultural dynamics of global games', *Sociology Compass*, vol 3, no 4, pp543–558

Ryan, G. (2005) 'New Zealand national identity', *Cricket and National Identity in the Postcolonial Age: Following On*, Routledge, London

Sabo, D. and Jansen, S. (1992) 'Images of men in sport media: The social reproduction of gender order', in S. Craig (ed) *Men, Masculinity and the Media*, Sage, London

Sabo, D., Jansen, S. C., Tate, D., Duncan, M. C. and Leggett, S. (1996). 'Televising international sport: Race, ethnicity, and nationalistic bias', *Journal of Sport and Social Issues*, vol 20, no 1, pp7–21

Saeed, A. (1999) 'The media and new racisms', *Media Education Journal*, vol 27, pp19–22

Saeed, A. (2003) 'What's in a name? Muhammad Ali and the politics of cultural identity', in A. Bernstein and N. Blain (eds) *Sport, Media, Culture: Global and Local Dimensions*, Frank Cass, London

Saeed, A. (2004) '9/11 and the consequences for British-Muslims', in J. Morland and D. Carter (eds) *Anti-Capitalist Britain*, New Clarion Press, Manchester, UK, pp70–81

Saeed, A. (2007) 'Media, racism and Islamophobia: The representation of Islam and Muslims in the media', *Sociology Compass*, vol 1, pp443–462

Saeed, A., Blain, N. and Forbes, D. (1999) 'New ethnic and national questions in Scotland: Post-British identities among Glasgow-Pakistani teenagers', *Ethnic and Racial Studies*, vol 22, September, p5

Sage, G. H. (1990) *Power and Ideology in American Sport*, Human Kinetics, Champaign, IL

Said, E. (1978) *Orientalism*, Penguin, London (republished 2003 and 2005)

Sailes, G. A. (1998) 'The African American athlete: Social myths and stereotypes', in G. A. Sailes (ed) *African Americans in Sport*, Transaction, New Brunswick, NJ, pp183–198

Sammons, J. (1988) *Beyond the Ring: The Role of Boxing in American Society*, Illinois Press, Illinois

Samuel, M. (2010) 'All other cheats pale in comparison with this lot', *Daily Mail*, 30 August

Sanghera, S. (2011) 'Formula One's race issue', *The Times*, 1 June

Sardar, Z (2006) 'Three lives – one identity', *Observer Guardian Online*, 6 February, http://observer.guardian.co.uk/osm/story/0,1699541,00.html, accessed 23 August 2011

Savage, T. (2007) 'Official: Test ace was poisoned and strangled'. *Daily Star*, 30 April

Searle, C. (1993) 'Cricket and the mirror of racism', *Race and Class,* vol 34, no 3, pp45–54

Seconi, A. (2008) 'Apology for "All white here" slogan', 21 November, http://www.odt.co.nz/news/dunedin/32697/apology-039all-white-here039-slogan

Selvey, M. (1992) 'Cricket commentary: Foul deed of a whistle-blower', *The Guardian*, 27 August

Sissons, R. and Stoddart, B. (1984) *Cricket and Empire: The 1932–33 Bodyline Tour of Australia*, Allen & Unwin, London

Sivanandan, A. (1986) *A Different Hunger: Writings on Black Resistance*, Pluto, London

Skillset (2009) *Employment Census*, http://www.skillset.org/uploads/pdf/asset_14487.pdf?5

Slot, O. (2007) 'Pakistan's World Cup failures weighed down by extra baggage on their return', *The Times*, 29 March 2007

Smith, D. (2009) 'Focus: Sport and gender', *The Observer*, 23 August

Society of Editors (2004) *Diversity in the Newsroom*, Report by the Training Committee of the Society of Editors, Cambridge, UK, October

Solomos, J. (2003) *Race and Racism in Britain*, 3rd edition, Palgrave Macmillan, Basingstoke, UK

Solomos, J. and Back, L. (1996) *Racism and Society*, Macmillan Press, London

Sparks, C. and Tulloch, J. (2000) *Tabloid Tales: Global Debates over Media Standards*, Rowman & Littlefield, New York, NY

Spracklen, K. and Long, J. (2010) *Sport and Challenges to Racism*, Palgrave Macmillan, London

Staples, R. and Jones, T. (1985) 'Culture, ideology and Black television images', *The Black Scholar*, vol 16, no 3, pp10–20

Steen, R. (2004) 'Whatever happened to the black cricketer? Oh my Daffy and my Devon', http://sites.google.com/site/bodaciouscom/whatever-happened-to-the-black-cricketer-

Steen, R. (2008) *Sports Journalism: A Multimedia Primer*, Routledge, Abingdon

Stoddart, B. (2006) 'Sport, colonialism and struggle: C. L. R. James and cricket', *Sport in Society*, vol 9, no 5, pp914–930

Stone, J., Perry, Z. and Darley, J. (1997) 'White men can't jump: Evidence for the perceptual confirmation of racial stereotypes following a basketball game', *Basic and Applied Social Psychology*, vol 19, no 3, pp291–306

Stone, J., Lynch, C. I., Sjorneling, M. and Darley, J. M. (1999) 'Stereotype threat effects on black and white athletic performance', *Journal of Personality and Social Psychology*, vol 77, pp1213–1227

Sugden, J. (1996) *Boxing and Society: An International Analysis*, Manchester University Press, Manchester, UK

Sullivan, M. (2007) 'Harry Potter drug did kill Woolmer', *The Sun*, 20 April

Sullivan, M. and Smith, E. (2007) 'Bob was large … he would be tough to strangle', *The Sun*, 23 March

Sutton Trust (2006) *The Education Backgrounds of Leading Journalists*, http://www.suttontrust.com/research/the-educational-backgrounds-of-leading-journalists/

Syal, R. (2001) 'Support England, Nasser tells young Asians', *Daily Telegraph*, 27 May

Syed, M. (2011) 'Is it wrong to note 100m winners are always black?', *BBC Online*, 27 August, http://www.bbc.co.uk/news/magazine-14679657

Sygall, D. (2010) 'Shirvo: It's not a skin thing', *Sydney Morning Herald*, 8 August

Telegraph and Argus (2002) 'City set to field first Asian player', 6 November

Temple, M. (2008) *The British Press*, Open University Press, Maidenhead, UK

Todorov, T. (1986) 'Race, writing and culture', in H. L Gates (ed) *'Race', Writing and Difference*, Chicago University Press, Chicago, IL

Tremayne, D. (2008) 'Hamilton suffers racist abuse by Spanish fans', *The Independent*, 4 February

Tumber, H. and Prentoulis, M. (2005) 'Journalism and the making of a profession', in H. De Burgh (ed) *Making Journalists*, Routledge, Abingdon

Turner, D. and Jones, I. (2007) 'False start? UK sprint coaches and black/white stereotypes', *Journal of Black Studies*, vol 38, no 2, pp155–176

Ugra, S. (2005) 'Play together, live apart: Religion, politics and markets in Indian cricket since 1947', *Cricket and National Identity in the Postcolonial Age: Following On*, Routledge, London

Van Deburgh, W. (1992) *New Day in Babylon: The Black Power Movement and American Culture, 1965–1975*, Chicago University Press, Chicago, IL van Dijk, T. (1991) *Racism and the Press*, Sage, London

van Dijk, T. (1993) *Elite Discourse and Racism*, Sage, Newbury Park, CA

van Dijk, T. (1998) *Ideology: A Multidisciplinary Approach*, Sage, London

van Dijk, T. (2001) 'Multidisciplinary CDA: A plea for diversity', in R. Wodak and M. Meyer (eds) *Methods of Critical Discourse Analysis*, Sage, London

van Dijk, T. A. (2009) 'News, discourse and ideology', in K. Wahl-Jorgensen and T. Hanitzsch (eds) *The Handbook of Journalism Studies*, Routledge, London

Vasili, P. (2000) *Colouring Over the White Line: A History of Black Footballers in Britain*, Mainstream, Edinburgh

Vyas, R. (2008) 'What do they know of cricket who only cricket know?', http://www.hindu.com/lr/2008/01/06/stories/2008010650030200.htm

Wacquant, L. J. D. (1992) 'The social logic of boxing in Black Chicago: Toward a sociology of pugilism', *Sociology of Sport Journal*, vol 9, no 3, pp221–254

Wacquant, L. J. D. (1995) 'The Pugilistic point of view: How boxers think and feel about their sport', *Body and Society*, vol 24, no 389–535

Wacquant, L. J. D. (2004) *Body and Soul: Notebooks of an Apprentice Boxer*, Oxford University Press, Oxford, UK

Wade, L. (2009) 'Semenya's makeover: Gender as performance', *Sociological Images*, http://thesocietypages.org/socimages/2009/09/12/semenyas-makeover-gender-as-performance/, accessed 2 August 2011

Wagg, S. (ed) (2004) *British Football and Social Exclusion*, Routledge, London

Wahab, A. (1989) *Muslims in Britain*, Runnymede Trust, London

Wall, E. (2009) 'Bet she's got one', *The Daily Star*, 22 August

Wallman, S. (1986) 'Ethnicity and the boundary process in context', in J. Rex and D. Mason (eds) *Theories of Race and Ethnic Relations*, Cambridge University Press, Cambridge

Ward, G. (2004) *Unforgivable Blackness: The Rise and Fall of Jack Johnson*, Pimlico, London

Wells, T. (2008) 'Lewis in racism storm', *The Sun*, 4 February

Wenner, L. A. (ed) (1998) *MediaSport*, Routledge, London

Werbner, P. (2005) 'Islamophobia: Incitement to religious hatred – legislating for a new fear?', *Anthropology Today*, vol 21, no 1, pp5–9

West Indies Players Association (2003) 'WIPA vehemently condemns NZ slogan', 20 November, http://www.wiplayers.com/home/index.php?option=com_content&view=article&id=124%3Awipa-vehemently-condemns-nz-slogan-and-call-for-its-immediate-and-unconditional-removal&Itemid=114

Whannel, G. (1992) *Fields in Vision: Television Sport and Cultural Transformation*, Routledge, London

Whannel, G. (2002) *Media Sport Stars: Masculinities and Moralities*, Routledge, London

Whannel, G. (2009) 'Between culture and economy: Understanding the politics of media sport', in B. Carrington and I. McDonald (eds) *Marxism, Cultural Studies and Sport*, Routledge, Abingdon

Wheeler, V. (2009) 'Sex-row runner has bit of both', *The Sun*, 11 September

Wiggins, K. D. (1989) '"Great speed but little stamina:" The historical debate over black athletic superiority', *Journal of Sport History*, vol 16, no 2, pp158–185

Williams, J. (2000) 'Asians, cricket and ethnic relations in northern England', *Sporting Traditions*, vol 16, no 2, pp39–53

Williams, J. (2001) *Cricket and Race*, Berg, Oxford, UK

Williams, O. (2009) 'Where the Premier League's players come from', BBC Sport, http://news.bbc.co.uk/sport1/hi/football/eng_prem/8182090.stm, accessed 7 July 2011

Wilson, N. (2010) 'White lightning shock awaits bolt', *Daily Mail*, 16 July

Winant, H. (2009) 'Thinking through race and racism', *Contemporary Sociology: A Journal of Reviews*, March, vol 38, pp121–125

Winter, H. (2003) 'England must answer charge over racist fans', *The Telegraph*, http://www.telegraph.co.uk/sport/football/teams/england/2399445/England-must-answer-charge-over-racist-fans.html, accessed 25 August 2011

Wonsek, P. (1992) 'College basketball on television: A study of racism in the media', *Media, Culture and Society*, vol 14, pp449–461

Wragg, J. (2007) 'Ohuruogu could to on the run for Nigeria', Express.co.uk, 9 August

Young, B. (2011) 'Lewis "has to learn to lose"', *The Mirror*, 1 June

Index

www.routledge.com/media

Journalism Studies
A Critical Introduction

Andrew Calcutt, University of
East London, UK, and
Philip Hammond, London South
Bank University, UK

Journalism Studies is a polemical textbook that rethinks the field of journalism studies for the contemporary era. It is the politics, philosophy and economics of journalism, presented as a logical reconstruction of its historical development. This book offers a critical reassessment of conventional themes in the academic analysis of journalism, and sets out a positive proposal for what we should be studying.

Organised around three central themes – ownership, objectivity and the public – *Journalism Studies* addresses the contexts in which journalism is produced, practised and disseminated. It outlines key issues and debates, reviewing established lines of critique in relation to the state of contemporary journalism, then offering alternative ways of approaching these issues, seeking to reconceptualise them in order to suggest an agenda for change and development in both journalism studies and journalism itself.

Journalism Studies advocates a mutually reinforcing approach to both the practice and the study of journalism, exploring the current sense that journalism is in crisis, and offering a cool appraisal of the love-hate relationship between journalism and the scholarship which it frequently disowns. This is a concise and accessible introduction to contemporary journalism studies, and will be highly useful to undergraduate and postgraduate students on a range of Journalism, Media and Communications courses.

Hb: 978-0-415-55430-5
Pb: 978-0-415-55431-2
eBook: 978-0-203-83174-8

For more information and to order a copy visit
www.routledge.com/9780415554312

Available from all good bookshops